T0367959

STORIES WE DON'T TELL

UNCOVERING GENERATIONAL SECRETS

**ANNA RAY
AND
ELIZA HARRISON**

WESTBOW
PRESS®
A DIVISION OF THOMAS NELSON
& ZONDERVAN

WestBow Press books may be ordered through booksellers or by contacting:

WestBow Press
A Division of Thomas Nelson & Zondervan
1663 Liberty Drive
Bloomington, IN 47403
www.westbowpress.com
844-714-3454

Because of the dynamic nature of the Internet, any web addresses or links contained in this book may have changed since publication and may no longer be valid. The views expressed in this work are solely those of the author and do not necessarily reflect the views of the publisher, and the publisher hereby disclaims any responsibility for them.

Any people depicted in stock imagery provided by Getty Images are models, and such images are being used for illustrative purposes only.
Certain stock imagery © Getty Images.

Scripture taken from the American Standard Version of the Bible.

Scripture quotations are from the ESV® Bible (The Holy Bible, English Standard Version®), copyright © 2001 by Crossway, a publishing ministry of Good News Publishers. Used by permission. All rights reserved.

[Scripture quotations are] from the New Revised Standard Version Bible, copyright © 1989 the Division of Christian Education of the National Council of the Churches of Christ in the United States of America. Used by permission. All rights reserved.

ISBN: 978-1-6642-3285-3 (sc)
ISBN: 978-1-6642-3286-0 (hc)
ISBN: 978-1-6642-3284-6 (e)

Library of Congress Control Number: 2021920002

Print information available on the last page.

WestBow Press rev. date: 09/29/2021

CONTENTS

To Troy and Annalise.
You made us mothers, and then you made us
warriors. We love you forever and always.

INTRODUCTION

When teenage mother Anna's firstborn son dies tragically from brain damage after a doctor's thoughtless mistake, she never anticipates how that loss might come back to haunt her years later. Yet when her granddaughter faces paralysis and a lifetime of seizures due to a medical mistake, she is thrown back into that place she faced when she was a young mother. Only now, Anna is witnessing her youngest daughter, Eliza, go through heartache and loss and the struggle to trust in God through it all.

This is the story of two women—mother and daughter—who share their stories of pain, loss, and grief. From the suicide of a loved one to a partial brain removal of a young child, these women are tested time and again. Through it all, as they expose their hearts, minds, and souls, their faith is strained to the point of breaking. This is a revelation of how very raw and emotional trials shape who they are not only as mother and daughter but also as children of God.

As they overcome bitterness, emotional pain, and betrayal, they struggle to find meaning. Through the uprooting of lives, God shows both mother and daughter how faithful He really is. Through their personal stories, God's mighty hand is revealed as He shows the way to love, forgiveness, and trust in the one who came to seek and to save the lost.

> You intended to harm me but God intended it for good to accomplish what is now being done, the saving of many lives. (Genesis 50:20 NIV)

1

Three-Generation Journey
of Medical Mishaps

Anna

2010

"Mom, are we cursed?" My youngest daughter's words strike me with an agonizing pain as I choke back my tears. I struggle to look at the fear in her eyes. What can I say to her when I, too, once faced what she is now going through as a young mother?

God, please help me. How many times have I told others we should not ask why things happened in our lives? How many times have I shared with others that we need to seek God as to what we need to do to get through these trials with His help?

But here I stand in the hospital lobby, silently asking God why my family has to go through tragedy due to another medical mishap. How many medical mishaps is my family to endure, one generation after another? *God, hasn't my family suffered enough?*

Someone recently remarked that my family's story is like modern-day Job. In the hospital lobby early that morning, such a statement does not bring me much comfort. I begin to pace back and forth in the large waiting area. Every so often, I glance over at my laptop, which I left in the chair I was sitting in earlier. Even now, I try to keep my emotional wall of defense intact.

Everyone in that lobby sits so stoically. How many others are anxiously expecting a doctor to come out and tell them there is no hope or their loved one has died? It is as if I am looking at expressionless mannequins. No one moves or smiles. Everyone sits there with blank stares. I wonder what they are thinking. *Is it about you, God? God, are you here?*

I notice the sun is casting a bright light in the lobby. The light reflecting on the marble floor is the only ray of warmth I feel at the moment. The Australian camera crew, who is here to do a documentary about my granddaughter, are gathered in the corner of the large room. They have moved their chairs in a semicircle and appear to be engaged in a serious conversation with the cameraman. Every so often, they glance my way and then look away. I turn and head back to my chair. What can we say to one another? *God, forgive me. I am failing miserably right now. This is new territory for me as I wait for the outcome of my granddaughter in surgery having half her brain removed.*

To be honest, I doubt there are many of us who would say, "Bring it on, God. I can handle this." When we are attacked from every side, there is a God who is there to comfort us in our hour of greatest need. I knew that to be true, but my flesh was weak. *God, You could perform a miracle right now and make it possible for us to walk out of here today. Annalise can be made well and whole again—her body completely healed. God, I do believe You are the healer. Remove this veil of doubt, fear, and worry that hovers over me.*

God gave Satan permission to test Job. *God, is this a test? If it is, I am really struggling right now.* Words such as *trial, test, perseverance,* and *stand strong* keep running through my mind. The educator in me is saying that if this is a test, then I am failing dismally.

God, You ask me to be strong. I am trying. Yet here I am facing another medical mishap, another child with brain damage, and possible death is looming over us once again. *God, how many times must I forgive those in the medical field who we trusted to heal and not harm and move on?*

God, I had finally let go of all the bitterness, anger, and hurt from my own loss. Now I feel this cesspool of past emotions welling up in me once again.

Here I stand in yet another hospital reliving the pain of watching my youngest daughter face the possible death of her own daughter. How can words bring comfort to my daughter? What can I possibly say to her? Having taken this same journey as a young mother, I utter the only thing that I know to say to my daughter, "All we can do is pray and trust God. In the storms of life, He is our only anchor."

That word *anchor*—hadn't I read somewhere that an anchor keeps us stuck in the same place? My mind searches for another word. *Rudder*. The word is rudder. A rudder on a boat keeps us moving, guiding us. *Oh, God. I am losing it. Why am I thinking such crazy things right now?*

My daughter just looks at me through her tears in silence. She then puts her hands over her face and sobs. She does not utter a word in reply. I feel like such a failure as a mother. *God, once again, here I stand unable to do anything to help my daughter or granddaughter. God, do something, please!*

I glance over at the group of people standing nearby, recording our every action and word. The Australian film crew has been following my daughter and granddaughter around the last several days, interviewing and filming them. *God, let today be about You and doing what only You can do to transform lives. God, we need a miracle now.*

Today, the environment in that waiting room is so tense. The surgical outcomes for other families remain uncertain. My granddaughter, Annalise, is in a surgical unit to undergo having half of her brain removed. Does anyone even know what that means? To me, this sounds almost like science fiction—to have a surgeon cut open her skull and remove half of her brain. Hadn't we already placed our loved ones in the hands of medical professionals whom we trusted? Only to have our lives turned upside down!

Once again, I look around the crowded waiting room. The air is heavy with fear, worry, doubt, and anxiety. So many individuals caught in the web of the impossible. So many times, I have prayed that others come to know a God who carries our burdens for us. How many times have I shared with others that God gives us a peace that surpasses all understanding if we lean on Him?

God, doesn't Your Word say my help comes from the Lord? Please, help us. Surround us with that peace that surpasses all understanding. We are to trust in You, and I am trying. Why do I feel afraid and full of doubt? God, I want to witness to others of Your goodness, mercy, and grace. I truly want to be what You created me to be. Is this what it means to be broken and let go, so You can perform a work in our lives? The words *not my will but Thine be done* echo in my heart.

To be honest, I am angry. I want to scream at God. *God, do whatever*

You have to do to me. I deserve to be punished for mistakes I committed in my life. God, You know all my past failures, but my children and grandchildren do not deserve to travel this road. I already lost one child. Isn't that enough?

God, I have clung to Jeremiah 29:11, which I call my 911 verse. "For I know the plans I have for you, declares the LORD, plans to prosper you and not to harm you, plans to give you hope and a future." *God, what kind of future is it when you spared my life due to my medical mishap but not the lives of my firstborn, my youngest daughter's husband, and now possibly my granddaughter?*

Suddenly, in my spirit, I hear God's voice asking me, "Who do you trust? Do you believe in me? Are you God? Who is in control?"

I take a deep breath and close my eyes. Wow! God certainly knows me and my dominant characteristics. My typical rebellious attitude of thinking things will not work unless I am in control. I have a real issue with trust due to my childhood. My belief in others is not one of my strong traits either.

There is nothing like God pointing out that my faith cometh by hearing and hearing by the Word of God. "So, then faith cometh by hearing and hearing by the word of God" (Romans 10:17 KJV).

My spirit quickens as I begin to pray for His will, not my will, to be done. I know only too well how my rebellious will wreaked havoc in my earlier life before I found a faith that surpasses all understanding.

My daughter stands slumped against the wall outside the surgery room doors. The tears flow down my cheeks as I walk over to embrace her. "Honey, God has this under control. Stand firm, knowing we are about to experience a miracle this day."

Annalise, her daughter, my granddaughter, is fighting for her life behind those surgery room doors due to yet another medical mishap in our family. *God, give us all the strength to hold on to Your promises. Give us the ability to forgive so we can all heal, not only physically but spiritually, mentally, and emotionally.* Do I have enough faith to do that if …? I shudder as I try to shake off the horrible thought of losing our precious Annalise. *Jesus, we need You during our hour of need like never before.*

Can I really forgive if …? We are fighting to forgive what has already happened in Annalise's young life. What did Jesus say about forgiveness? I hug my daughter and then quickly turn and head back to the lobby. I have to be strong for her; I fight back the anguish welling up inside me. I sit back down in the hospital chair and search the scriptures on my computer until I find Matthew 18:21–22 (NIV). "Then Peter came to Jesus and asked, 'Lord, how many times shall I forgive my brother when he sins against me? Up to seven times?' Jesus answered, 'I tell you, not seven times, but seventy-seven times.'"

Forgive? How many times must I forgive for these medical mishaps? What was it that Jesus told Peter about forgiveness—to forgive seventy times seven?

Lord, I know there are excellent doctors who are committed to healing and caring for the sick, but this is the third generation of my family to experience these medical mishaps. When is it enough? I know in this life there will be trials and tests. Lord, I utterly understand that. I know how Your hand of protection has been with our family at other times. But God, this has really hit us hard this time. God, I am struggling.

I just know in spite of all that was going on that God is here whispering to me those verses I read so often. "I have told you these things, so that in me you may have peace. In this world you will have trouble. But take heart! I have overcome the world" (John 16:33 NIV). "We are hard-pressed on every side, but not crushed; perplexed, but not in despair; persecuted, but not abandoned, struck down, but not destroyed" (2 Corinthians 4:8–9 NIV).

A wave of peace comes over me as I feel the Lord's presence. He is reminding me that He is fighting this battle as His Word defeated the enemy who is coming against me. I take a big sigh. "Oh ye of little faith," I mutter to myself.

How many times has Jesus forgiven me? I sit here in this hospital lobby chair and glance around at others nearby. I am questioning if all that is happening is due to my own rebellion and disobedience at one point in my life. Even while dying on the cross, Jesus cried out, "Father, forgive them for they do not know what they are doing" (Luke 23:34 NIV).

Old emotions well up inside me as memories come flooding back. Old hurts seem to attack me as I sit in the hospital lobby. Satan certainly is doing his best to attack me in my weakest moments. Doubts seem to swirl around me. As I sit here in the hospital chair, I know there is a spiritual warfare being waged against me and my family. The enemy is doing his best to bring me to my knees and cry out against God. *Maybe if you had listened to your mother, your family would have been spared from all this pain you have brought upon your family all these years.*

Leave me alone! My spirit cries out against the attack coming at me from the evil one. *Not this time! You are not going to win this time. My God is greater!* What is that verse about resisting the enemy who tries to rob your faith?

"Resist him, standing firm in the faith, because you know that your brothers throughout the world are undergoing the same kind of sufferings. And the God of all grace, who called you to his eternal glory in Christ, after you have suffered a little while, will himself restore you and make you strong, firm, and steadfast" (1 Peter 5:9–10 NIV).

I drop to my knees and begin to pray to the only one who has our lives in His hands, and that is God Himself. I begin to go through the entire alphabet from A to Z, praising Him with every name I know, beginning with Abba Father, Almighty God, my All in All, Adonai, Awesome God, the one full of Agape Love. I keep on praising Him until I finish every name to describe God that I can think of from A to Z. When I finish my alphabet of praise to the Lord, I begin the Lord's prayer, pouring out my heart as I pray:

Our Father, *My Father,*

Who art in heaven, *Even though you are in heaven, I know you are here beside me right now.*

Hallowed be thy name, *Father I have praised you with every name I know from A to Z.*

Thy kingdom come, thy will be done on earth as it is in heaven, *Father, please help me to do Thy will and Thine alone; help me to go where You want me to go and do what You want me to do.*

Give us this day, *Father God, thank You for each breath I take, each brain function I have, each organ that functions, and the ability to spend quiet times with You.*

Our daily bread, *Father, I thank you for the times when You provided for my needs when I had little, enough, and plenty. I hunger for that daily bread that only You can provide. I thirst for that living water that will quench my thirst for You. Help me to understand each word, verse, chapter, and book of Your Word. Teach me to listen when You speak. Teach me to hunger for more of You.*

Forgive us our trespasses as we forgive those who trespass against us, *Father, help me to love others as You love me and help me to forgive others as You have forgiven me.*

Lead us not into temptation, *Father, please protect my heart, mind, and soul from all that is unholy and unrighteous. Father, keep the evil one from trying to rob my heart, mind, and soul by planting the seeds of doubt, fear, and worry within me.*

But deliver us from evil, *Father, please cleanse anything within me that would dishonor You in what I say, do, think, or act upon. Cleanse this cesspool of pain, agony, unforgiveness, anger, and doubt swirling around me and inside of me.*

For thine is the kingdom and the power and the glory, forever and ever. Amen.

After I finish bombarding heaven with my prayer, a peace comes over me once again. *Jesus, Jesus, Jesus.* I keep saying my Lord's name over and over again because demons have to flee at the sound of his name. *Jesus, Jesus, Jesus.* A calmness and peace wraps around me, and I feel the incredible presence of God covering me with his Shekinah glory.

He heals the brokenhearted and binds up their wounds. (Psalm 147:3 NIV)

Let everything that has breath praise the LORD. Praise the LORD. (Psalm 150:6 NIV)

So begins a story of redemption and forgiveness that can only come from letting go and letting God have His way in our lives. The path of forgiveness is not an easy one for me and comes after overcoming many trials, tests, and perseverance. I will forever be grateful to a loving and merciful Lord who never gave up on me when I was unlovable and unreachable, determined to bask in the miry clay of disobedience, rebellion, and pride. Looking back, I know I have no one to blame but myself for choosing to go against the will of God. For years, I tried to blame others for the emotional pain I encountered in my life. But those reactions are in themselves a crutch to avoid taking any action to reach out to God to rescue us.

> He healeth the broken hearted and binds up their wounds. (Psalm 147:3 NIV)

> He will wipe every tear from their eyes. There will be no more death or mourning or crying or pain, for the old order of things has passed away. (Revelation 21:4 NIV)

> No temptation has seized you except what is common to man. And God is faithful; he will not let you be tempted beyond what you can bear. But when you are tempted, he will also provide a way out so that you can stand up under it. (1 Corinthians 10:13 NIV)

2

Up on the Roof

Eliza
June 2010

I was on the roof.

Below me, Annalise was getting her head sawed open, and the waiting room chairs felt like jagged stones against my back. The women who were there as my surgery day support system kept giving me looks that were so sad and pathetic I just needed a break. My mom, Annalise's babysitter Jan, and my best friends, Monet and LeAnn, sat in the chairs around me, forming a circle of protection and love. I know they all meant well and were there because they loved me and loved Annalise, but what I needed wasn't going to be found in the sympathetic looks they were feeding me.

I told everyone I had to use the restroom and would be right back.

I found the door to the stairwell that led to the hospital's roof. I paused for a moment and stared at the door before trying the handle to see if it would move. To my surprise, it not only moved but opened. I quickly scanned the hospital's pristine hallway, and, finding nothing but stainless-steel trash bins scattered every few feet along the gleaming hallway, I stepped inside and quietly closed the door.

The climb up the stairs went quickly, and with every step higher, I was convinced that someone would appear and scold me for being where

I knew I shouldn't be. When I turned the knob to the door marked Roof Access, I was certain an alarm would sound. It didn't. The door opened silently. The only sound was a gust of wind that blew the hair from my face as I stepped onto the roof.

It was a warm day in Los Angeles, but at this height, there was enough of a breeze to make the temperature comfortable. It wasn't cold, but I was shivering. I had been so hyperfocused on Annalise's needs and hadn't given much thought to why certain moments of my life would cause me to stop breathing, to shiver from phantom coldness in the air, to entertain how easy it would be to jump into the abyss of darkness.

I stared at the church of Scientology. The blue façade and gold script of the church's sign was oddly calming. I wondered if I jumped now, how long it would take for anyone to realize. I folded myself over the side of the cement wall that rose to just above my waist. If I fell, my body would land directly on Sunset Boulevard. I felt the weight of my body against the stone wall and the moment of weightlessness as my feet lifted from the ground. Blood and wind rushed in my ears. I closed my eyes. At any moment, I could easily give up control and give in to the pavement below me. Thoughts of my broken body on the pavement below danced in my head, how my bright red hair would look against the red of my blood as it oozed out of my cracked skull.

Do it. Do it. Do it. The words floated in my head. *Just let go. Drop.*

My phone rang. "Bittersweet Symphony," my ringtone, disrupted the thoughts of ending my life.

It was Jan, Annalise's twenty-year-old babysitter who, along with her family, had come out to wait and pray with us. "Eliza? Where are you? They have an update on Annalise."

I had answered the phone while still upside down. My voice momentarily caught. "I'll be right down." I put the phone in my back pocket and forced my body upright. My feet touched the concrete, and a rush of dizziness caused me to see spots of blue light.

You had your chance. Now you'll have to live through more pain.

I drew a deep breath and felt the wind on my face. They were at the halfway mark; Annalise had another five hours of surgery to go. I couldn't jump, not now, not ever.

The fact that I had been able to gain access to the roof so easily wouldn't dawn on me until years later. When visiting that same hospital lobby, I'd once again see the door and try the handle just to see if it would turn. It wouldn't.

3

The Unwanted,
Redheaded Sin Child

Anna
1964 and Earlier

"You make your bed, you lie in it," my mother screams at me during one of our very heated arguments when I demand at the age of seventeen to leave home and marry the young serviceman. Little do I know how my life will turn into a bed of thorns. Yet I know in my heart that through it all, I set my course of disobedience. It will be my own rebellion and disobedience that lead to the consequences of my actions until the LORD finds me.

I am not at the point in my life where I am receptive to the verse in the Bible that talks about honoring my father and mother. I am not at that point in my life where I believe or embrace the verse in Romans 8:28 (NRSV): "We know that all things work together for good, for those who are called according to his purpose." Now, looking back over my life, I stand absolutely in awe at the journey I took over the highest mountains and lowest valleys of life. The song by Helen Baylor, "If It Had Not Been," is a reminder of *Where would I be if it had not been for the Lord on my side.*

I do not know it at the time, but the Lord's plan is to teach me forgiveness, beginning with my mother. My mother—the woman who never really forgives me for being born, until much later in my life.

I will become an adult before I understand that forgiveness is not an option for the believer. If we harbor feelings of hate, bitterness, and anger, we remain the victim. I must be honest and say that even after becoming a Christian, it was easy to embrace the fruits of the spirit mentioned in Galatians 5:22, such as love, joy, and peace. Words such as *patience* or *longsuffering* are more difficult to embrace, and I struggle with how they do not seem to fit with words like *love, joy,* and *peace.* As a seventeen-year-old, I am not ready to forgive my mother. I am angry with her believing that she robbed me of knowing who I really am. I feel like she owed me the chance to know my real father. I feel she does not deserve my love, trust, and respect.

> Children obey your parents in the Lord, for this is right. Honor your father and mother, which is the first commandment with a promise, that it may go well with you and that you have a long life on earth. (Ephesians 6:1–3 NIV)

I admit that it took me an awfully long time to understand the verses in Galatians about the fruits of the spirit that mentioned patience and self-control. I struggled to embrace those words. "But the fruit of the Spirit is love, joy, peace, patience, kindness, goodness, faithfulness, gentleness, and self-control" (Galatians 5:22 NIV).

God has a work to do in my life, changing a broken and bitter heart of a seventeen-year-old girl. "I will give you a new heart and put a new spirit in you; I will remove from you your heart of stone and give you a heart of flesh. And I will put my Spirit in you and move you to follow my decrees and be careful to keep my laws" (Ezekiel 36:26–27 NIV).

In Max Lucado's book, *God Will Use This for Good: Surviving the Mess of Life,* he states that "God will like Moses, train us, test us and teach us." These words make me think about the way a soldier prepares for the battlefield.

Along this journey of life, we often want our life to resemble a bed of roses where everything is worry-free and carefree. But if we really think about it, Moses could have never led his people to the promised land without the training and testing he endured. Joseph would have never ended up saving his people from hunger and starvation had it not been for the trials he endured and the training he received while serving in Pharaoh's court.

While our trials may not be as paramount as what the disciples or other biblical individuals faced, those stories in God's Word are there to help us overcome the spiritual, emotional, physical, and financial woes we encounter. As I watch and read about the many things unfolding in our nation today, I try to control myself from verbally attacking others. It is easy to revolt against those who will do all they can to undermine those who do not embrace their political agenda.

I know the blame game all too well. My life, beginning with my conception, is full of placing the blame on someone else rather than taking responsibility for one's actions.

"How many times am I going to have to pay for my sin?"

During my mother's ranting and beating, I can never understand why she keeps saying those words all the time. Does she feel guilty as a mother for beating me but does it anyway?

I cower in the corner of my bedroom as my mother screams hysterically at me. The emotional pain is worse than the physical pain as she repeatedly beats me over the back with a broom handle. The pain of the beating is nothing compared to the pain in my heart. I know that if I cry, the beating will stop, but I refuse to let her see me cry. Why does she call me her sin child?

A sin child, in the Catholic Church, was defined as "the aftermath of having unmatrimonial sex. If two people have sexual intercourse without getting married and the female becomes pregnant, the child would be called a 'sin child.'"

After each beating, my mother collapses in her favorite living room chair with her hand over her heart. She sits there in that chair for the longest time and struggles to breathe. There is no door between my bedroom and living room, so this allows me to sit against my bedroom wall and stare at her. *Why does she hate me so much?*

Oftentimes, clumps of my hair are lying on the floor beside me. During my beatings, she grabs my hair as she bangs my head against my bedroom wall. She yanks my hair so hard it feels like my scalp is going to tear away from my head. She threatens to burn my red hair off my head.

I don't know what hurts worse afterward, my burning scalp or my aching back and legs.

> See that you do not despise one of these little ones. For I tell you that in heaven their angels always see the face of my Father who is in heaven. (Matthew 18:10 ESV)

> For you formed my inward parts, you knitted me together in my mother's womb. I praise you, for I am fearfully and wonderfully made. Wonderful are your works; my soul knows it very well. My frame was not hidden from you, when I was being made in secret, intricately woven in the depths of the earth. Your eyes saw my unformed substance; in your book were written, every one of them, the days that were formed for me, when as yet there was none of them. (Psalm 139:16 ESV)

When others ask her why I am always so black and blue, she tells them I am clumsy and fall a lot. Part of that story is true about my falling a lot. As a little child, I had to wear special shoes to strengthen my ankles in order for me to walk. Even as a young teen, my ankles would sometimes give way, and I would fall suddenly. I cannot count the number of times I have stood on a street corner, waiting to cross the street, and suddenly fall into the road.

I hate my red hair and feel like I am abnormal in some way. My mother is always threatening to burn my red hair off my head. I dread the times she grabs my hair in her hands and yanks me around in a circle. She uses such violence and yanks me so hard that handfuls of my red hair are left in her hands.

But it is not only my mother who makes me self-conscious about the color of my hair. While growing up, the kids at school taunt me with such sayings as "I'd rather be dead than red on the head. Redhead, wet the bed." I felt like an outcast during the early years of elementary school. It would be years before I would come to really like my red hair, knowing that I am in a very select group of people in the world with such a hair color.

When the truth comes out years later about the true source of my mother's anger toward me, I am kind of relieved to know I am not the only one she hated. Did I say the *truth*? The truth of how I was conceived would never be told. My mother would go to the grave never sharing with me what really happened in her life before I was born. We made our peace with each other later in my life. However, her becoming pregnant with me would be a topic she refused to say much about. She refused to discuss the details about my biological father as well.

> For whatever is hidden is meant to be disclosed, and whatever is concealed is meant to be brought out in the open. (Mark 4:22 NIV)

According to my mother, she had nothing to do with what happened to her. She called her getting pregnant with me a terrible mistake of her being served a date-rape drug by an airman she had dated. But the story never really seemed credible due to the very brief and different versions she sometimes uttered about my biological father, a man I never met. The only real thing I knew about him was that I inherited his red hair. She made that obvious point each time she got angry with me and threatened to burn that red hair off my head.

> The tongue has the power of life and death, and those who love it will eat its fruit." (Proverbs 18:21 NIV)

Every time I tried to ask her about my real father, my mother began to cry hysterically. So I backed off and learned not to ask any more questions about him. However, from an incredibly young age, I did learn some interesting points about my real father indirectly from my mother during her rantings and beatings. But those tidbits of information began to make some sense much later during my teen years. In the meantime, my mother led me to believe that I was to blame for the beatings she inflicted upon me.

4

Secrets and Lies

Anna
1955

My mother is so intent on keeping the truth from me regardless of the trauma I experience on a trip we take today. I am eight years old, and I believe she wants to give me up for adoption. My mother and father said they were taking me on a trip for the day. I am so excited because they want to spend time alone with me. I never remember us spending time together without my two brothers and sister tagging along.

I remember the time they tried to sneak off on a trip with my siblings and leave me home. I remember how hurt I was when I discovered them loading everyone except me in the family car and driving away. They left me home with some relatives to look after me. I ran as fast as I could to catch up with the car, crying for them to stop. The last image I saw as they drove away was my brother looking out the back window, laughing and waving as the car sped down the road.

So, imagine my excitement now, three years later, to learn it is my time to go on an outing with my parents by myself. Now it is my turn to wave goodbye to my siblings and go on a trip with my parents. I don't even know where we are going. It is just fun to go off on an adventure with my parents all by myself. But part of me is fearful at the same time. My parents are acting kind of weird and avoid looking at me or talking to me. My father's mother just the day before told my parents they need to get rid of me. I am excited but afraid where we might be going. I sit in the back seat of the car and do not make a sound. I will be a good girl.

We arrive a short while later in a city I have never been. My parents are noticeably quiet as my father parks the car in front of a large white building. My mother takes ahold of my hand and leads me up the sidewalk. I wonder why we are going into this big building. It doesn't look like a fun place to go. Although I think it might be fun to skip up and down those big steps.

I gaze up at the huge white pillars on each side of the stairs. My mother looks down at me. "Don't you even think about it." She squeezes my arm as we ascend the large steps with big white pillars on each side. She can probably tell what I am thinking.

"Where are we going?" I ask as I glance up at my mother and father.

Silence. My parents say nothing and continue up the large steps. My father opens a large door, which leads into a huge room with more big, round columns. I have never been in a building this big before, except for church. This building looks scary, and I can't understand why my parents want to come here.

Soon, we are seated on a large bench in this big hallway. My feet cannot even touch the floor, and I begin to squirm. My mother reaches over and squeezes my arm hard. I continue to wonder what we are doing in such a strange place and where we are going. I know to be quiet and just wait. I am just glad to be with my parents on this trip, even if it seems like a strange place to be.

I look over at my parents and wonder why we are all dressed up in nice clothes to come to this place. The only time we ever dressed up in fancy clothes was one time when we were going to church at Easter. We never made it to church that day. A large bird swooped down and pooped on my mom's dress as we stood outside that morning. That incident made my mother so mad that she refused to go to church, and we went back home. She beat me that day for laughing at something she said was not funny.

Eventually, a woman comes walking down the long hallway and motions for us to follow her as she opens the doors to a large room. She waves her hand for us to go inside. My mother sits me down in a large chair at a big table. It is the biggest table I have ever seen, and it has lots of chairs around the table. *A lot of people must eat at this table.* I look around and notice that there are other people sitting at the table with us. I wonder if we are going to eat with them.

These people don't look very friendly. They keep staring at us as we sit down. They look down at a bunch of papers a few times. Everyone just sits and stares at one another for the longest time. No one is talking.

I become easily bored as I wait for what is to happen next. I keep glancing at the door, fully expecting someone to bring us some food soon. I am hungry. My mother said we are going to get something to eat while we are on this trip. What is it taking so long?

The room is very big with all sorts of pictures on the walls of scary-looking men. I don't like those pictures. I don't like this place.

"Anna, the judge is talking to you!" My mother nudges me and gives me one of her looks that means to pay attention. "She doesn't listen very well," my mother replies to the scary-looking man sitting at the end of the table.

I look down the long table at this man my mother called a judge. The man smiles briefly at me as he proceeds to talk to me. "Anna, do you want to be adopted?"

"Adopted?" I begin to cry. My parents are giving me away. They lied about taking me on a trip together and going out to eat. I don't want to stay in this place.

I turn and grab ahold of my mother's arm with both of my hands. "I promise to be good. Please, don't give me away. I promise to be good." I am now sobbing uncontrollably.

The judge looks over at my mother rather sternly. "Does she not know why she is here?"

My mother mumbles something to the judge, and the next thing I know, we are heading out of that large room with the big table.

I can't stop crying. I expect someone to come along any minute and snatch me from my parents. As soon as we get outside that big building, my mother squeezes my arm hard. My mother yells at me to stop acting like a baby.

"Are you giving me away?" I plead as I wipe the tears away. I don't want to make her angrier. "I promise to be good. I promise I won't run away anymore."

Is it really running away when I always end up trying to find my mother? That one time I ran away was scary, but most times I know where I am going. Is it so wrong to look for my mother when she leaves me with strangers? When our house burned down, why did the whole family go off and leave me with our neighbors?

"OK, now let's get something to eat," she replies as she leads me and my father across the street into a little restaurant. Sitting in a restaurant is something we have never done before as a family, just me, my mother, and father.

There was the time my mother once took me to a restaurant after she bought me a dress for my first communion. But she never showed up at church to see me in that dress when I made my first communion vows. A nun at the convent is always there with me at church. Sister Xavier is such a blessing in my life and treats me like her daughter. Every day after school, I run to the convent to help Sister Xavier with her chores. One day, I am going to become a nun just like Sister Xavier.

My parents are quiet during the meal. I try to sit there quietly and eat my food. I want to show my mother I can be a good girl, so she won't give me away. For a few moments, I am happy, until we finish eating. Surely, they wouldn't feed me if they are going to give me away.

"Are we going home now?" I look out the restaurant window and stare at that big building across the street. I don't want to go back there. I am ready to go home.

"No, we have to go back there because you made a big fuss by crying. If you want to go home with us, make sure you sit there and be quiet. If the judge asks you any questions, just say yes and nothing else. Do you understand me!"

"Yes," I reply as I fight back the tears. I don't want to go back there. My mom is squeezing my arm really tight.

"Just remember what I said," my mom growls at me as we cross the street in front of the big building.

Then my mother is leading us back to the big building and back into that room with that man they called a judge.

"Did you tell her?" the judge asks rather sternly as he looks first at my mother and then at me.

"Do you understand what adoption means?" The judge stares at me with eyes that look like a big, scary bear.

"Yes," I reply and quickly look over at my mother for her approval.

My mother mumbles something to the judge. She speaks so low that I don't hear what she says to him, but soon we are on our way out of that scary place.

"Am I going home?" I ask.

"Yes," she replies. She glares at me as she pulls me down the big hallway. Her fingers dig into my arm, but I am only glad to know she isn't going to give me away.

I nearly cry again, but this time it is because I am not going to be adopted. Little do I know that the man I call my father is the one who is adopting me. I never learn this truth until it slips out during an argument with my father, who I later call my adoptive father, many years later.

My mother continues to pull me down the hallway. Soon we stop at a desk where a woman at a typewriter hands my mom a paper. "Look over the information and let me know if it is correct," the woman says.

"All except her middle name," my mother replies as she hands the sheet of paper back to the lady.

The lady looks up at my mother and lets out a deep sigh. "How should it be spelled?"

"Without an E," my mother replies as she looks down at me.

"Is her middle name now spelled correctly?" the woman asks as she holds up the paper once again.

"Yes," my mother says.

"Does this mean you are keeping me?" I ask as I look up at my mother.

"Yes," my mother replies. "As long as you behave," she says in a low voice.

Years later, I will embrace the verses that talk about how God had plans for my life even while I was being conceived in my mother's womb. I was not an accident. I was created by God for a purpose. I was chosen by God. You loved me even when I was unlovable.

> In Him we are also chosen, having been predestined according to the plan of him who works out everything in conformity with the purpose of his will. (Ephesians 1:11 (NIV)

This is what the LORD says—he who made you, who formed you in the womb, and who will help you: Do not be afraid, Jacob, my servant, Jeshurun, whom I have chosen. (Isaiah 44:2 NIV)

Your eyes saw my unformed body; all the days ordained for me were written in your book before one of them came to be. (Psalm 139:16 NIV)

We arrive back home that day, and nothing is ever mentioned again about that trip. It will be several years before the truth about that day is revealed. When the truth eventually comes out, I am furious that my mother led me to believe she was going to give me away. As the years unfold, I learn that my mother was a broken, hurting soul who never found the peace of God in her own life.

5

Unforgiving Spirit

Anna
1963—Earlier

Ironically, I resemble my adoptive father more than I do my mother. Everyone comments how much I look like him. We are both tall, slender, and fair skinned. He has blond hair and blue eyes, while my hair is red and curly. My mother is short, heavyset, and olive skinned with dark brown hair and eyes. I do have my mother's dark brown eyes.

Throughout my mother's life, my red hair is a constant reminder to her of the man who is my biological father, a fact that I learn indirectly from my paternal step-grandmother who resents her son having to raise a child who is not his own. She wanted her son to give me up for adoption, not adopt me as his own.

"You are never, ever to go to the airbase. Don't ever let me catch you dating an airman, a southerner, or a Protestant!" my mother yells at me as she shakes her finger in my face. Some of these things don't make any sense because she met my adoptive father, the man I knew most of my life as my father, when he was in the army. My adoptive father is also a nonpracticing Protestant. His only redeeming trait is that he is a northerner from Massachusetts.

I do not understand why my mother makes such a fuss about religion when she never steps foot in a church other than for a baptism, wedding, or funeral. And only a Catholic church at that! My adoptive father tries to take me and my siblings to church when my mother is in the hospital after the birth of her fourth child. When she learns my adoptive father takes us to a Protestant church, she yells and screams at him so much that he never steps foot in church again. Even more ironic are her actions; she pushes me and my oldest brother out of the house every week to attend Catechism and church, but she never attends church herself.

Later in life, when I accept Jesus as my Savior and become a Christian, I share my salvation experience with my mother. She is visiting me and my family in Arkansas. We have reached a point in our lives where I have gained her admiration due to my achievements. I have acquired a nice home, good education, and good job. She admires those things. I hear from relatives about how proud she is of me. We have reconciled our relationship with each other, and things are good between us. Until I become a Christian, I have learned to never discuss the one forbidden topic—my birth father. However, it becomes obvious that the topic of religion is also a source of contention with my mother.

All goes well with my mother's visits until it comes time to attend church on Sundays. Her headaches always flare up on Sundays when I ask her if she wants to go to church with me and the family. She never reaches the point where she will step foot in a Protestant church, except for one time, and that is when my oldest daughter gets married. At the time, I ask her if she believes in an eternal place of torment for nonbelievers. She looks at me with cold, steely eyes. Her face grows taut, and I know she is angry at my daring to ask her such a question.

"Torment." She practically screams the word at me. "My torment has been right here on earth."

Tears flood my eyes as I hurry my family out the door for church, leaving her to brood in her own created world of anger and bitterness.

Why is it that individuals twist scripture to justify sin? "For a time is coming when people will no longer listen to sound and wholesome teaching. They will follow their own desires and will look for teachers who will tell them whatever their itching ears want to hear. They will reject the truth and chase after myths" (2 Timothy 4:3–4 ESV).

Yes, she has in many ways created her own torment. She is angry for so many things besides me. She never cleans her house, and to say it is filthy is to put it mildly. At one point, the neighbors even call the Board of Health to her house because it is that dirty. Even before I am old enough to start school, I attempt to clean the house and do the dishes.

For most of my life at home, I come home from school to find the kitchen table and sink full of dishes. The floors are littered with trash, and the beds are unmade. I can't understand why she allows us to live like this. Her mother, my maternal grandmother, is completely the opposite.

I escape to my maternal grandmother's house every weekend, where I sleep on freshly starched and ironed sheets. My grandmother keeps her house so clean that she even covers the living room furniture to avoid any dirt from soiling the upholstery. Her house is spotless, and she edifies what I learn later in a home economics class about "a place for everything and everything in its place."

I am so thankful for a maternal grandmother who encourages me to keep my room at home clean and neat. I make my bed every morning before leaving for school and pick up all my dirty clothes. To this day, I cannot stand any clutter in my home—sometimes much to the chagrin of family members.

My mother is generous to others in so many ways. There are family members who share with me how my mother provides them with food and clothing. My mother loves her mother with all her heart and will do anything for her. She often deprives herself of things to help others. She goes without so many things in life, such as decent clothing. Others see my mother as loving and generous. What can I do to make her go to church with me? Her pain runs deep, and this leads to her avoiding any attempt to find comfort in things of a spiritual matter.

> There is a way that seems right to a man, but in the end it leads to death. (Proverbs 14:12 NIV)

> Enter by the narrow gate. For the gate is wide and the way is easy that leads to destruction, and those who enter by it are many. (Matthew 7:13 ESV)

I look back on the times we spent together when she visited me and my family in the various areas of the U.S. we lived in. Our relationship is always guarded. While we have made peace with each other, there remains a wall between us. I often wonder if she looks at me and sees in me the man who is my biological father. Does she find it a strange coincidence that I am raising my family in the South and rearing my children in the Protestant religion?

After her death, some pictures are found that offer clues to just how deep her emotional pain ran within her heart, mind, and soul. If only she could have found peace and let God do a work in her life. I will always regret that I was unable to reach beyond that emotional wall and help her find the peace that only our Lord can give us.

My mother was determined to keep secrets from all of us. She kept her feelings bottled up inside her. These secrets brought her and others so much emotional hurt and pain. Buried deep inside her were so many deep-seated issues. She was never able to let go of the guilt that held her enslaved.

However, she gave birth to me and endured the ridicule and shame of having a child out of wedlock. She bore the emotional pain of being labeled as sinful in the eyes of her family and church during a time when such an action was looked down upon. She endured the embarrassment of giving birth to me in a home for unwed mothers who were treated as sinful women.

Learning more of her story after her death, I know God's hand was upon my life from the moment I was conceived. Things could have turned out so differently if it had not been for God protecting me while I was being formed in my mother's womb.

6

Rebellion and Revenge

Anna
1960–1965

The verse in James 4:16–17 (NIV) very accurately describes my season of rebellion and scheming: "As it is, you boast in your arrogant schemes. All such boasting is evil. If anyone, then knows the good they ought to do and doesn't do it, it is sin for them."

There are often little things said at family gatherings that eventually make me suspicious about my mother and the man I know as my father. An aunt blurts out at a family gathering that my parents married after I was born. But I always keep these suspicions to myself—until my father and I get into a pretty heated argument when I am thirteen years old. I do not understand why my father won't let me go on a date with this sixteen-year-old boy I met who has a car.

"You are not going on a date with someone in a car!" he yells at me. This reaction of his is surprising to me. My father rarely disciplines me. It is always my mother who takes charge of discipline when it relates to me.

"I am going to go!" I yell back at him.

"Go to your room. That guy is too old for you!" he yells back at me.

I don't know what makes me scream the words that spew out of my mouth. All of my pent-up anger comes flooding to the surface as I lash back at him. "Who are you to tell me what to do when you and Mom didn't even get married until after I was born!"

I become frightened when I see the look on his face. He comes toward me and raises his hand to hit me but then stops himself. He screams, "I may not be your real father, but as long as you live in my house, then you will do what I say!"

Not my father? I gasp. His words hit me like an explosion set off inside my heart.

Behind me, I hear my mother scream at him. I turn to look at her, and she collapses in a chair, screaming and crying.

"What is he saying?" I scream at her as the tears stream down my face. I try so hard to choke back the sobs escaping my lips.

"How long am I going to have to pay for my sin?" This is her standard response every time she beats me. After that day, I will hear it every time I approach the subject about my biological father. The secrets will die with her.

Now I know for the first time why she calls me her sin child. The lies, the secrets, and her refusal to talk about it are the beginning of my wanting to cause her the emotional pain I feel as a nobody, a nothing. I come to think of myself as the child nobody really wants.

If you are reading this and have been a child who was abandoned or neglected or unloved, please know that you are loved. You were created by a heavenly Father who loves you and desires the best for you. It took me a long time to come to this realization and accept the blessings on my life by a Father who loves me.

> For you who created my innermost being; you knit me together in my mother's womb. I praise you, for I am fearfully and wonderfully made. Your works are wonderful. I know that full well. My frame was not hidden from you when I was being made in the secret place, when I was woven together in the depths of the earth. Your eyes saw my unformed body. All the days ordained for me were written in your book before one of them came to be. (Psalm 139:13–16 NIV)

At the time, the words *sin child, unwanted, unloved,* and *mistake* fill me with such bitterness. Looking back, I am so thankful for a God who saw within a young girl a life that was worth saving. And I will always be grateful to a God, who protected me from even more foolish stunts during my season of rebellion. I know that God was watching over me when I was determined to plunge headlong into disaster.

> The thief comes only to steal and kill and destroy. I have come that they may have life and have it to the full. (John 10:10 NIV)

I am determined after that incident to cause my mother the same emotional pain she inflicts upon me. So I set out to get even with her the only way I know how. I begin to sneak off to dances at the airbase, located seven miles from my house, every Saturday night. I lie to my mother about where I am going.

I know she will never suspect me of walking seven miles each way to the airbase at night. Besides, no one is allowed on the airbase for the dances unless they are eighteen years or older. I am only fifteen years old and lack the proper ID. I did say proper ID. A senior at the high school I attend knows I want to go to the airbase dances, so she lends me her ID. Friends joke about how much alike we look, so it is easy to pass for her when I show her ID at the airbase security gate entrance.

My life begins to revolve around the Saturday-night dances at the airbase. I love the attention I get from all these lonely airmen. My only desire is to have fun and dance with them, nothing more. I live for the Saturday-night dances at the base. I love to dance to the rhythm of rock 'n' roll music and am quite a good dancer. I usually win one of the top three awards during contest nights. There is something about that music that allows me to release all the pent-up emotional pain in my life. But those dances are not my only escape; they are simply my fun and carefree escape.

It is a time when we are all trying to escape the emotional toils of life. Little do I realize that these young men are facing going off to fight for their country in the Vietnam War. I am so caught up in my own issues that it never dawns on me what these young men are thinking or feeling. The dances and the music are a way for us to momentarily forget the emotional pain and torment that loom over us.

Thankfully, I excel in my schoolwork and love the challenge of learning and being recognized for these accomplishments.

During the week, school is my escape. I am always the first one to awake each morning, other than my adoptive father, who leaves at the crack of dawn for work. As soon as I hear the door close as he heads to his factory job, I jump out of bed and get ready for school.

Usually, there is no milk in the house, so I drink my steaming cocoa water, which is flavored by dipping a piece of bread slathered with mayonnaise into the cup. Some mornings, there is no bread in our small cupboard.

Every evening on the way home from work, my father stops at the next-door bakery bread outlet and buys ten loaves of day-old bread for a dollar. How can my family eat so much bread every day? But with two adults and seven children, and having some neighbor kids over, it isn't that much of a surprise.

Those loaves of bread also attract some little critters in the night, such as mice and cockroaches. It isn't unusual to put my hand into a loaf of bread, and my fingers encounter a mouse eating its way through from the backside of the loaf. On those mornings, my appetite takes a sharp nosedive. My mind conjures up all sorts of diseases if I eat that bread, not to mention mice poop and cockroach droppings.

> I have been young and now am old; Yet have I not seen the righteous forsaken, nor his seed begging bread. (Psalm 37:25 ASV)

Each morning while it is still dark outside, I make my three-mile walk to school around six o'clock. On good days, I look forward to a nice, hot school meal at lunchtime. However, the school day drags by during those time I don't have any money to pay for lunch. On those days, I sit alone in an empty classroom during lunchtime. My stomach aches as I sit there breathing in the wonderful smells wafting my way from the cafeteria below.

"Laugh and the world laughs with you. Cry and you cry alone." My accounting teacher will sometimes look at me during class and quote this saying as he walks by my desk. I like to be recognized for my achievements. I work extremely hard to earn the respect of my teachers. I will never forget the first time I made a 100 percent on an exceedingly difficult accounting exam. My accounting teacher pauses at my desk as he hands me my exam. "I always knew you had it in you," he says.

I believe this man had an influence on my life that led to my becoming who I would eventually be.

As I look back, I see the incredible ways God used so many individuals to impact my life. Even during the most difficult times, we go through trials and testing to eventually be a blessing to others. "Praise be to the God and Father of our Lord Jesus Christ, the Father of compassion and the God of all comfort, who comforts us in all our troubles, so that we can comfort those in any trouble with the comfort we ourselves receive from God" (2 Corinthians 1:3–4 NIV).

Even during those hungry days at school, I knew that my hunger for being accepted was being fulfilled during school hours. This, too, was a time in my life in which I was learning a life lesson that would shape my life forever. God was preparing the younger me to become the future educator He desired me to be.

My mother prepares a meal for us each night. She enjoys eating and prepares large evening meals of meat and potatoes for the family. Our meat often consists of wild game. My adoptive father's love of hunting and fishing—deer, rabbit, squirrel, fish—makes for some interesting meals at our house. Then there are the times he brings home an abundance of meat from the family farm. He helps his mother slaughter the cows, pigs, and chickens she raises on her fifty-acre farm. No matter how much food my mother prepares for the evening meal, there are never any leftovers to make sandwiches for the following day. We always have extra people and kids in our neighborhood and tenement building partaking of the evening meal with us.

Those early times of going without food during school hours lead me at the age of fourteen to take a job during the summers on a tobacco farm. Every morning, I board the farm bus to begin the journey to an assigned tobacco farm. The bus is crowded with the faces of tenement kids from my neighborhood. We are bused across the state line into Connecticut to begin our hot and grueling days of work. The days under those tents are excruciating, with the hot sun boiling down upon us.

I end up with tobacco poisoning on my hands and arms, which results in boils and swollen, oozy skin, but I need to work. My summer job means having lunches at school all year and some nice clothes to wear. I have to buy my own lunch each week while working on those farms.

I cash my check each week and sock my money away in my bedroom drawer. Each day, I take out just enough money to buy lunch the next day. This system works for a while. Every evening, the work bus drops us off after a typical twelve-hour workday. Exhausted, I rush home to clean the tobacco grime and dirt off my face and body. Then I walk to the little market nearby to do my food shopping for the next day.

But one day, everything changes. It is early in the week, and enough money is put aside for the entire week, as always. I reach into my bedroom drawer for my stash of money, which I keep hidden under my clothes. I feel nothing. I panic as I remove all my clothes to discover an empty space where my money is kept. The money is gone. I begin to cry. What am I going to do? Where has my money gone?

Out of the corner of my eye, I spot my mother standing behind the curtain outside my bedroom. This curtain serves as my bedroom door. From the look on her face, I know she has taken my money. She denies it, but I know it to be so. My mother is not a very good money manager. When it comes to money, she has no idea how to budget.

We are living in a six-floor tenement in the city because our home in the suburbs has been foreclosed. The utility company has placed a quarter meter outside our apartment because my mother failed to pay the electric bill. When the lights go out, we have to place a quarter in the meter if we want electricity. Most of the families in the six-story tenement building struggle to pay the bills and put food on the table. Yet the men somehow find the money to buy alcohol.

Money and my mother are not compatible. My adoptive father often goes to work with sandwiches slathered with nothing but butter, yet he never complains much. But I do know that he puts aside a little money in the bank from his paycheck each week. His practice of saving is a lesson learned after he failed to insure our first home. Our first house was totally destroyed in a fire on Christmas Eve when I was four years old. Our second house was foreclosed three years later when my mother spent the mortgage payments on other things.

After my money comes up missing, I open my very first checking account the next week. The missing money taught me to be fiscally responsible. What was meant for wrong turned out to be a blessing, teaching me a lesson that has lasted a lifetime. The time of working on that tobacco farm teaches me the value of work habits and a determination to pursue life's goals. During that time, I also realize I do not want to see others go hungry. Even though I save up enough lunch money for my lunches all year, I withdraw just enough savings to cover my expenses each week.

I still find myself not eating at school two times a week. There is a girl in my neighborhood who begins walking to school with me. I learn that she never has any money for lunch and goes hungry every day. At first, she asks me if she can borrow enough money for lunch one day. She promises to pay it back but never does repay me the money I loan her. Soon, I realize she cannot repay me. I could just stop loaning her money for lunch. However, I know what it is like to be hungry at school, so I come up with a plan. I give her money to eat two days a week, and I eat three days a week. I never see her again after that first year. Eventually, I learn from some kids at school that she has dropped out.

I wish I had been wiser with some other choices I made in life on a personal level. How could I have failed to follow God's will rather than my own in areas of willful rebellion, impatience, and a wayward heart? I sought acceptance and approval from others but not God. I believed in God but did not have a relationship with God. Yet, even as I look back on a gift I received one Christmas; I believe God was giving me a glimpse of what my future would be like someday. God believed in me and saw something in me that was worth saving.

> And God is able to make all grace abound to you, so that in all things at all times, having all that you need, you will abound in every good work. As it is written, He has scattered abroad his gifts to the poor, his righteousness endures forever. Now he who supplies seed to the

slower and bread for food will also supply and increase your store of seed and will enlarge the harvest of your righteousness. You will be made rich in every way so that you can be generous on every occasion, and through us your generosity will result in Thanksgiving to God. (2 Corinthians 9:8–11 NIV)

Christmases at my house are sparse in terms of presents. With one sister and five brothers, our parents struggle to provide each of us with a gift. I usually get a new nightgown for Christmas. But this year, we receive presents from our local parish. I will always remember this Christmas. I receive a beautiful red sweater, a gorgeous, red-and-black, pleated wool skirt, black tights, and a pretty red necklace. The outfit is beyond anything I have ever worn. I can't explain it, but my feelings each time I look at this outfit or wear it are beyond materialistic.

Years later, the memories of this Christmas will come flooding back to me. God was telling me something. I went on to earn a doctorate from a state university with a red logo the color of that sweater. I later became an assistant vice president at a leading research university with a black-and-red logo the color of that pleated wool skirt. One may say it is mere coincidence. I choose to believe that even then my path was being laid by the One who saw me before I was born and to whom I would bring glory. I was not a mistake. I was not a sin child. I was God's child, and He sent His angels to watch over me, even when I did not deserve His mercy, love, and grace. He loved me just as I was, right where I was.

Now to him who is able to do immeasurably more than all we ask or imagine, according to his power that is at work within us. (Ephesians 3:20 NIV)

"For I know the plans, I have for you," declares the LORD, "plans to prosper you and not to harm you, plans to give you hope and a future" (Jeremiah 29:11 NIV)

7

Nick

Eliza
May 2003

When I am not in class, I am busy working one of several jobs. Since my major is broadcast journalism, I thought that it would be beneficial for me to get some experience while on campus, so I applied for and was hired as the Arts and Entertainment editor for the university newspaper. I've also been asked to host a weekly segment reporting on higher education news for the university news station. My other on-campus job is working as an assistant at the teaching center in Crusader University, which is run by my mother. I assist teachers in need of technical help, with photocopying, or who need to leave messages for my mother, who is usually held up in meetings.

On my off days from school, I drive roughly one hundred miles round-trip to work at a day spa (also owned by Mom), where I wrap people up like mummies in a mineral mixture, with the goal of eliminating toxins and inches. I know what this sounds like—entitled and nepotistic. However, I can assure you that while it is my mom who got me two of my four jobs, working for her is not easy. She is a tough businesswoman who expects me to be professional in all things. If anything, I think she is harder on me than she is on any of her other employees, as she expects great things of me.

Most days, I feel as if I fall entirely short of great things. My focus is scattered. I have three roommates who party until the early-morning hours and can't seem to understand why I would ever *want* to be at work by 9:00 a.m.

I've also recently broken up with my fiancé, a man I had been living with. I came to realize that it would never work out long-term.

And now I am keeping a huge secret from the one person who will see this secret as a flat-out lie. My mother.

The week after breaking off my engagement, Nick began making the rounds to my office more frequently.

Nick is a professor at Crusader University. I've known him since I was sixteen years old, having been the chaperone of choice for my mother to the university holiday parties. But we never connected on more than superficial greetings during the holidays. It was while working on campus that Nick and I got the chance to talk on a frequent basis. He noticed that I was the new assistant in the center, and since then, he's been coming in nearly every day. At first, he would ask me to help him with the copier or to look up some information for him. But eventually, these visits turned into just visits, with no apparent purpose apart from chatting with me.

During one such visit, we started talking about cars. I drive a silver Honda Civic hatchback, and he mentioned that was no kind of car for a beautiful girl to drive. I didn't know about beautiful girls, but I kind of loved my Civic. It was small and cute and got me from point A to B and never broke down.

Nick was considering selling his car and asked if I wanted to see it. He said he would give me a good deal on it. I said, "Sure," and after my workday was over, I went to the parking garage with him to take a look. It was a white convertible, and like many other twenty-something girls, I thought having a convertible would be *super cool*.

"Why don't we go get a beer?" Nick asks as I sit in the driver's seat of the convertible.

"I can't. I have plans." I think of the Italian student who works as a photographer at the university paper with me. We've gone on a few dates here and there, and while it has never been super romantic, we do enjoy each other's company. (Enjoying each other's company means we hang out, get coffee, listen to music, I listen to his accent, and then we have sex. It wasn't love, but it was fun.)

"What are your plans?" Nick asks.

"I'm going out with a friend around six." I look at my watch. It is just after three.

"We have time. Just one beer." Nick keeps a respectable distance. "We can talk about the car. You want it, right?"

I hesitate. There is a slight alert sensor going off in my brain. I push the feeling to the side. I don't know exactly how old Nick is, but it's obvious that he's substantially older. Nick has kids close to my age and at one point even tried to get me to go out with his oldest son who attends university with me. There is no way he's trying to hit on me. He used to work for my mother when she was the department chair of the School of Business, and now he is just trying to win brownie points by being nice to me.

"Come on," he insists again. "You have time. It's just one beer. I promise."

"OK, fine," I relent. "Just up the street at Carmel Hill. I'll meet you there."

I get out of the driver's seat and hand Nick his keys. I stride away toward the direction of my Civic, parked one floor below.

Carmel Hill is a steakhouse on the hill next to the university. It has an upper crust feel and appeals to the university professors because of its proximity to campus and its decent menu. They have a bar area that looks out onto the freeway, which is where we decide to sit. Nick orders two Sam Adams, without asking me what my preference is.

As we sip the beer, I try to keep the conversation around the car. Nick has other ideas. He asks about my classes and the work I am doing on the school newspaper. I tell him about being the Arts and Entertainment editor, which allows me to attend several movie screenings and roundtable interviews with famous actors and directors. I tell him about meeting Billy Crystal and Robin Williams and how genuinely kind they were. He seems interested in this and asks me about other actors I have met and who my favorites are. He tells me about growing up in Iran and how he loves music and dancing.

At one point, I get up to go to the bathroom, and when I return, there is a fresh beer waiting for me. I call him on it and tell him that I can't stay for another because I need to leave in order to meet my date in time. He pushes and says, "It's only one more," and promises, "We will definitely go after this one."

Around five o'clock, I tell him I absolutely have to go. It is then that he reaches across the table and grabs my hand. I look up at him, my head starting to pound. The first thing I think is, *I hope he doesn't mean it as a come-on.*

I quickly remove my hand from underneath his, grab my purse, and stand up. "I really have to go," I say.

"No problem. Let me walk you out."

We walk out into the bright sunlight. I dig my sunglasses out of my purse, and as I do, Nick takes my arm and spins me around to face him. The motion causes several items to fall out of my purse. He pushes me up against the door of my car and plants an open-mouthed kiss on me. I am in shock. He doesn't stop, even though my mouth remains closed.

After a few seconds of this, he pulls away.

"I'm sorry," he says. "I just can't help myself."

I don't know what to say. Here is a man I've known since I was a teenager, who worked for my mother, who is substantially older than I am. I can't think of words to say, so I just look at him.

He seems to be drunk off of two beers. His face is flushed, and he's giggling.

To break the awkwardness, I say, "It's fine. I, uh … have to fight the traffic," sweeping my hand in the direction of the freeway.

"OK, gorgeous." He places his hand on the side of my face. "I'd like to take you to lunch tomorrow. Can we?"

He is still pressing up against me, preventing me from getting into my car.

The next day is Saturday, and I could make up any number of excuses why I can't meet. My brain, on the other hand, can't frame a single excuse into words, so I agree to meet. "Sure, lunch sounds good."

Satisfied with my response, he backs away. I jump into my car, give a weak wave, and drive off in a stunned haze.

I make it back to my place at 6:45 p.m. LA traffic is horrific on a good day, and by the time I get home, my date has come and gone. I call him and apologize, but my head is still reeling from my encounter with Nick. My date is angry, after driving an hour in traffic and finding me not at home.

He's now driven another hour back. I apologize again and head off to bed early, where I lie there staring at the ceiling and thinking of what I should have done. I should have pushed away. I should have told him I wasn't interested. I should have covered my head. I finally drift off to the sounds of my roommates hammering and sawing on something in the backyard.

On Saturday, Nick calls me at nine thirty in the morning. I tell him I don't feel like going out. Nick insists.

"Come on. It's Saturday, and I'm going to take you for some Iranian food. It's so good, and I've already made a reservation. You have to come," he says.

Lunch turns into dinner. That dinner leads to a movie, which leads to wine tasting, which leads to more dinners. Within a very short period, we are officially a couple. The caveat is we are a couple that few others know about.

I've tried to explain how I allowed myself to be romanced by a man nineteen years my senior. This does not make sense to a lot of people. I get that. I have no defense, other than to say that I am an adult. I am fresh out of a horrible relationship with a man who did not respect me, and suddenly there is this older man who pays attention to me, gives me compliments, and lavishes gifts and fancy meals upon me. I am besotted.

Because of Nick's position as my mother's former employee, I am afraid to tell her about our relationship. This is horrible because my mother and I are incredibly close.

I've been lying to her about who I'm involved with, but a weekend trip to Las Vegas will force the truth to come out.

Since I am in charge of the entertainment reviews for the university newspaper, I often get invites to events such as movie screenings and art shows—and on this particular occasion, a trip to Las Vegas. I've been invited by Harrah's to come out and see local Vegas celebrity Clint Holmes's new show and interview him after.

I invite Nick to go with me, and we drive from LA to Vegas on the third weekend of July. If you've never been to Vegas in July, it's incredibly hot—like walking on the surface of the sun type of hot. This weekend was no exception. The car overheated on the way to Sin City, but Nick and I made the best of it. Because of the heat, all I felt like drinking was water and Gatorade.

On Saturday night, we see Clint Holmes perform, a fantastic show that highlights his career and his family life. At one point, Clint introduces a surprise guest in the audience, his mother, who at one time was an opera singer. She stands and gives an emotional performance of "Summertime." I am deeply touched by the stories and the bond he has with his mother, and I am moved to tears.

After the show, we are directed backstage to meet Clint. I am nervous and emotional. I tell Clint how much it meant to see his mother on stage with him and tell him through tears how great it was to hear her sing.

Once the interview is over, I feel immediately embarrassed. *Why was I crying?* I have done at least a hundred interviews with celebrities at this point. I even met Al Pacino and didn't blubber a bit. To take the edge off, I order a cocktail but feel nauseous immediately after drinking a few sips. I blame it on the Vegas heat and tell Nick that I am only drinking water for the rest of the trip.

The next day, we pull onto the freeway to head back toward Los Angeles. While sitting in the passenger seat, I become ragingly nauseous. I make Nick pull over at the closest stop, an Arby's restaurant. I jump out of the car, run to the bathroom, and throw up. Once I am done vomiting, I walk out of the bathroom and order a large roast beef sandwich with curly fries and a Diet Dr. Pepper.

Nick stares at me as I walk back to the car, carrying my bag of food. "Are you OK?"

"Weirdest thing," I say, tossing a fry into my mouth. "I threw up, then got hungry. Oh, and I think I should drive. Your driving is making me carsick."

"OK, but I think your driving is worse than mine," he says, staring at me as he walks to the passenger side.

"Yeah, right," I reply and make a sweeping motion with my hand toward the desert landscape. "How could anyone live here? It's so hot!" I say, turning the air-conditioner on high and pointing the vent at my face.

"You're sure you're OK?" Nick asks. His eyes narrow as he watches me shove a handful of fries into my mouth.

I give him a look and shrug. "Yeah, I guess it was just car sickness."

"You get that a lot?"

I think as I chew. "No. Huh, as a matter of fact, this is the first time I've ever been carsick. Must be the heat. Or your driving."

We pull onto the freeway, and I finish my meal. About an hour later, while Nick looks through one of his notebooks (he keeps these little notebooks that have phone numbers and random notes inside of them. At any given time, he has two to three of these notebooks in his bag and consults them frequently.) I suddenly have a rather curious thought.

"Hey, Nick?" I say.

"Hmm?"

"You don't think …" I pause, trying to choose my words carefully. "That I'm, like, pregnant. Do you?"

Nick jerks his head toward me. "No way."

"You sure? Because I was just thinking. I got really sick but was immediately hungry. And I never get carsick. Like *ever*."

"There's no way, Eliza," Nick says, looking at me with a smirk.

Nick previously mentioned that he'd had a vasectomy years earlier, after the birth of his third child. whom he had with his ex-wife. The chances of a vasectomy not working were slim.

"OK, I'm just wondering if I should check," I say.

"It's not possible unless you slept with someone else." His gaze is on me, intense and questioning.

"You know I haven't," I insist.

I haven't been intimately involved in that way with anyone since Nick and I started spending all of our time together, almost two months ago. I can tell he is irritated by the conversation, so I drop the issue. I also make a mental note to get a pregnancy test at the university clinic first thing Monday morning.

What do I feel God was teaching me in this season? I believe he was teaching me about the dragon hiding in my desires. My desire to be loved, to be taken care of, to have comfort, and, yes, one of the fiercest dragons of all, my desire to have sex. The temptations I was facing, the sexual relationship with a man who was nearly two decades my senior, overtook me. I knew that I shouldn't, but I wasn't thinking beyond the immediate feelings I was facing. Genesis 4:7 speaks of "sin crouching at the door. It desires to have you, but you must rule over it." It took me many years to come to terms with this idea, that sin is like a wild beast crouching at the door, waiting to pounce.

8

Pee and Mortadella

Eliza
July 2003

I find out about my pregnancy during a break between my morning and afternoon classes.

Typically, after class, I head over to the *University Times* newsroom to either check my mail or hang out and chat with friends, the cool and dimly lit office giving a welcome reprieve from the orange fluorescent glow of the campus hallways. But today, I have other plans. I walk across campus to the health office. I have never been to the health office before, so I am surprised to see that it truly resembles a doctor's office. I give them my student ID and take a seat in the waiting area. I look around, trying to figure out if any of the other girls are waiting there for the same reason I am.

After filling out the required forms, I am given a small, clear plastic cup.

"You don't need to fill it up; we just need about a tablespoon worth," the nurse says, directing me to the bathroom down the hall.

I clean off the seat, sit down, and place the cup under me. How much is a tablespoon of pee?

Once I finish, I place the cup inside a cubby-like shelf that is accessed via a sliding door from inside the bathroom. Whatever the result, yes or no, I'm ready to know. About thirty minutes and one pregnancy test later, I am called into a private cubicle-sized office.

"Well, honey. You are pregnant." The nurse looks at me with concern.

I smile.

She stares at me for a moment. "So, I assume since you're smiling, this is good news?"

In that moment, all I feel is happiness. "Yeah, it is. I didn't expect it, but yeah. Good news," I say, instinctively touching my belly.

The nurse raises her eyebrows. "All right then. I'm happy you're happy." She hands me the paper that shows the positive test outcome. "You might want this. You have a doctor?"

"Not yet."

"I suggest you get one. Any idea how far along you are?"

In my head, I do some quick menstrual math. Did I have my period last month? I know I had it in May, but what about June? "You know, I'm not sure. Maybe a month?"

"Get a doctor. There are clinics you can go to."

After high school, I was disillusioned by the prospect of college. I'd taken a year and a half off after high school and had worked temp jobs for extra money. As an educator, my mother was less than thrilled.

"You need to go to school, Eliza, my mom would say. "You need to take care of yourself. Don't rely on someone else to take care of you. You need school."

"Mom. It's fine. I don't even have a clue about what I want to go to school for," I would reply.

"So, you go to community college and figure it out."

So, I did. I went to Orange College and took classes that would transfer over to a university, and I took some that were just killing time. I joined the rowing team and found out how strong my body could be. My coach once told me that I was the one who brought the aggression to the boat, forcing the other girls in the skull to fight through the pain and go for the win. With every stroke, I would grunt as the oar drove a cut through the water as we'd row through our patch of sea in Newport Beach. After two years and taking every class I could, I got into Crusader University.

I'd wanted NYU but couldn't afford it and didn't have the grades to get in. So, Crusader it was.

That was four years ago, and now at twenty-five years old, I am still in school, no longer covered by my parents' insurance, and pregnant. That terrifies me, but I figure I'll either get another job to pay for private insurance or go to a clinic. It isn't the end of the world.

I am the poster child for naivete.

Walking out of the clinic, I stare at the paper in my hand. Under my name and student ID number, it reads:

Pregnant: Positive

Nick is just getting out of his first class of the day. He has a short break until his office hours. I dig my phone out of my backpack and dial his cell.

He picks it up on the first ring.

"Hey there." His voice is low, almost a whisper.

"Hey …" I can tell he's not alone and wonder if he's with a student. I also realize I have no clue what to say and don't want to tell him this news over the phone. "Can you meet me, really quick?"

There is a short pause as he considers my request. "Sure. Are you OK?"

I laugh. "Am I OK? Uhm … yeah. I just need to talk to you."

"OK. I'll meet you at the coffee cart."

"Sounds good. I'll grab a table."

I have about ten minutes to rehearse what I am going to tell him. It crosses my mind that he might not believe this is his kid, considering he had a vasectomy and will essentially say the same thing he said on the way back from Vegas. I shrug it off. If he doesn't believe that this is his kid, we can get a paternity test. The thought of him denying that this is his child makes me a bit angry. I am still riding high on this anger when he strolls up to the table.

"Hey. How are you?" he asks, keeping a respectful distance.

We are always a bit formal while on university grounds. The thought of another teacher or student seeing us together can cause a stir that neither of us is prepared for. I realize that in a few short months, I won't be able to hide anything.

I smile at him and slide the paper across the table. He examines it as if he is grading a term paper.

"Oh, wow." He massages his jawline and stares at me.

"Yup. Wow." I bite my lip, like I always do when I am nervous.

"Are you hungry?" He asks, looking back at the coffee cart. "Want a mortadella sandwich?"

My eyes are wide. "That's it?"

"What?"

"That's all you have to say. I'm pregnant." The words come out as a hissed whisper.

"I know," he says calmly.

"And you want to know if I want a sandwich?"

"I thought you might be hungry," he says, pulling his wallet from his pocket.

"Well, I am hungry." I steal a glance at the line, making sure no one is overhearing our conversation. "But I want to know what you're thinking."

"Listen, we can't really talk about this here. I want to hug you, and we can't do that. Can you come over? We'll talk tonight?"

I look around again. The campus is packed, as per usual for a Monday afternoon. This obviously isn't the place for a heart-to-heart.

Nodding my head, I agree. We split the sandwich and sit in silence for the ten minutes it takes to finish it.

9

Do We, or Don't We?

Eliza

This wasn't how I expected this night would go. I knew it wouldn't be exactly like the movies, where the mother-to-be shows the expectant father the pregnancy test—the two lines marking out a specific moment in time where there is a positive charge in the air, and the future is filled with thoughts of baby coos, baby cuddles, and baby socks (they're so tiny!).

I am old enough to decipher fantasy from reality, but I didn't expect to end up crying on the bathroom floor of my lover's home.

"Eliza. We need to figure this out," Nick says through the painted white bathroom door.

"You want me to give it up. I can't even believe you," I say through sobs.

"I just think we need to look at all of our options," Nick says, his reply muffled by the closed door.

I pull myself up off the floor and splash cold water on my face. My cheeks are blotchy, and my eyes are rimmed with red. My fingertips lightly caress my stomach. It is relatively flat now, but in a couple of months, it will be hard to hide.

"Eliza, please open the door."

"I can't believe you," I repeat.

Nick lets out an audible sigh. "Eliza, all I'm saying is I think we should talk about this. Please open the door and talk to me."

I blow my nose and open the door. Nick's frame fills the small doorway.

"Hi," he says, reaching out for me.

I nudge his hand away and push past him to sit on the couch.

"Let's talk," I say.

Nick gives another sigh and sits next to me.

"Boosie," he says, using his nickname for me. *Boos* means kiss in Farsi and is pronounced like *loose*.

I stare at him, saying nothing.

"Listen, please. Can you do that?"

I shrug my shoulders.

"It's not that I don't want this baby. It's just that it's a surprise."

"Well, yeah!" I exclaim. "I'm just as surprised as you are. And before you even think to say it, this baby is yours. It *has* to be. I haven't been with anyone else since we started dating."

"Did they say how far along?" he asks.

"I won't know for sure until I can see a doctor."

"OK." He reaches out to take my hand, and this time I let him. "You want to have it?"

I nod, and as I do, I feel the tears begin to start again.

"OK. Then we will have it." He says it so casually, as if he were agreeing to adopt a kitten. He kisses my hand, then my forehead. "We will have this baby, and it will be beautiful, like you."

"Are you sure?" I ask through tears. "Really sure?"

"Yes. I know I want you, so I also want this baby." He pulls me into his chest. "Our baby."

"This is kind of insane, right? I mean, how did this even happen?" I ask.

He stares at me blankly.

"I just always thought vasectomies meant that, you know …" I make a small scissor motion with two fingers. "Snip and that's it."

Nick pushes out a small laugh. "I've been reading about it, and I guess sometimes vasectomies just don't take."

"So strange," I say, studying his face.

"Mm-hmm," he replies.

10

Like Mother, Like Daughter

Anna
1964–1965

For over a year, I am able to carry out my little charade and keep my mother from learning the truth about where I really go every Saturday evening. That is, until I meet this charming airman who is quite handsome with a contagious smile. He looks like a cross between Elvis Presley and Jimmy Dean. When I learn that he is a southerner and a Protestant, those facts really pique my interest. Yes! This airman fits the bill perfectly. He is someone my mother will not approve of me dating.

This young airman is not exactly my type. He is not that great a dancer; we spend more time talking than dancing. However, he does not hesitate to let me know just how interested he is in me. There is an immediate sexual attraction to him, but I am not about to end up like my mother. In a way, my playing hard to get makes me even more desirable to him. In the beginning, I have no interest in getting seriously involved with anyone. I am young, and I want to have fun—which means going to dances and partying. But dating him will upset my mother. I figure if she wants to keep secrets about my biological father, then I can keep my own secrets.

He who plots evil will be known as a schemer. (Proverbs 24:8 NIV)

For a while, I keep our dating a secret. Then quite by accident, my mother discovers where I am going every Saturday. The easiest way for me to walk to the Air Force base leads me past my uncle's house, my mother's brother. This uncle lives less than a mile from the base. I am usually incredibly careful as I pass by his house. I always walk on the other side of the road and duck behind the trees whenever possible. But this one evening, the entire family is standing in the front yard as I pass by very quickly. The trees obviously do not camouflage me well enough. They call my name, but I keep walking. I hope my ignoring them makes them think they are mistaken as to who they think they saw walking by their house. But word quickly gets back to my mother anyway. My uncle wastes no time in asking my mother if she is aware that I attend the dances at the Air Force base.

Wash and make yourselves clean. Take your evil deeds out of my sight! Stop doing wrong. (Isaiah 1:16 NIV)

The confrontational scene with my mother about my disobeying her is brutal. She screams at me and calls me all kinds of ugly names. I strike back at her with accusations about her own past. I threaten to run away or even worse—unless she lets me date this airman. In the end, she relents and agrees for me to date him. She lays down the rules for my seeing this young airman. I can see him only at our house and in her presence. This arrangement works for a while because I agree to my mother's greatest desire. My seeing him means I stop attending the dances at the airbase.

Turn away from evil and do good, seek peace and pursue it. (Psalm 34:14 NIV)

Get rid of all bitterness, rage, and anger, brawling and slander, along with every form of malice. Be kind and compassionate to one another, forgiving each other, just as in Christ God forgave you. (Ephesians 4:31–32 NIV)

However, things are about to escalate again when this young airman proposes to me right after my sixteenth birthday. His surprise proposal makes my mother livid. I expect her to demand that I stop seeing this young man. To my amazement, my mother does not try to break us up directly. She tries to get other friends, family, and neighbors to talk me out of my plan to marry this guy. Her sneaky attack strategy only fuels my anger and rebellion. I am determined to marry him before my eighteenth birthday unless my mother promises me something in return. There is only one way I will give her what she wants, and that is her telling me the truth, the whole truth, about my biological father.

> Do not say, "I'll pay you back for this wrong!" Wait for the LORD, and he will deliver you. (Proverbs 20:22 NIV)

> Do not say, "I'll do to him as he has done to me; I'll pay that man back for what he did." (Proverbs 24:29 NIV)

> Make sure that nobody pays back wrong for wrong, but always try to be kind to each other and to everyone else. (1 Thessalonians 5:15 NIV)

I tell my mother that I will not marry my young airman on one condition—if she tells me all about my biological father, I will break off the engagement. My mother refuses to reveal anything. So I tell her I want to get married before I turn eighteen. After many threats back and forth, my mother relents and signs for me to get married. His parents, too, must consent for him to marry since he is not of legal age either.

So begins our journey in planning our wedding. We participate in marriage counseling sessions with my local parish priest. My young future husband and I go shopping together to find me the perfect wedding dress. Looking back, it is so ironic that it is him and not my mother who shopped for my wedding dress with me. He buys the gown for me off a sales rack at a local department store.

Three months before my eighteenth birthday, we are married in the Catholic church. My parents give us a nice little reception at a small reception hall in a nearby town, attended by my family and our friends. After the wedding, we head south to meet his family.

I have never been out of the Northeast before, so the trip is a real adventure and quite a culture shock. I see a sign posted at a laundry window that reads "Whites only." This wording comes as a shock to me; I am confused as to where everyone washes their colored clothes. This is the mid-sixties, and racism is foreign to me when it relates to people's skin color. I have grown up with a mother who is adamant about my not having anything to do with the Irish and Polish, which I have never heeded.

I am so relieved to be on my own and begin my new life. I long for my independence and freedom. No longer do I have to live with a mother who calls me her sin child when no one else is around. But life is about to take me on a journey I would never wish on anyone. Just as I convince myself that I am now free to live my life on my terms, I am about to fall flat on my face. That part in the marriage vows, "For better or worse …"

What is about to happen in my marriage is partly due to my own rebellion and disobedience. So many signs were there regarding my relationship with my young airman, even before we married. Because I was so lost and focused on getting revenge, I chose to ignore the danger signs.

So, if you think you are standing firm, be careful that you don't fall. (1 Corinthians 10:12 NIV)

All I did was change my residence, but my heart is still hard and bitter. The so-called victory of my revenge is about to leave me crushed and broken. Even in the midst of my anger and bitterness, God was there warning me and trying to redirect my path, but I refused to listen. God gives us free choice, and, as Eve in the Garden of Eden, I desired to feast on what would bring me chaos and even more heartache.

Above all else, guard your heart, for everything you do flows from it. (Proverbs 4:23 NIV)

It would be years before I would come across the following verse, which allowed me to embrace the realization that I was not anyone's sin child but a child of God.

You made all the delicate, inner parts of my body and knit me together in my mother's womb. Thank you for making me so wonderfully complex! Your workmanship is marvelous—and how well I know it. You watched me as I was being formed in utter seclusion, as I was woven together in the dark of the womb. You saw me before I was born. Every day of my life was recorded in your book. Every moment was laid out before a single day had passed. (Psalm 139:13–16 NLT)

11

Wedding Bells and Hamburgers

Eliza
July 2003

Nick convinces me that the best idea is to get married in order to obtain health insurance to cover the baby. I am afraid of the stories he's been telling me about Medi-Cal and going through the motions of being pregnant without the safety net of a large insurance corporation under me, so I consent to marry him immediately. He buys me a two-carat diamond ring from a friend of his who works in the Diamond District in Los Angeles. The ring makes me feel secure and wanted. I know how this sounds to an outsider (gold digger), but it means a commitment to our marriage and our new family and shows me that Nick is in it for real.

And, truth be told, the engagement and pregnancy are a temporary distraction from a huge issue that I have yet to face.

I want to tell my mother the truth about my relationship with Nick. I've rehearsed what I want to say to her many times, but I am finding it incredibly difficult because not only is he so much older than me, but she is his former boss.

The clock runs out for me to come clean when an overzealous gossip divulges the information to her. She confronts me about it over the phone.

"Are you crazy?" she yells. "He's an old man! We're practically the same age!"

I go completely silent; my brain has lost the ability to form complete thoughts.

"Eliza, you have to end this. He could be fired for dating a student."
The thought of this finally frees my ability to speak. "Mom, I was never his student."

"It might not matter! I am so angry at the both of you. How could you even do this? Were you not thinking?" Without waiting for an answer, she adds, "I know what he was thinking. That he'd get this young thing. It makes me sick. You need to end this now."
"Mom, I ..." I want to tell her about the baby and the engagement, but I'm scared.
"I can't see you right now. I'm sorry, but this is just too much," she says. "I'm so embarrassed! My daughter is sleeping with faculty. I can't believe you." She hangs up.
I don't hear from her for a week, after I call her to confront her about giving my now changed phone number to my ex-fiancé. When my ex called from a number I didn't recognize, I picked up and listened to five minutes of self-righteous indignation about how he expects me to come crawling back to him. When I hang up the phone, I'm incensed. Then I call my Mom.
"Why would you give him my new number, Mom?" I ask.
"Because you need someone to tell you that you're making a huge mistake, and since you won't listen to me, I thought you might listen to him."
"Mom, that was totally wrong. I changed my number because of him, and now he has it! What are you thinking?"
"I could ask the same of you!" she yells into the phone. "Eliza, you keep making ridiculous mistakes, and now this? Are you out of your mind?"
"It's my life! Just let me live it!" I yell.
"You want to live your life? Fine. Go ahead, but I won't be here to watch. Good luck."
"What does that mean?" I ask.
"You're on your own." She hangs up.
Now she refuses to talk to me or have anything to do with Nick or me.

She doesn't know about my pregnancy. I haven't summoned the courage to drop yet another massive bomb on her, and now she isn't speaking to me.

The clock is ticking on the pregnancy, and Nick and I have decided to get married soon so that I can get on his insurance.

Soon means we will be married in a courthouse in California the same week I find out about the pregnancy. It isn't the ideal setting for a wedding, and I cry in the bathroom. While sobbing in the bathroom, I see what I feel is a bad omen. As I open the door to the first toilet stall, it is smeared with drying blood. It looks like a crime scene, and I back away, horrified.

After a few minutes, I muster the courage to locate Nick in the courthouse and do what we came here to do. I dry my tears, and we say our vows. We pledge to love and support each other for a lifetime, and once the ceremony is through (a total of ten minutes), we are back in the car, headed to our now marital home.

The sun is extremely bright, one of those gorgeous Southern California summer days. I look lovingly at Nick, studying his face as he drives.

Nick turns to look at me for a moment and gives a quick smile. "Listen, you'll probably want to take that off for now." He grabs my hand and gives my wedding ring a jiggle.

I'm confused. "What do you mean?"

"Just put it in your purse for now. My daughter is coming over, and I don't want her to see it."

I pull my hand away from his and look down at the ring. It's a gorgeous square-cut diamond, and it gives off a blinding sparkle every time the sun hits it. "Don't you want to tell her the truth?" I ask.

"Boos. Don't be difficult." He sighs deeply and turns into the drive-through for Jack in the Box. "I'll get you a cheeseburger. You'll feel better after you eat something."

I hesitantly twist the ring from my finger and place it in my purse. I reach for my sunglasses and put them on, hoping they will hide the shame that I now feel about this marriage. My thoughts begin to race, and I wonder how long I'll be expected to hide the news of our nuptials.

12

The Reception

Eliza
September 2003

Our official wedding reception was held at one of the nicest Persian restaurants in Orange County. There were buffet tables of delicious Iranian food, an open bar, and a DJ, who had been instructed to play a mix of Persian and American songs for our mixed audience of Persian and American guests. At the end of the evening, when one of my friends commented about the music, I realized that the DJ only played Persian music the entire night, because Nick told him that nobody wanted to hear the American songs. Out of the ninety-six people at our party, only sixteen were my friends and family. Nobody at the reception knew about my pregnancy outside of those sixteen people. My father, who hadn't really been a strong part of my life for many years, was there, having split up from his second wife. My brother and his fiancée were there, as were my sister and brother-in-law. My cousin and his girlfriend had flown into California from Massachusetts for the occasion. I'd told them of my pregnancy at the airport, after my cousin who knew me far too well made a statement in jest about this being a shot-gun wedding as we waited by the baggage carousel for his luggage to arrive. The news was met with shock but also with excitement and love.

The one person who was notably absent, by all in attendance, was my mother. She lived a mere twenty minutes away from the location where I stood in an ecru, empire-waisted gown. She hadn't talked to me in two months and had vowed to never speak to me again because of my involvement with Nick.

It wasn't entirely unnoticed that I went the entire day without drinking so much as a glass of champagne. Aside from the obvious absence of my mother, it was the one thing that was commented on the most during the party. As I sipped Diet Coke or water with lemon, I would just smile and say I was "just trying to be good." I was three months pregnant under my wedding gown, but not a soul in Nick's circle of family or friends knew. Following the party, I think they were beginning to get the idea.

Pretty soon, I couldn't contain the fact that my belly was swelling rapidly. None of my jeans fit, and I was wearing sweatpants everywhere. Nick didn't want me to buy maternity clothes and didn't want me to wear them around his kids, because he still hadn't gotten around to telling them the news.

I've been hiding my pregnancy from them for six months. Nick is going to finally tell his children tonight and asks if I would go to the bookstore for a few hours while he breaks the news to them. It feels as if I am hiding out, but in reality, I am glad to not be there. I'm not sure what the reaction will be, and if it is a negative one, it's probably better that I'm not there.

As I leave the house that night, I ask Nick what his plan is for telling his family.

"Are you going to tell them that the baby is three months' premature?" I say with a smirk.

"I mean, they won't ask," he says, his expression completely serious.

"Nick, that's the first thing people ask," I say. "They will want to know how far along I am."

He gives a quick shrug and opens the car door so I can climb in. My belly has begun to pop, and I move the seat back in order to comfortably fit behind the steering wheel. Nick stares at my discomfort and laughs. "They might ask. But I won't tell." He gives me a quick kiss and closes the door.

13

Death of Firstborn

Anna
1966

After we married, my young husband and I began attending church most Sundays. One week, we attended the Catholic church, and the alternating week we attended a small Protestant church. This practice of alternating between the Catholic and Baptist churches went on for quite a few years.

Even as a child growing up, I loved going to church and felt drawn to spending time in a place of worship. I knew even then that there was something special about worship. I went to church even when we lived in predominantly French Catholic neighborhoods, where the sermon was in French and the mass in Latin. From a very young age, I was drawn to the peaceful environment at church.

I remember telling my mother that I wanted to go to the Irish church because the sermon was in English. She adamantly refused my request and threatened me with severe punishment if I disobeyed. As stubborn and rebellious as I could be, I am amazed that I listened to her on that matter. Maybe part of it was that I knew everyone in my predominantly French Catholic neighborhood church.

Even as a young child of five years old, I woke up before dawn each Sunday, dressed myself, and headed off to church alone, regardless of the weather conditions outside. For a short time, we lived in the suburbs, and I went to church with a neighborhood family. When my family moved back to the city, I went to church alone. One would think those early church years would have kept me from becoming the rebellious and vengeful person I was for a time. But church does not make one holy; only by giving our lives to our Lord do we learn to experience joy in our lives. Only by a relationship with our Lord are we made whole. What does the Lord's Prayer say about "Forgive us our trespasses as we forgive those who trespass against us"?

Even then, I believe God was working in my life for what was to come. I stand amazed at the times He protected me and let no harm come to me growing up. All those nights I walked the dark streets alone, beginning at the tender age of three and four years old. Many times, during my family's tragedies later in my life, I asked God why He spared me. Why would He heal and protect me when my life seemed to turn upside down, but not others'? Why had God protected and healed me but allowed my loved ones to suffer?

Job asked God for answers. Job never got his questions answered but came to realize his limitations and stopped quarreling with God. I will never know the answers to my questions until I get to heaven. All I know is that my God is in control, and His ways are perfect. For me, letting go and letting God be the pilot of my life is something I must constantly bring under submission to Him. My one regret is that I did not realize this sooner, to avoid the pain and anguish my thoughts, words, and deeds inflicted upon others during my state of brokenness.

> Can a man be of benefit to God? Can even a wise person benefit him? (Job 22:2 NIV)

The saying that ignorance is bliss pretty much sums up my relationship with my new husband. Looking back over our courtship and marriage, I reflect on the many, many times I either chose to ignore issues or failed to see the obvious signs. The blame is not entirely his to bear. At every point in our courtship, I make choices. One of those choices is to ignore certain obvious signs. I want to be happy for once. I have convinced myself that avoiding any confrontation spares us both from a lot of unhappiness. I allow my own shortcomings to cloud my judgment, and in many ways,

I enter our relationship with plenty of emotional baggage. Our marriage begins with three people in the relationship: my husband, myself, and my mother.

I am so focused on proving to myself that my mother can't hurt me anymore that I am oblivious to what is happening around me. I feel such power in believing that I am in control of when and if I want to communicate with my mother that I isolate myself from other issues brewing in my life. The desire to have complete control regarding my relationship with my mother is delusional at best. I fail to honor the Lord's commandment to "Honor your father and mother, so that you may live long in the land the LORD your God is giving you" (Exodus 20:12 NIV).

In so many ways, I am still a child and not an adult. The verse in Ephesians 4:14 (NIV) sums up how we are to grow up and are not meant to remain as children: "Then we will no longer be infants, tossed back and forth by the waves, and blown here and there by every wind of teaching and by the cunning and craftiness of people in their deceitful scheming."

> Do not be deceived. God cannot be mocked. A man reaps what he sows. (Galatians 6:7 NIV)

> Each one should test his own actions. Then he can take pride in himself without comparing himself to somebody else, for each one should carry his own load. (Galatians 6:4–5 NIV)

God calls us to settle and reconcile our relationships with one another, but during this period of my life, I allow the enemy to harden my heart even more. I am only hurting myself with my anger, and things slowly go from bad to worse. I do not realize it now, but I will look back in regret at the years I threw away and the pain I brought upon my life and others because of my bitter feelings.

> You may tear out your hair in anger, but will that destroy the earth? Will it make the rocks tremble? (Job 18:4 NLT)

> Therefore, if anyone is in Christ, he is a new creation. The old has passed away; behold, the new has come. All this is

from God, who through Christ reconciled us to himself and gave us the ministry of reconciliation. (2 Corinthians 5:17–18 ESV)

When my heart was grieved and my spirit embittered, I was senseless and ignorant; I was a brute beast before you. (Psalm 73:21–22 NIV)

Three months after we are married, I discover I am pregnant with our first child. I am beyond thrilled and make a vow that I will be the loving mother I miss not having for myself. Many family members will be surprised to hear these remarks because, to them, my mother is a loving and generous individual. They never see the side of the woman that makes her strike out at me in anger and bitterness. Never in my wildest dreams could I imagine becoming like her, harboring such anger, bitterness, and agonizing emotional pain in the months ahead. But to be honest, those seeds are already planted in me.

Years later when I become a Christian, I also come to understand that my mother's bitterness is a result of her own pain and hurt in her life. While she never shared the root of that pain, I come to a point where I can forgive her and love her. Once I walk the agonizing emotional path of my own life, I weep for the pain I caused my own mother. All I can do when that time comes is love her and forgive her and ask her to forgive me.

Once again, I am getting ahead of the story of my journey as a soon-to-be young mother.

My pregnancy goes very smoothly, and I breathlessly await the day my baby will be born. The due date comes and goes, but still no baby. *This child is certainly taking its sweet time being born.* Little do I realize that the time is a gift from God to carry this child a little longer in my womb, where it is safe and secure.

After I pass my three-week overdue date, the doctor decides it is best to induce my labor and bring this much-awaited baby into the world. So, on February 2, four days before our first wedding anniversary, I am admitted to the air force base hospital to deliver my baby. The day is agonizingly slow as I am prepped, and the inducement process begins. Nothing seems to work. This baby is simply not ready to be born. Finally, after ten long hours, the doctor states that we will begin the process again tomorrow and start afresh. Well, around nine that night, I begin to go into labor. The nurse comes running into my hospital room and then runs back out to call the doctor. She reappears with a shot for me, and my labor pains eventually subside.

During the evening, I lie in the hospital bed and think about how ironic it is to find myself at the same airbase where it all began, first for my mother and then for me. While we both met our airmen on this very base and attended the same dance hall, things turned out differently. She, as a single mom, gave birth to me in a home for unwed mothers. I am about to bless my husband with our first child in a hospital building across the street from where we first met.

The next day, the process begins again. This time, the labor is intense, and the delivery is not an easy one. As I lie on that delivery table, I can see the sweat on the doctor's brow. He seems to be struggling with the forceps as the baby is birthed. As soon as the baby is born, I can tell by the doctor's and nurses' facial expressions that something is wrong. There is no sound from the baby. I start crying, begging them to tell me something. *Is my baby alive? What is wrong?*

Silence. Long, long periods of silence. Finally, the doctor says the baby is having some initial problems, but he seems to be OK. "You have a boy," he says, without looking directly at me. Something is wrong. I can sense it.

"Is my baby OK?" I try to raise my head off the delivery table to see what is going on in the corner of the room. I want to see what the nurses are doing to my baby.

"Your son needs some oxygen but is stabilized." The doctor refuses to look at me.

Time suddenly seems to spin out of control after that. I am wheeled back to my hospital room. A nurse comes in to say the baby has been placed in an incubator and is being attended to by the medical staff in the nursery. The hours slip by as I wait for more reports on my baby. "When can I see my baby?" I ask the nurses on call.

"Soon" is the reply. I begin to cry and am told I am disturbing the other patients in the room. I look around at the other two women who hold their babies in their arms. I want to know why I can't have my baby. Soon a nurse appears in the room and gives me a shot. The next thing I remember is waking up hours later to be told that my son is experiencing some difficulty.

A priest enters my room to inform me they are giving my son last rites. The hospital staff does not think my son will make it through the night. I cry. I scream. I want my son. *Why, God? I am going to love this child and be a good mother to him. God. Why is this happening?*

> My God, my God, why have you abandoned me? Why are
> you so far away when I groan for help? (Psalm 22:1 NLT)

Then, it seems like God hears my prayers because the next thing I know, I am told my son is stabilized once again. The Air Force hospital is transferring him to an intensive pediatric ward at another hospital in a nearby city. My heart aches for my child. I had only a glimpse of him for a brief moment in the delivery room. My arms ache to hold my son. *God, please let me hold him.*

About then a different priest enters my hospital room and informs me that my son is being given last rites. *What is he saying?* The hospital staff just told me my son is doing better. I start screaming in hysterics. *Why, why is this happening?*

My screaming brings the hospital staff running into my room. They tell me to control myself. Control myself! Where are they taking my son? Have they lied to me? What is this priest doing here?

After much confusion, it is discovered that this priest was supposed to be there a day earlier when my son was in distress. I lay my head down on my pillow and sob. I want out of this place. My heart aches so badly, and every part of my being longs to hold my child in my arms.

> When you pass through the waters, I will be with you;
> and through the rivers, they shall not overwhelm you;
> when you walk through the fire you shall not be burned,
> and the flames shall not consume you. (Isaiah 43:2 NIV)

Later, I learn that the intern assigned to take my son to the pediatric hospital has trouble starting the oxygen tank attached to the incubator. I am told there are some tense moments in the ambulance when they almost lose my son on the way to the new hospital. The very people assigned to protect my son could have been partly responsible for him dying due to their inability to give him oxygen.

Finally, four days after my son is born, I am able to visit him in the intensive pediatric ward. I reach out to him in the enclosed incubator and touch him with my rubber-covered hand. How I long to hold him and let him know his mother is with him. I have never seen a more beautiful baby in all my life. He is perfect in every way. I smile as I look into his little blue eyes. My eyes widen in surprise to see he has red hair, just like his mama.

My heart just nearly bursts open with a love for this child that I never imagined possible. The tears run down my cheeks as I sob openly like I have never done before. It is like a dam just bursting open and overflowing. I never remember feeling such raw emotions before for another human being. I feel more alive than I have ever been in my entire life. *So, this is what real love is like.*

That feeling of love keeps getting stronger and stronger in the next few weeks as I hold my child in my arms. He begins to recognize my voice and cries for me to hold him. The nurses tell me he certainly knows his mama's voice. I love hearing those words. I look forward to the day I can take him home. He seems to be getting stronger every day.

His nursery room at home is ready for him to occupy as soon as he is well enough to leave the hospital. The room is equipped with a new crib, bassinet, small dresser, and toys. I long for him to come home so I can take him for walks in his new carriage. I cannot wait to dress him in his adorable little boy outfits. Looking back, I wish I would have cherished the time together more rather than wanting the time to pass quickly so we would take him home.

Life is about to take a cruel turn. When my son is three weeks old, we are informed that he has suffered brain damage due to his head becoming lodged in the birth canal during the birth process. Initially, the hospital staff says he should be OK other than the brain trauma, but a new problem has arisen. My son has spinal meningitis, and the illness is spreading quickly to the brain. The doctors are doing everything possible to stabilize him. Less than one week later, my son is dead. *Oh, God, why?* I do not want to live without my son. *Please, God, help me! Why would You give me someone to love so much, only to take him away from me?*

Again, life has a way of rising up and hitting one squarely in the face when least expected. At this season in my life, I do not have a strong faith foundation to rely on God to help me through it. Just when you think things cannot get any worse, they do. As I mentioned earlier, there are other things going on in my life, which I either choose to ignore or fail to see. My husband and I finalize arrangements with the local funeral home in Massachusetts to fly our son to Arkansas to bury him. We decide to bury him in my husband's family cemetery. Our plan is to move to Arkansas when my husband is discharged from the service. He wants to be close to his family and pursue a job with the family business, owned by his grandmother. This is quite a move for a girl who has lived in Massachusetts all her life.

After my baby dies, I cannot bear to stay in our apartment. I sob uncontrollably just seeing the nursery our son was to occupy when he was released from the hospital. So, my husband and I stay at his best friend's house. The next few days are a blur as we complete funeral plans and travel plans to take the baby's body back to Arkansas. I am so numb with grief and barely notice what is going on around me. My husband's best friend's wife is pleasant but seems somewhat distant. I believe it is due to the circumstances swirling around all of us. However, as we are preparing to leave their apartment for the airport, my husband takes me aside. He tells me he feels the need to bear his soul to me.

"I love her," he says. I look at him strangely. What is he saying? His words don't quite register with me. He must see the confusion on my face, so he takes ahold of my arm as he repeats his earlier statement.

"I love her," he says again. Her? Is he calling our son a 'her'? Is my husband so distraught with grief that he is not thinking clearly?

"You love who?" I ask.

He blurts out his best friend's wife's name. I stand there and stare at him. I am numb with grief from losing our son, and he has the audacity to say such a thing. I feel nothing at that moment but somehow know this to be so. How can he?

I look away from him as my eyes scour the apartment for a glimpse of the woman who has my husband's heart. I see no sign of her. Somehow, she manages to stay out of sight until we leave for the airport on our trip to Arkansas. Somehow, so many things that took place over the last year confirm my suspicions that I chose to ignore. She was supposed to be my friend. Once again, another betrayal.

I am emotionally numb with an overwhelming grief as I stare out the window of our plane on the tarmac. I choke back the tears as I watch my son's casket being loaded onto our plane to take him to his final resting place in Arkansas. I want to die. *God, I don't want to live.*

Getting through my son's funeral is the hardest thing I have ever encountered in my young life. No one should have to bury their child. Life is not supposed to happen that way. I barely hear the pastor's eulogy. I look briefly around the crowded little room at the funeral parlor and realize I know no one except for my husband and his parents. None of my family made the trip from Massachusetts for the funeral. When the service is over, I get up from my seat and move toward my son's casket. I look down at my baby son and feel the urge to scoop him up in my arms. I want to take him out of this place. I cannot bear the thought of placing him in some cemetery. *Please, God, take me.*

The entire time we are in Arkansas, I can barely bring myself to talk to this man who has the nerve to call himself my husband and my son's father. How can he be so callous and profess his love for someone else with all we are going through? We never speak of his love confession again during the time we are in Arkansas, but it will once again rear its ugly head immediately upon our return trip home to Massachusetts.

My husband's best friend and his wife pick us up at the airport. How dare she have the nerve to meet our plane! Instead of taking us right home, we end up at a bar and restaurant for dinner. I sit there in numb silence as they eat and drink a few drinks. Then the band starts to play, and my husband jumps to his feet and takes the hand of this woman as he leads her to the dance floor. I watch in silence for a few minutes as he dances and holds her close. Suddenly, I feel violently sick. We have just buried our son. How can he be so callous and uncaring? How can he have the audacity to hold another woman in his arms and profess his love for her? I barely make it to the restroom before I get violently sick to my stomach.

In a few minutes, this so-called friend comes into the restroom and tells me that my husband wants to go outside alone with her. How can she do such a thing to me? She is a young mother. Doesn't she have any remorse or guilt for what she is doing to me? Why is her own husband being so nonchalant about what is happening? I do not want to admit to myself that she is everything my husband finds attractive. She is quite petite and pretty with a deep southern accent. She is soft-spoken and very girly with her soft demeanor. Suddenly, I recall how she openly flirts with him. How could I be so blind not to see the way he looks at her and looks for excuses to be near her?

I am sickened by the lies and the betrayal. This woman is supposed to be my friend. I feel betrayed by the two people I came to trust. All the lies and deceit of my past come flowing out as if a cesspool inside me has just exploded. I lash out at her in that restroom. Whatever I said causes her to run for the door. In a few minutes, I find myself in the back seat of their car with my husband as we head home.

From that moment on, our married life takes on a strange turn of indifference on my part. I pretend not to see or choose to ignore the obvious in our lives. I decide to make a life for myself within our life at large. I build an emotional wall around me, determined that no one will ever hurt me again. Our relationship has never been one of communication with each other. After our son's death, the rift in our marriage grows even wider. Part of it is my own willful pride not to admit to the hurt I feel from being betrayed. Part of the problem is my feelings of inadequacy and unworthiness. I keep my feelings bottled up inside of me. The cesspool of bitterness, anger, and emotional pain continues to fester within my heart, mind, and soul.

I convince myself that I am experiencing what so many female relatives in my large Catholic family have endured. Most of us know about the men in our families who have a wandering eye for women other than their wives. The rumors are rampant about their affairs and infidelities. My generation watches as these women endure this unfaithfulness in silence. These women adhere to their vows of "for better or worse … until death do us part."

But what they are teaching us is wrong in so many ways. My mother's words: "You make your bed; you lie in it." Period!

Even during this period of my life, I am not fully aware yet how God is using what is transpiring to draw me closer to Him. After the death of my son, I really don't want to live anymore. I never entertain the idea of doing something like taking my life. I am just so brokenhearted that I feel dead inside. To be honest, the mere task of facing each day is a survival struggle. In a strange way, what follows next leads to me finding someone else to focus my bitterness on besides my spouse, my mother, and my former friend. The enemy is not content to know I am in a survival mode. He wants me to stop calling out to God and to let go of what little faith I still cling to.

I arrive home from the agonizing trip to Arkansas in time to keep a scheduled medical appointment. At first, I wonder why I even consider keeping this appointment. What is the use in showing up for my six-week checkup with the doctor who delivered my son? Why should I put myself through this? For reasons unknown, I keep my appointment.

Again, life is to take another turn. The exam is routine. This is the first time I notice just how young this doctor must be. He seems nervous and almost apprehensive to examine me. I notice that two other nurses keep entering and exiting the room. They appear to glance at me, then at the young doctor. Something seems strange. The doctor seems aware of my loss and doesn't say much. After my checkup, the doctor comes back into the exam room with tears in his eyes. "I am so sorry," he says. I choke back my tears. His sympathy will not bring my son back. I look away. But his next words will alter my feelings for an exceedingly long time.

"I never thought about your going into labor that night after trying to induce your labor. When my nurse called me and told me you were in labor, I told her to give you a shot to stop the pains. I was at a dinner party and saw no need to return to the hospital. I never expected the baby's head to become lodged in the birth canal and lead to brain damage. I am so sorry. Please, know that I did not expect you not to be able to have a child by natural birth and need a C-section. From now on, always insist on a C-section when giving birth."

I gasp and quickly stumble off the examining table. I had to get out of here. He saw no need to stop partying and come check on me! *This man is admitting to the reason my baby is dead.* I feel such a surge of hate and bitterness overcome me like nothing I have ever felt in my entire life. His words will impact the person I become for years to come.

In a very twisted way, this doctor's apology to me is one reason my marriage will survive. I have someone else to whom I direct my anger and bitterness. It is easier to convince myself that love is overrated and all men are incapable of faithfulness and real love. But to be the one responsible for the death of my son is unforgivable. My son died because he did not feel the need to leave a dinner party. And as for more children, I have no intention of that happening again.

There are days when all I can do is stare out the living room window of my fifth-floor apartment at the street below. There is one particular day that is forever etched into my memory. I stand looking out the living room window of my fifth-floor apartment. I stare at the snow swirling around outside. I look down at the icy street below. Not a single car is on the street. The snowplows come through, and the snowbanks are piled several feet high. Many cars lie buried beneath these huge snowbanks. But then a movement on one of the snowbanks catches my attention. Down below, I spot a little child crawling around on top of the snow. I shudder just watching this young child.

What strikes me is the fact that this child is out there all alone in below-freezing temperatures. The child has no coat or shoes on. I continue to stare at this child who appears oblivious to the environment and the frigid temperatures. All I can do is watch this child in disbelief. I wonder how this child is allowed out in this weather, barefoot and unprotected.

Then I get angry. I begin sobbing and crying out to God. "Why, God? Why did You let this happen? Just look at that child in the snow! Where are his parents? How could You let these irresponsible people have a child but take mine away? I would have cared and loved my child and protected him. How could You do this?"

God never answers me that day. I cry and cry as I lie huddled on the couch that day. In my agony and grieving, never once do I find it in my heart to maybe do something about helping that poor child on the snowbank. That memory will stay with me forever. In due time, I learn a valuable lesson. Healing only comes from helping others less fortunate than ourselves. Our pain is eased when we walk alongside those who face trials we once faced and by sharing our testimony with them.

I also believe that God tried to get my attention that snowy day, but my heart was hardened, and my eyes were glazed over. There was only one person who could eventually save me from myself, and that person is Jesus Christ.

As the months pass, relatives whisper to one another about how well I am coping with my son's death. I am not coping with it. In one year, I lose my child due to a medical mishap, my husband informs me that he loves someone else, and I am pregnant again. My heart has waxed cold and indifferent. I build a shell around me that no one can penetrate.

Life becomes so lonely, so very lonely. I spend days alone in my darkened, empty tenement. My young husband rarely comes home, except to sleep, and this will set a pattern for our relationship as we go forward. To the outside world, we appear a loving couple who are spotted at church together on Sunday. This too will become our pattern for years to come.

Some years later, friends and family ask me how I managed to overcome all the trials in my life. That part of the story is yet to be told.

14

Nick Is Cheating

Eliza

December 2003

Healthwise, the first six months of pregnancy have been smooth sailing. I was having morning sickness, which was really like all-day sickness, but every doctor visit has gone well. Most of the time, I am being seen by nurse practitioners, who report that everything is healthy and fine. We have also found out that we are going to have a baby girl! Truth be told, this news makes me cry for a few days when I hear it, primarily because I have been missing my own mom so much. However, I am trying to focus on the positive, and this mind shift has made all the difference. I am excited about the prospect of having a gorgeous little girl in my life.

Since we have a few months until the baby is born, we've decided to take a trip to Seattle to visit Nick's family. The day after we fly into Seattle, it is decided that we will take a daytrip into Canada. Nick, his children, and I, along with his parents, his sister, and her family, drive three hours to the Canadian border and into Vancouver. We spend the day walking through the city and make a stop at Roots, which is a new favorite clothing store. I buy our baby girl the most adorable snowsuit that she will be able to wear the following year. It is a brown, suede zip-up one-piece, with white Sherpa lining. It is one of my favorite things that we have bought for our

71

baby girl, and I can't wait to see her bundled up in it for her first Christmas. I know it's a year away, but I'm just so excited.

Nick's family and I have been getting along really well. This includes Nick's children from his previous marriage, two adult sons and his teenage daughter, who have made the trip with us. Nick's preteen niece has spent most of the time by my side, as she loves hearing about my experiences interviewing celebrities. She asks me questions about who I've met, and we chat for hours on end about music, movies, and trends. His mother and sister have been cooking every single day, and we delight in the spoils of their efforts during dinner. I have become extremely relaxed and really feel as if Nick's family will truly be my family as well.

Nick has been so attentive to me during this pregnancy. He always makes sure I have a place to sit down, checks frequently to see if I need anything, and has been so loving. He knows that I've been craving fresh slices of tomato and turkey on mayonnaise-slathered lavash bread, so he has made sure that there are plenty of these items in the fridge during this trip. I told him it wasn't necessary, that the baby could go a week without her special sandwich, but he insists. It's sweet of him, and I feel so cared for and doted upon.

After a week of relaxation and fun, we return home to California. Nick's classes resume on Monday, and as usual, Nick is rushing out of the house to get to the university on time. He is especially loving this morning, even getting up early to surprise me with breakfast. We eat together in an easy fashion, and before he rushes out of the door, he makes a final check of his email to ensure there are no cancellations in his schedule. He runs to his car and then back inside to give me a quick kiss before rushing out the door again.

I clean up the kitchen table and put everything away. I don't have school until later on this evening, so I decide to watch a TV show and check my email on the computer we share. As the TV plays in the background, I jostle the mouse to wake the computer screen. It automatically opens to Nick's work email account. I'm about to switch over to my Yahoo account when a subject line catches my eye.

Subject: *Nice seeing you …*

I stare at it for a few seconds, debating on whether or not I should open it. Curiosity wins, and I click the email open.

Inside, what I read makes my entire body go numb. It is from an admin at a sister school. She wrote to my husband about how she was thrilled to be able to see and spend time with him. How good it felt to connect sexually with him. She went into detail about how good it felt to give him pleasure and how sad it made her to know that he's been trapped in a marriage by a young girl who's gotten herself pregnant. She questioned why he had been involved in a sexual relationship with someone else while he'd been in one with her. She said that she'd forgiven him and didn't care about the marriage he's now in, although she did wish that he hadn't felt the need to get married. The email ends with a series of flowery sendoffs and an expressed hope to see him again soon, perhaps even the following week, where they could meet as usual at her house.

I read the email over and over again, searching for clues of a mistake. Surely, it couldn't be true. She stated that they met a few days before we left for Seattle. She said he'd been complaining of a sexless and passionless marriage. *But Nick and I have sex regularly, and he frequently tells me that this is the happiest he's ever been. He has a nickname for me, Boos, which means kiss in Farsi. He tells me I remind him of a beautiful doll. That he is so lucky to have me and our baby in his life. That we make him young. That we make his life complete.* And yet here is this woman repeating words that he's apparently said to her about how awful his life is. Images of the week we'd just spent flash in my brain: walking hand in hand in the snow, being wrapped up in his large overcoat when I got cold, eating with his family and learning words in Farsi, kissing and cuddling at night, his caresses leading to more, falling asleep in each other's arms. That was real, wasn't it?

That evening, I skip class. When Nick arrives home, I pepper him with questions about the email I found.

"How could you?" "Is this true?" "Are you unhappy?" "Are you cheating?" "Did you tell this woman these things?"

He denies everything. Even going so far as telling me that this woman, who he found old, fat, and ugly, was completely delusional.

"She said you met her last week, that she performed a sexual act on you, on her couch!" I cry. "You're telling me that she made *all* of it up?"

He grabs my shoulders, "Boos, please. You know me." He stares at me, his face stern. "You know I wouldn't want anything but you and our baby." He moves his hands to my swollen stomach. "You both are my life. Please believe me. This woman means nothing."

"Did you do it?" I ask, tears streaming down my face.

"No," he says firmly.

"I just want the truth. Just tell me the truth." I'm exhausted, and the stress of this is making me nauseous.

"I said no, and that is the truth. This woman is a psycho." He makes a crossing motion with his arms, signifying that he's had enough of this conversation.

In my heart, I know he's lying. I know that what this woman wrote to him in her email is the truth. In that moment, I recognize that the man I married is capable of betrayal without remorse. That lesson has stayed with me, not only throughout our marriage but in relationships beyond the marriage. Over time, I become jaded because of this, thinking that all men are capable of deceit, even in the case of my own father. Emerging from the cloud of this will take many years of learning through God's Word and massive amounts of therapy.

15

Welcome to the World, Annalise

Eliza

February 2004

I often wonder why God gave me a mother's heart, if His only intent was to repeatedly break it.

If I'm being honest, it has taken me a while to adapt to the fact that I am now a mother. I mean, yes, I went through pregnancy and morning sickness, craved frozen peanut butter and jelly sandwiches, and experienced the utter terror and joy of bringing my daughter into this world.

Since her birth, I have held her at night, fed her, bathed her, folded tiny clothes, and placed them methodically into dresser drawers, but it just feels a bit unreal. I'm in charge of this tiny human, and that terrifies me.

It isn't that I don't love Annalise. I love her with every fiber of my being. It's just that life and all of its "Are you kidding me?" moments got in the way, interrupting the ideal image of motherhood I had created in my mind.

I assumed it would be a lot of park visits where I would push her on the swings, encourage her to tackle a tall slide, and catch her in my arms upon her victorious descent. In between sliding and swinging, there would be sniffles and perhaps the occasional bout of the flu, but that would be the exception, not the rule.

I suppose that I did have that particular brand of peaceful domesticity with her for the first year. The moments of bonding, of lazily rocking her and absentmindedly adoring her. I was basing my expectations of motherhood on a single picture-perfect year, followed by years that tested not only my strength but Annalise's too. The latter years turned that idyllic first year into scenes from a movie that you saw once and texted the whole way through. You get the basic idea of what it was all about, but you can only remember flashes of the story you saw when you were actually paying attention.

And, as I've come to realize, I wasn't trusting. I didn't trust my abilities as a mother. Didn't trust in what the future would look like. Didn't trust that God had my daughter and me in His hands. It's the old cliché, calling myself a Christian and believing that yes, somewhere, there was this spectral being that I called Father but never grasping what that actually meant.

My heart wasn't open to His love, so my heart wasn't open to love of any kind. The twenty-something version of me would scoff at this notion, would want to save face and protest angrily that I knew love and felt love. But here's the thing: I didn't really know love because I didn't understand love. Not until I got to the point in my path with Christ when I was able to grasp the gravity of how a parent could sacrifice their only child for the sake of love would I even begin to feel the softening of my heart.

February 18, 2004

Today I have a routine doctor appointment. My baby shower is this weekend, which is being hosted by my best friend, Monet. She and I met a few years ago in one of our shared elective courses, Voice 100: Intro to Singing. Monet sang "La Vie en Rose," and I sang "Edelweiss." Our shared love of foreign love songs merged a bond that exists some twenty-plus years later.

While today's appointment is routine, I want to bring up the swelling in my hands and feet. I have had to remove my wedding rings because my fingers look like sausages. My legs are so swollen that it feels as if the skin might rip, and the cuffs of my socks are digging into my ankles, leaving deep red marks. This has been going on for a month, and while I've been to the doctor's office for regular checkups and have been mentioning to the nurse practitioners that the swelling in my ankles has made it painful to walk, they've written the swelling off as excess weight gain. "Too many peanut butter sandwiches" were the exact words I was told on my last visit. I wish I had never mentioned that I was craving frozen peanut butter and jelly sandwiches, but they had asked what I was eating.

Today, I plan to be firm—to ask if there is something they can recommend to reduce the swelling, even just a little bit.

I arrive at the office and check in, only there is a problem. My usual nurse practitioner is out ill, and apparently they tried to call to reschedule, but I never got the call. After protesting that I'd already driven all the way there, the front desk clerk is allowing me to see one of the doctors on staff.

When I walk into the back, the doctor is obviously rushed. He looks me up and down. He looks at my chart. He grabs one of my hands.

"How long have you had this swelling?" he asks.

"I'm glad you mention that," I say, looking at my wrists. "It's become really hard to walk, painful even. Can you recommend something for the swelling?"

He looks at my chart again and repeats his question, "How long have you had this swelling?"

"Oh, uhm … about a month," I reply.

He lets out an exasperated sigh. "Have you seen any doctors at all—or just nurses?"

I shrug. "You know, it's been primarily nurses. The one I was meant to see today is out sick."

"You're thirty-six weeks today?" he asks.

"Yeah, my baby shower is this weekend," I say, smiling, my hand resting on my belly.

"You have to go to L&D, immediately," he says, writing a note on my clinic papers.

I nod my head. "Uh-huh. OK. Uhm, what's that?"

He keeps scribbling. "What's what?"

"LND?" I ask.

He stops writing and stares at me. "L and D. Labor and delivery."

I shake my head. "Oh no, I'm only eight months. My shower is this weekend," I repeat, sure that he's made a mistake.

He hands me the paper and points to the notes he's written. "Labor and delivery. Go there now. You're having this baby today."

I take the slip of paper and nod my head. It's possible that I managed to squeak out an "OK," but I can't remember for sure. As I walk to my car, I call Nick.

"Yeah? What's up? I'm in a class," Nick whispers into the phone.

I pause. "Just wanted to let you know that I'm on my way to the hospital."

"OK, for your appointment?" he asks.

"No, I just left my appointment. The doctor wants me to go to labor and delivery. He says I'm having the baby today."

Audible shuffling and the creaking of a heavy door travel through the phone.

"Now? You're sure?" Nick asks.

"I'm on my way there now."

"OK. You'll probably have to check in and get a room when you get there."

"I mean I guess. I'm not sure what to expect," I say.

"So, just let me know when you're settled and what room. I'll be there after my classes."

"OK." I pause. "Can you cancel your last class? I mean, I need you there."

"I'll see what I can do. Don't worry. I have to go. I just walked out, and they're getting restless."

Before I can respond, he hangs up.

I insert the address for the hospital on the slip of paper into my GPS and wait for it to calculate the route. It is a typical sunny day in Southern California, and even though it is February, the sun radiates through my car windows. The heat on my face is soothing. I look down at my swollen belly and speak to the baby who is causing all of this fuss.

"It's me and you, I guess." I look at the clock in my car—almost 1:30 p.m. I kiss my fingertips and rub the kiss onto my belly. "Let's do this, kid."

February 21, 2004

What was meant to be a same-day delivery has turned into a several-day ordeal. Upon my arrival to labor and delivery, I was tested for toxemia and preeclampsia. The protein in my urine, combined with the swelling of my limbs and high blood pressure means that I'm in a waiting period while the doctors attempt to stabilize me. I've been given no food for days, only IV fluids. I'm not hungry though; apparently whatever is in those clear plastic IV bags is keeping me satiated. The nurses have been checking my blood pressure every hour and have banned me from watching TV or having the lights on in the room for more than an hour at a time. I've been sleeping a lot, mostly because I'm bored.

Nick has been working, and I've given him instructions to go and buy a car seat since it seems that we will need it soon. He came by earlier this morning on his way to work. He brought the nurses bags of chocolate and told me that it's so they'll take better care of me. The obstetrician on staff says that they are thinking of inducing my labor today. The induction will be done via another IV medicine. The doctor on call says that it will work quickly. Apparently, they just hook it up, and voila … baby.

February 22, 2004

"Oh. My. God! Someone needs to get me an epidural, right now! Ow, ow, ow!" I scream while repeatedly pushing the call button.

The nurse responds to my distress call all too casually. "You only need to push it once, honey. If you push it multiple times, you're just turning it off and on."

I look at the button. "Oh. Ohhhhhh!" I wince as a wave of pain hits. "Please give me something. This hurts!"

"Not all fun and games, is it?" she says.

I shake my head, unable to speak as I ride this recent contraction.

"I can give you something for the pain once we find out how dilated you are. The doctor got my page and should be here in a few minutes."

"Minutes?" I squeak.

"I know. Let's see if we can breathe through it." She takes hold of the hand that isn't using the bedrail as a brace and rubs my back. "That's it. Breathe. Breathe. Deep breath in, slow exhale out."

My breaths are not coming as easily as hers are, but we make it through the contraction, and once it has passed, I feel a deep surge of relief pass through my body. I lie back onto the pillows to fully embrace the moment of peace. A familiar face appears at the doorway. It's the doctor I met two days ago.

"Still here?" he asks, pausing to rub sanitizer onto his hands.

I nod. "Mmhmm."

"Well, what do you think? Are we having this baby tonight?" he asks, approaching my bedside.

"I think so. Contractions have started," I say.

"Great. Let's see how dilated you are." He takes a few seconds, and then says, "Well, you're about two centimeters."

"Only two? How many do I have to be?"

"I'd like to see you at about seven."

"Seven! How long is that going to take?"

He smiles at me and looks at the clock. "It all depends. I'm going to give you something to help with the dilation." He says something to the nurse, and she nods her head.

"Isn't that what the drip is for?" I ask, motioning to the IV in my arm.

"We started you on the Pitocin, yes. But I just want to see if we can get this to go a bit faster."

Both he and the nurse leave and return. He washes his hands this time, places gloves on, and shows me a little white ball that he explains will be inserted inside of me and will help speed things along with the dilation. The process takes about thirty seconds.

When the doctor is done, he says, "I'll be back in about an hour, and we'll see where you are."

Six hours later, my cervix has only dilated to four centimeters. The doctor returns to let me know that they've decided to stop the Pitocin drip.

My mind flashes to my mom and all of the stories I've heard over the years about her firstborn son. That doctor had stopped the induction, and the baby's head became stuck in the birthing canal.

I speak up. "Isn't that dangerous?" I ask the doctor. "I mean, inducing my labor and then stopping it? Can you be sure that the baby hasn't started to come through the birth canal yet? I don't want her head to be crushed."

The doctor tips his head at me and looks amused. "Where did you hear that?"

"My mom, her first child. That doctor induced my mom and then stopped it, and the baby died." I give him the CliffsNotes version, wanting him to reconsider or at the very least take my family history into account.

His face softens, and the amused smile disappears. "I'm so sorry to hear that," he says. "You're not dilated enough for the baby to begin her way through the birth canal. I'm thinking of your safety as well as hers."

I don't reply. I can't. I'm thinking of my mom and this baby girl alive inside of me. I simply nod.

February 23, 2004

It's 12:30 a.m., and Nick has been steadily feeding me ice chips as they are the only thing, along with the steady stream of medication from the epidural, that are keeping me going at this point. Once the induction was officially stopped, it didn't take long for my contractions to begin again on their own. I've been contracting since 2:30 p.m. yesterday, and it only feels like a matter of time before this kid makes her official world debut.

I push with each contraction and would probably stop and marvel at the body's innate ability to perform this miraculous feat if I weren't actively trying to just get this baby out of me. This sentiment is something that I've told the doctor about ten times in the past five minutes.

"Get it out!" I scream.

"You're doing great, Eliza," The doctor replies. "Just keep going."

This is a different doctor from the day before. This doctor is young, pretty. She has dark brown hair, dark brown eyes, and olive skin. I tell her at one point just how pretty she is, which makes her laugh.

"Come on, Eliza," she says over my cries. "You're almost there. I can see her head."

The nurse asks me if I want a mirror so I can see the head. I swipe her hand away and give her a look that says, "Come at me with that thing, and I'll murder you." My vagina and I are just fine. We don't need to see each other in our rather savage states, thank you very much.

The head comes, followed by the shoulders. Then, with a single push more, I feel Annalise's body slide out of me.

The nurse says the time; it's 1:41 a.m. Annalise is small but long—4.5 pounds, 21.5 inches. She's early at thirty-seven weeks, which worries me, especially because she doesn't make a single sound. The doctor tries to focus my attention back to her so I can pass the placenta. But my focus is on the activity going on behind me, where Nick is now standing. The baby isn't making a sound—no crying, nothing.

"Is she OK?" I am crying, worried, and tired from the hours of labor. I finally hear a small mew, like the sound a kitten would make.

Nick says, "She's fine, Eliza. She's so beautiful."

The nurse appears by my side, presenting me with a white blanket. Inside, I see the smallest face I've ever seen. Annalise's eyes are open. She's quiet and staring at me.

Sobs catch in my throat. "Well, hi there," I say to her. "You have such a little face, gorgeous and so little." I kiss her forehead. Nick kisses me. The nurse snaps a couple of photos with a Polaroid camera. They remain, to this day, two of my most treasured photographs.

The nurse allows me a few moments with Annalise and then says she wants to put her in the warmer.

"The warmer? Like a burrito?" Nick jokes.

"Yup, just like a baby burrito," the nurse jokes back.

Annalise is quiet, small, and perfect.

16

Car Seat

Eliza
February 26, 2004

Nick goes back to work the morning after Annalise's birth, while she rests in the pediatric intensive care unit. I'm slowly regaining my strength after the bout with toxemia and having dangerously high blood pressure. Nick returns to the hospital around eight in the evening, carrying a rotisserie chicken from Costco and a dozen roses. He stays for an hour before he starts making excuses for why he has to leave. "I have to be at work so early," "I need a shower," "I've been working all day," "I'm so tired." As if he is the one who just gave birth to a tiny human.

It hurts me deeply that he isn't at the hospital with me. I am already in an emotional state because of the surge of postpartum hormones rushing through my body, and the loneliness I'm feeling forces me to lie in bed in the darkness of my room and cry. I've just given birth to a tiny and fragile little girl, my mother still isn't talking to me, and my husband has better things to do than spend his time with me and our daughter in the hospital.

Annalise, even though she is small, is doing extremely well—well enough in fact that the doctor deems it perfectly fine for us to go home after the third day. I am ecstatic and so ready to get home—the idea of being with my daughter and my husband, playing out the Rockwell-like scene of a family I have been fantasizing about. When I call Nick on his cell phone to give him the great news, he is less than thrilled.

"But I'm working," he says.

I am stunned at his reaction and think, *What does he mean?*

"Nick, they are letting us go," I say, thinking he doesn't understand what I'm trying to say. "They're releasing us from the hospital. Letting us go home."

"I can't tonight," he says. "Tell them to let you stay one more night."

Tears well up in my eyes. I want to go home. "I don't think it works that way, Nick," I say.

"Yes, it does. Just tell them you'll stay one more night. Tell them you don't feel well." His tone is firm.

The tears are now streaming down my face, and my throat is burning. "I don't want to stay another night. Please hear me. I've been here for over a week."

"Eliza. You're staying." He sighs deeply on the other end of the phone. "I have to go teach. I have to work. I'll pick you up tomorrow."

He hangs up, and I inform the nurse on call that I am not feeling well and need to stay another night. I crawl back into the bed, turn off the lights, and cry.

The next morning, I visit Annalise in the intensive care unit. I love holding her, and the nurses decide it will be OK for her to stay with me in our room because of the impending discharge. The afternoon hours go by painfully slowly. I am waiting for Nick to arrive at the hospital, and the nurses obviously are too because they keep coming by every half hour to ask me when my husband will be picking us up. Finally, after 8:00 p.m., Nick shows up. It has begun to rain, and Nick, who just purchased a car seat, pulls the car to the front entrance. According to hospital policy, Annalise and I are pushed in a wheelchair out to the front entrance. I thank the nurse and rise from the chair with Annalise in my lap. Nick opens the back door of the car to reveal a large box lying where the car seat should be. He hasn't even bothered to take the car seat out of the packaging. It is cold and now pouring rain, and here he is picking us up a day late, with a car seat in a box.

The nurse is visibly annoyed. "You didn't take it out?" She is a large woman, and I secretly wish that she would smack him for me. "How were you planning to get the baby home?"

Nick laughs nervously. "I just picked it up. I didn't have time to …"

I cuddle Annalise closer to me in an attempt to protect her from the chilly breeze sweeping through the roundabout in front of the hospital entrance.

He pulls the box out of the car and begins to fumble with the thick tape keeping it securely closed. He tears into the tape with one of his keys, finally releasing it from the box. He lifts the car seat, which is wrapped in sealed plastic, and steals a glance at the nurse and me, as if to say, "It's coming along nicely, right?" We both return his glance with flat expressions.

He finally frees the car seat from its plastic encasing and stares at the two pieces that are included. He doesn't know what to do with the base, doesn't understand how the actual seat fits into the base or how to secure the base with the seat belt. The nurse, who has grown so annoyed with him, wheels Annalise and me back into the lobby so that our newborn won't get sick from the cold. She then walks outside, says something to Nick that I can't hear, and grabs the car seat base from Nick.

I watch as Nick stands back as the nurse installs the car seat. He looks over at me staring out at him through the lobby's glass doors. He smiles at me, and I don't return the smile.

The drive home from the hospital is during a torrential downpour. I am nervous because there is a rain-created water attraction on the freeway that leads to our home in Cerritos. Annalise is so small that she fits haphazardly into the car seat, her tiny head bobbing around as the car sloshes through puddles. I sit in the back with her, holding the sides of her head the entire way home, hoping she won't slip out of the car seat restraints.

When we finally make it into the house, our home phone is ringing. It is the hospital asking us to come back because they have forgotten to remove the security bracelet from Annalise's ankle. I look under the blankets, and sure enough, there it is. After white-knuckling it the entire way home, I am not about to turn around to repeat the journey.

"No way. You can tell them they can come here and get it. Some security system!" I scream to Nick.

"The nurse says if she doesn't get it back, she'll be fired," Nick replies, holding the phone receiver in his hand.

"They should have known to remove it. Look how hard it's raining! No way, Nick."

I grab a pair of scissors and cut through the band circling Annalise's foot. My hands tremble as I do so, a mixture of fury and nerves. It snips off easily, and I slam it on the counter.

"Here. They can come and get it." I carry Annalise upstairs and place her in our bed. Her crib is next to my side of the bed, but right now, I just want to lie down with her and look at her. She is sleeping so peacefully, the evening's dramatic events having no influence on her rest whatsoever.

17

A Bed of Thorns

Anna

1967

Upon my husband's discharge from the armed services, we move to Arkansas. A northern Catholic girl being immersed in his Southern Baptist family is a cultural adjustment to say the least. We take up residence in his grandmother's home upon our move to Arkansas. So much has happened in our family in the previous year—my son dies in February, his grandfather dies in March, and my young husband's father suffers a debilitating stroke in July. We are all tired, emotionally and physically. What is going on with our family?

After having been on our own, I am less than thrilled about living with relatives again, particularly a relative I barely know. We begin a somewhat cordial relationship; we are both headstrong, independent women. Later, I realize how trivial those conversations that we called spats were. She cannot embrace my being Catholic and from the North. I do not understand her stance on what I call her southern haughty attitudes about social and cultural issues. I try to be understanding, as she, too, is trying to recover from losing her husband.

She thinks her grandson practically walks on water. Daily, she reminds me how lucky I am to have such a catch. If only she knew.

"He could have married a doctor or lawyer's daughter," she often says to me.

"Well, he wasn't exactly the son of a doctor or lawyer," I say. Once again, I lash out in emotional pain. How dare she think I am not good enough for her grandson! Her attitude toward me just makes me stronger. I am determined to prove her wrong.

The family adjustment proves difficult enough and I discover that living in the South is a culture shock. I try to acclimate myself to the food, accents, and relationships. But my biggest fear is the upcoming birth of my second child. Will I give birth only to find myself having to bury another child beside my first child? I dread every day that passes that brings me closer to my baby's due date. I dread every doctor's visit.

"What is wrong with that doctor? Is he delusional?" I scream at my husband and his grandmother.

My visits to the doctor leave me frustrated and angry. I share with this doctor all that happened in my first pregnancy. I stress the urgency of my need to undergo a C-section to deliver my next child. He is adamant that no such action needs to be taken. I become more and more agitated the closer I get to my due date. Once again, I am three weeks late, but this time the doctor says he prefers for nature to take its course.

"Take its course," I cry out during one of my visits, which are now weekly. "I already had one child die due to a doctor's mistake. Are you so set on your ways that you will have blood on your hands also? I can't go through that again!" I scream at him.

Well, I go into labor on my own, and it is long and drawn out. I scream at everyone, begging someone to listen to me, to help me. The medical staff must think I am a crazy person. When they learn I am a Catholic, a nun is sent to sit with me in the labor room until it is time for the baby to be delivered. All her presence does is give me someone else to verbally attack.

"Don't just sit there and do nothing! I lost one baby and am about to lose another due to their incompetence," I scream at the nun. She continues to sit there very calmly and do her knitting. Her silent demeanor only makes me grow more agitated. I am my own worst enemy. I am so consumed with worry and fear. My emotions spiral out of control by anticipating the very worst scenario is about to happen to my unborn child. I am uneducated regarding the simplest Bible verses, and no one else volunteers to pray or to recite such verses as "So do not fear, for I am with you; do not be dismayed, for I am your God. I will strengthen you and help you; I will uphold you with my righteous right hand" (Isaiah 41:10 NIV).

After six hours of labor and exactly one year and eight days after I gave birth to my firstborn, I give birth to a dark-haired, olive-skinned little girl. Immediately upon seeing her, I tell the nurse she has brought me the wrong baby. There must be some mistake. I expected a little redhaired, fair-skinned child.

The nurse looks at me very strangely. "Miss, your child is the only child that was delivered today. This is your child."

"Are you sure? Are there other babies in the nursery? Maybe you brought me the wrong one."

Once again, this nurse gives me this wary look as she places my daughter in my arms. "There are no other babies in the nursery. You are the only one who gave birth today."

I look down at this baby in my arms. All during my pregnancy, I felt certain I would give birth to a little redhaired boy. But in my heart, I know that God has a different plan. And that plan is to love this little girl God created. I am not to think of her as a replacement for the son I lost. This little girl is uniquely made and about to teach me some valuable lessons about what it means to be her mother.

About then, the doctor who delivered my daughter comes walking into the room. "Your daughter is healthy, and the delivery went very well," he says softly. This poor man has been subjected to my many emotional tirades, so he treads very gently in my presence.

I begin to cry. "I am so sorry, but this past year has been a terrible journey; I was so afraid. When you would not listen to me, I said some terrible things to you."

He pats my shoulder as he looks down at my daughter in my arms. "I just came up against a strong Yankee woman."

"Well, obviously not strong enough because you didn't listen to me!" I jokingly reply as tears stream down my cheeks.

With that said, we make our peace. Over time, I realize just how great a person and doctor he is in the community. A few years later, he passes away due to an incurable illness.

Even through this period leading up to the birth of my daughter, God is using others to show me, teach me, and train me. To this day, I never fail to be amazed at the individuals God sends our way to minister to us, pray with us, or share a word of knowledge with us when we need it most. During these times, I come to see how He takes us through times of trials and testing to prepare us to minister to others who face similar trials. It took me a long time to realize just how much God equips us to serve as His hands and feet in ministering to a lost and dying world. What Satan intends for evil, God turns around and uses for good.

18

Trouble with the In-laws

Eliza
March 2004

At one point, Nick mentions the possibility of his parents moving in with us, "to help out with Annalise." This is not something that I want. Although I want to have a good relationship with his parents, the culture and language barrier (they speak little English, and I speak zero Farsi) make it difficult to imagine living under the same roof.

Also, there was an incident that has put me off of wanting to allow his mother to be too involved in our home life. When Annalise was about three weeks old, his mother, sister, preteen niece, and cousin all came to visit and stay with us in our home. I was looking forward to it as I was a new mom, as I felt it would be great to have some additional help. Aside from Nick, I had no reprieve. My mom and I were still on shaky ground, and I wasn't about to ask her for help. I thought having the women in my husband's family come to visit was a great idea, as I envisioned being able to take a shower and share some of the responsibility for the three weeks they would stay with us.

I should've known something was up when Nick started staying at work past his late-evening class, not coming home until eleven thirty or midnight almost every night. Every morning, Nick would get up with Annalise and bring her downstairs to sit with his mom or sister. They'd make tea and speak animatedly in Farsi. When I would make my way into the kitchen, the chatter would cease, and all eyes would be on me. Since I didn't know what they were saying, I would ask.

"Good morning. How'd everyone sleep?" I'd ask, looking from face to face. Several times, my question was met with no reply. I'd look to Nick to fill in the blank stares. "Is everything OK?" I'd ask him.

"Yes, it's fine. We were just talking about making something for dinner," he'd say, turning his back to me.

"Oh, that sounds good," I'd say, smiling. "Anything I can help with?"

At that point, I'd get a laugh. "Oh no, it's an Iranian dish. We make it, you eat it."

"OK. Uhm. Great. I love Iranian food."

"Yes, you love food," his sister said.

I laughed weakly, wanting to dive right under the kitchen flooring and reemerge in Australia.

Over the next three weeks, the tension only got greater. Not only was I getting practically no help with Annalise, but I was expected to cater to them as well. Most evenings, when Nick returned home, he would find me in a ball on the bathroom floor, tears streaming down my face.

"What happened now?" he'd ask, annoyed at my emotional outbursts.

"I can't do anything right! They told me to get rid of all the clutter, which by the way is mostly yours, and when I told them that the clutter was yours, they said that it was my responsibility to throw it away." I looked up at him and sniffled. "I mean, if I did that, then you'd be mad at me!"

He sighed. "It's not that much longer, Boosie."

"Nick, I have a three-week-old baby. I'm trying to take care of her, and I thought they were coming here to help, but all they want to do is have me drive them from one place to another, and on top of that, I get lectured all the time about cleaning and cooking," I ranted. "I mean, come on. This is insane. And to top it off, you're not even around! You get to escape to work, while I'm stuck here with your family! I can't do this anymore."

The second I mentioned him not being around, he started to get angry. "Are you kidding me? I'm doing this for you! I work so I can support this young wife and baby."

"What? Nick, I never asked you to work more," I said. "I'd rather you be here. I miss you. Annalise misses you."

He stood up. "You don't understand anything. This life you expect from me takes money. I have to work like a dog just to support you."

His words cut me. I sat on the bathroom floor, stunned into silence.

Hearing his outburst, his sister appeared in our bedroom doorway and knocked quietly. "Bahram?" she said, using his Iranian name. "Is everything all right?"

He nodded his head and looked down at me. "Yes. I'll be down in a minute. I need some tea."

She responded, "I'll make it for you," and walked away.

He looked down at me, still seated on the floor with my crossed legs pulled up to my chin.

"You should come down, have some tea," he said.

"It's late, and I've had enough." I couldn't bring myself to look at him.

"Enough tea, or what are you saying?"

I sighed. "Just … enough."

"Go to bed then. Maybe in the morning you will feel better." He planted a kiss on the top of my head.

I crawled into bed and listened as Farsi was spoken downstairs. They could have been talking about anything, but I did hear my name a couple of times and so assumed that the topic of conversation wasn't the weather.

The next few days, the routine was the same. Nick would leave for work and return home late. I took care of Annalise and tried to avoid confrontations with his family. Luckily, they had a rental car and began taking day trips. Even luckier for me was that I was not invited to accompany them. This meant I had large portions of my day back and could focus on my schoolwork and being a mother without the scrutinizing looks.

After three weeks, I was ready to have my house to myself. I was stressed, not getting along with my husband, and desperate to feel comfortable again. The day that my husband's family was scheduled to leave, I decided to book a manicure and pedicure. They had a rental car to return and didn't need me to drive them to the airport. Nick had said his goodbyes before leaving for work that morning, so I made the appointment for the afternoon, thinking they'd leave by at least three. They didn't actually tell me when their flight was, but they'd rolled their suitcases into the entryway, and I assumed the end was near. I told them that I was heading out and wished them well on their return flight home.

My mother-in-law asked quizzically where I was going, and I told them that I was going to get a manicure, all via a quick translation from my sister-in-law. She then proceeded to say that they had time and wished to come with me to the nail salon.

Fifteen minutes later, we were on our way to the nail salon. On the way, my mother-in-law voiced her desire to not go to the nail salon but instead to Target, which was again translated through my sister-in-law. I mentioned that I had made appointments for everyone and that I couldn't cancel with such short notice (also, I really was perturbed at the entire idea that I'd been duped into this apparent bait and switch). His mother insisted, so I dropped her off at Target, and the rest of us proceeded to the nail salon.

In the middle of the manicure, my hands wrapped in paraffin wax, my sister-in-law's phone rings. It's my mother-in-law, and she wants to be picked up from Target. I ask the manicurist how much longer, and she says about thirty minutes, which gets a collective scoff from both mother-in-law and sister-in-law.

Confused, I tell my sister-in-law, "It's only thirty minutes, and then we can all go pick her up together."

"No, no." She laughs. "She's waiting outside. You should go get her and come back to finish up. We'll save your seat for you."

I raise my waxed hands, demonstrating that now is not a good time.

"You can have them take that off. It's not a problem," my sister-in-law replies.

Inside, I'm screaming. Outside, however, I say, "Sure," ask for the wax to be removed, and relay the information to my manicurist, who looks utterly confused.

"You're coming back?" the manicurist asks.

"I sure hope so," I say half-jokingly.

"We'll be done soon ..." she says.

"It's my mother, she's waiting outside," my sister-in-law interjects.

The manicurist points at my sister-in-law. "Your mom?"

"Yes."

"Why don't you go pick her up then?"

I choke out a laugh.

Sister-in-law glares at the manicurist. "Because I don't have the car."

"I could give you the keys," I offer.

"I can't right now. My hands?" She holds her paraffin-dipped hands.

I look at the manicurist, who offers a snort in reply.

"I'll be back," I tell her. "I'm going to leave Annalise here, OK?" I motion to Annalise, who has been sleeping peacefully through this entire exchange in her stroller.

"No problem. We can watch the baby for you," my sister-in-law says with a smile.

"Thank you so much." I jog to my car. I want to hurry and return before Annalise wakes, so I can finish my manicure.

I drive to Target, where my mother-in-law is waiting with an armload of bags. I help her put them in the car, and we drive wordlessly back to the nail salon. She doesn't want to come in and instead wants to sit in the car with the A/C running. I don't object.

We all finish our manicures, mine obviously being the last to complete, and we return home. On the way, everyone is talking about the manicures, and my sister-in-law exclaims that she's never had a professional one done before but enjoyed it.

The manicure and Target stops took longer than they'd expected, and when we return home, they have little time to spare before they need to leave for the airport. My mother-in-law and sister-in-law both tell me what a wonderful time they had, and even though I am sure they're lying, I return the sentiments (even though I am also lying).

My sister-in-law then says, "My mother has a surprise for you."

I look from her face to my mother-in-law's face, and they are both glowing. It is then that a large cardboard box is presented to me. I take the heavy box and set it down on the kitchen table.

"You didn't have to get me anything," I say.

My mother-in-law makes a motion for me to open the box, and smiling at her, I lift the flaps to open it.

What I see utterly confounds me. The smile disappears from my face. I look from the box to my mother-in-law, back to the box, and then back to her again. I say nothing.

Excitedly, she begins to speak Farsi, and my sister-in-law translates.

"She says it's for you to clean the way Bahram likes it."

I do nothing but stare at her, feeling a rush of heat building at the top of my shoulders.

My mother-in-law, taking my silence as a cue, begins to lift cleaning supplies from the box. She takes out a pack of Brillo pads, some heavy-duty green and yellow sponges, Ajax powder, and Lysol disinfectant and then presents me with her piece de resistance—a handwritten note with carefully drawn diagrams. It's an illustration on how to clean.

She urges me to take the note from her, which I do. I look at it, and the heat that began at my shoulders has now engulfed my neck and entire face. I stare at the carefully drawn pictures of pots and pans, toilets, counters, and floors.

I'm speechless.

My sister-in-law translates again. "My mom says that you have to really scrub on the pots to get them clean."

I smile tightly. "You know, those pots and pans belong to your son. They were like that when I moved in here," I reply.

My words are translated, and upon hearing them, my mother-in-law's face changes. She goes from smiling to grim. "You clean," she tells me.

I look at the microwave clock. "Time to go, I think," I say to my sister-in-law.

She nods and says something in Farsi to her mother.

After the bags are loaded and my mother-in-law is in the car, my sister-in-law comes back into the house. She motions toward the box of cleaning supplies.

"I'm really sorry about that. She was only trying to help."

I let out a loud laugh. "Right. Well, better be on your way."

She gives me a tight smile, hugs me quickly, and kisses Annalise. "Tell Bahram we said goodbye."

I watch from the front door as they pull away and drive out of sight. For the first time in weeks, I feel a sense of relief and walk back inside. I take one look at the box, still sitting on the kitchen table, and laugh for ten straight minutes.

When Nick returns home that evening, the earliest he's been home in weeks, I tell him about the box and its contents.

"Your mother gave me this surprise when she left, but I really think she meant it for you," I say, motioning to the box.

He looks inside and crinkles his face. "What is this?"

"Cleaning supplies," I say, taking out the handwritten note. "And these are detailed instructions on how to clean."

He studies the note. "Wow. Well, I'm sure she was just trying to help."

"Help with what? Help to make me angry? Help set the women's movement back fifty years?"

"I'm her oldest son. I'm sure she just wants to make sure I'm taken care of."

"Excuse me? You're a grown man. You're almost old enough to be my father. And she wants me to take care of you?"

He looks at me and makes a choking noise. "Come on, don't say things like that."

"This is offensive! Why aren't you more upset?"

"Let it go. You don't have to do anything with it. Throw it out if it makes you feel better."

"You're missing the point."

"What's the point?"

"This is offensive. I mean, to say she has a surprise and then give me a *giant* box of *cleaning supplies*? That's insane."

"She's just old-fashioned, Boosie. Let it go."

"Never again. I won't be treated like that ever again," I say, taking the note and throwing it in the box. "You talk about my mother? This, my friend, takes the whole cake."

"Don't even. Your mother is terrible. She wanted to get me fired."

"Seriously? You still have a job, and ..." I say, motioning to the box once more, "I'm pretty sure she never surprised you with *cleaning supplies!*"

He looks at me and opens his mouth to reply, but instead of words, laughter pours out of his mouth.

I look at him, just standing there laughing, and shake my head. Then I begin to laugh. He reaches out and pulls me to him, cradling my head to his shoulder.

He stops laughing and holds me tightly. "Boos, you never have to clean anything," he says, his voice low.

"Can I get that in detailed writing? With pictures?" I ask jokingly.

What do I feel God was teaching me in this season? I believe that I was being taught that I cannot control every situation. In the time that I spent with my husband's family, I encountered several personality types, many of which were aggressive and downright rude. Looking back, I see a young woman who was trying to figure out who she was and gain the confidence she needed to take on this new role of motherhood.

What God put in my path were people I was forced to deal with because they were part of my husband's family. What I wish I'd done better was to recognize that whatever irritations I was feeling were beyond my power to resolve. I needed to lean on God in those situations to make things better, to have peace within myself.

In hindsight, it was a short season in which I was placed in front of my in-laws, and not every visit with them was this hostile. There were several of his family members who were extremely warm and welcoming. If I'd known then what I know now, I would have grumbled less. Now I understand that part of maturity is living through the difficult seasons and learning from them. Not every battle will be won, but then again, not every battle needs to be fought.

19

An Era of Emotional Pain and Unforgiveness

Anna
1968–1971

Life becomes extremely busy in the next few years. Looking back, I can see God's hand of protection on our family in so many ways. We leave Arkansas and move to Ohio as our young family settles on starting a new life. But tragedy is to strike again one snowy Saturday afternoon while out shopping with my husband and daughter. It is rare we spend much time together other than a Sunday, so this day, it was meant for my husband to be with us. Our feisty little one-year-old girl is an escape artist when she is in her stroller, so I often carry her across busy streets.

Today, we have her stroller loaded with shopping bags, so I have her straddled across my hip. Just as we are about to cross a busy street, a car comes speeding down the road. The car is traveling much too fast for such slippery road conditions and slides right through the red light. Fortunately, I see the car headed straight for my daughter and me.

I will never forget that car being unable to stop. The car skids directly to the very spot I stand with my child. Instinctively, I know that car is going to hit us. My only reaction is to jump back. My daughter is in my arms. We are going to be killed unless I get out of harm's way. Then we suddenly go airborne for a brief few seconds.

The car hit the curb where we stood just moments before. When I jump back, I slip on the ice and fall with my daughter still in my arms. That fall on the ice tosses me backward a few inches farther away from the car.

Normally, my daughter is sitting in her stroller, but I made the decision to carry her that day. She is a little escape artist now that she has recently learned to walk. After our shopping trip, we took a shortcut to head back to the car with the packages. We found it easier to load them in her stroller and carry her. That decision likely saves both of us. The stroller is knocked sideways, and the packages spill out into the street.

The car avoids hitting us, but my fall catches my daughter's leg under me. Her leg is fractured due to my falling on her leg. My little daughter, just a year old, ends up in the hospital with her leg in a sling for the next couple of weeks. It is months before she learns to crawl and eventually walk again.

Just about the time life seems to be back on track after my daughter's accident, I discover I am pregnant again. There is no way I can be pregnant again; I tell my doctor. "How can I be pregnant? You told me my uterus was flipped upside down and getting pregnant again would be next to impossible."

"Well, it looks like the impossible happened," the doctor replies.

Life becomes terribly busy once again when we are transferred from Ohio to Illinois one month before our next child is due to be born. Once again, I feel this incredible dread wash over me. How can I suddenly change doctors at this late date in my pregnancy? This whole thing is insane. Once again, I become consumed with worry and fear. *God, could it happen again?*

Thankfully, the month goes by extremely fast. I find a doctor recommended highly by those in the community. Just before Christmas that year, I give birth to a healthy baby boy. My heart lurches when I see him. The baby that I hold in my arms is a little redhaired boy. I cannot come close to describing the emotions I feel upon seeing him for the first time. I have to consciously tell myself that this is not my firstborn child. This child is his own person.

In the days ahead, this thinking is put to the test when it comes time to name my little boy. His paternal grandparents say I should give him the name of my firstborn son. Anger rages up inside of me! How could they dare to even suggest such a thing? This baby will have his own name. He is not a replacement. Finally, I relent a little and give my son a name that carries his father's initials, even if he will not have the label of Junior after his name.

Looking back on those days, I see how our little family continues to lead a life that from all appearances to the outside world appears to be a perfect, happy family. The children and I lead our own lives, which revolve around a world of "mom and the kids." Their father uses work as an excuse for being absent from the home during the week, using the home as a place he slips into during the night to sleep. On Sundays, we go to church together. A good way of describing our church life is that we show up. I am still a nonpracticing Catholic who attends a Protestant church. My husband goes through the motions of going to church.

Once again, our little family uproots and moves to yet another state. I am growing weary of moving from one state to another with my husband's job. This time, we move to Kansas and settle in a cute little community. Our time there goes by so fast, and we once again find ourselves settling back in Arkansas. My daughter is four years old, and my son is two years old. To be honest, I never thought I would live in Arkansas again. But this time I am older and a little beaten down by life's trials. So, this becomes just one more thing to endure and bear, I tell myself. In a way, I feel relieved knowing that my firstborn is not far away, in a little cemetery close by.

I am glad for the fact that my children will be living near their father's relatives. I know how much I love my maternal grandparents. I want my children to have a relationship with their grandparents as well. It will be nice to have relatives around since the kids and I are by ourselves all the time. Their father's ritual of never being home continues with our living closer to his family. The only change is that our Sundays now include visiting with his family after church every week.

For a season, our lives roll along somewhat smoothly despite the marital issues always brewing under the surface. I finally feel like life is as close to normal as it can be in my world. During one of our return trips home after visiting the grandparents, we come upon a box in the road. We almost drive around it, until the children yell, "Kitty, kitty." We stop the car and retrieve the box. There inside this box is a litter of five tiny kittens. Apparently, someone dumped the box in the middle of the road.

Well, we load the box of kittens in the car and take them home. The children are delighted because they now have both dogs and kittens, all strays who somehow came to live with us. Again, life is about to take another turn for us.

Early one morning, my two-year-old son comes crawling into the kitchen where I am preparing breakfast. "Why are you crawling on the floor like a baby? You are a big boy now," I say as I lift him to his feet.

"Mommy, hurt," he cries out as his legs give out underneath him and he crumples to the floor.

I lift him again, thinking he is playing jokes on me, which he often does. Even at two years old, he has become one little prankster. And to be honest, this is a trait I so love about him because it brings such joy to all of us.

Once again as I lift him and let go of him, he falls to the floor. My heart lurches because this time I can tell he is not playing any game. He screams out in pain.

I scoop him up and get the two children ready to rush out the door to the emergency room. My pulse is racing as I fight back the tears so as not to frighten the children.

After several hours of tests, my son is admitted to the hospital and hooked up to an IV. My child has contacted cat fever. He is unable to walk; the poison has spread into his lymph nodes.

The medical team at the hospital informs us that my son has what is called cat scratch fever. They inform me that fortunately we sought medical attention in time before he developed even more threatening symptoms, such as encephalitis (swelling of the brain) or endocarditis (an inflammation of the lining of the heart), both of which are lethal and difficult to cure.

My heart lurches as I sink into the chair beside my son's hospital bed. My son could have died due to what we thought was a harmless little kitten. He is always prone to running high temperatures when he isn't feeling well. A few days earlier, I thought he had a mild cold. The symptoms earlier in the week did not prepare me for what transpired. I was clueless as to what was wrong until the weakness in his body set in.

What kind of mother am I? My child could have died. I came close to being responsible for the cause of my son dying, due to my naivete.

God, thank You for Your hand of protection upon my child.

After the cat episode, we had to find new homes for these little fur babies. Once again, this was a reminder how sensitive my son is to his environment. He is the one who always runs the high fevers when he comes down with even a simple cold. He is the one who is extremely sensitive to the algae in the lake and has to sit on the bank and refrain from going in the water.

All that kept running through my mind was how close my son came to dying because of something that seemed so harmless, bringing home some stray kittens.

> Be alert and of sober mind. Your enemy the devil prowls
> around like a roaring lion looking for someone to devour.
> (1 Peter 5:8 NIV)

20

Mom Becomes Grandma

Eliza
March 2004

I finally reconnect with my mother, when she sees me pushing the baby stroller across campus (where she and my husband both work, and where I attend school). She yells my name, saying it only once, with the same tone she used on me so many times when I was a teenager. "Eliza!" I freeze, my hands grasping the stroller tightly. My daughter is only a month old and sleeping in her cocoon of blankets with the stroller canopy closed. She walks briskly over to me. "Let me see your baby." I hesitate, not sure if my own mother means to do my child any harm.

Gingerly, I pry open the canopy, revealing to my mother for the first time my daughter, her granddaughter. Annalise is sleeping peacefully, blissfully unaware of my rapid heartbeat and perspiring upper lip. Her hands are framing her face, her tiny fists on either side of her tiny pink mouth. My mother is silent. I look from Annalise to my mom, who is fighting back tears.

My mother doesn't say a word; instead she just nods her head once, as if she is a guard in the queen of England's infantry, the head nod signaling a performance of her duty.

"I'm running to a meeting," she says to me, her eyes still misty.

"Yeah, I was just going upstairs to Nick's office."

She motions to Salazar Hall, where Nick's office is located on the sixth floor. "I'm going to the dean's office." (Located in the same building, first floor.) "Let me get the door for you."

I'm confused by her willingness to do anything for me, even if just to hold open a door. I have a brief concern that she might slam the door on the stroller. "Thanks." It's all I can say.

She holds the door for me, and I walk my separate way to the elevator. The canopy of the stroller is still open. I push the call button for the elevator car and stare down at Annalise. Tears are forming in my eyes, and I'm biting my tongue in an effort to stop them.

My mother calls out to me suddenly. "Wait!" She runs to my side, where I stand frozen once again. "Let me just …" She reaches down with extremely gentle fingertips and touches Annalise's blanketed chest, the gentle rise and fall of her baby breaths barely noticeable. "I just wanted to see her again."

I look at my mother's face. A tear is gliding down her cheek. She wipes it away.

She looks up at me and says a quick yet sincere "Thank you."

"No problem." It's all I can say. Months of silence and hostility ended with an interchange that lasted all of five minutes. Annalise is the glue that has brought us together again. We don't talk about what happened; we just let it go. It seems that this is the best way. We won't talk about it in detail until nearly fifteen years later.

21

A Family

Eliza
Summer 2004

It's difficult, but I put the woman who sent the sexual email to my husband on the back burner in my mind—not forgotten but set aside so that I can focus on motherhood. It may sound biased, but Annalise really is the most gorgeous baby. She has wisps of golden hair, pudgy pink cheeks, long legs set upon the most adorable baby feet (one of which had the cutest little dot; "That's where God dotted you with His paintbrush," I'd tell her), and eyes that actually sparkled. Even as an infant, Annalise seems to have a wisdom far beyond her age, as if she's been living a life for millennia instead of months.

In addition to motherhood, I've been finishing up my bachelor's degree. Between class coursework and nighttime feedings, I am exhausted. I adore Annalise and enjoy my classes, but I missed my Mom and the bond we once shared. I missed being able to call her and discuss my professors, who she knew from being a part of the university staff. It had become awkward to be on campus since I knew that Nick and I had become the topic du jour for campus gossip. It wasn't any easier for Nick. My mom was essentially his boss, and it didn't bode well that he'd gotten the associate dean's daughter pregnant out of wedlock—not to mention the nearly twenty-year age gap.

At home, when it was just Nick, Annalise, and I, we were distracted by the daily routine of raising an infant. It was a comforting loop of sleep, eat, poop, bath, repeat. The trips to the Cerritos library, Cerritos Town Center, and Sunday-afternoon trips to Costco became a part of the regularity. I'd push Annalise in her stroller around the sun-warmed pathways as we darted in and out of retail stores.

Looking back, I realize how lonely I was. True, I had friends, but they were neck deep in university life—study sessions, nights out, parties, bars. My current situation (married with a baby) didn't fit in with that anymore. As much as I loved my daughter, it was difficult to accept that maybe this was all that my life would be. I'd had dreams of pursuing a career in broadcast journalism and had been working toward that goal. Now, as Nick's wife and Annalise's mom, that dream had vanished. In its place was a dream that consisted of living day by day and constant insecurity.

I wasn't unhappy. I was just unsure. I knew that I was a mother and wanted to be the best mother I could be. I knew that I was a wife and wanted to be the best wife I could be. But there was so much insecurity in me that I started using crutches to help me cope. The first was shopping. I came home with shopping bags at least twice a week. Target, ULTA, Sephora, TJ Maxx. If it had shelves of goods illuminated by fluorescent lighting, I was there, typically with Annalise in tow.

Nick began to comment about my spending. The remarks were dropped innocuously at first, a mention of how many bags were being hauled in from the car. Then he'd begin showing me the credit card bill, raising an eyebrow at a $250 Target run. Eventually, the small mentions became stern lectures, then full-blown arguments. I'd stop for a week; the only purchases were those made with Nick on our Sunday Costco run. It was then that I began using the time between Annalise's naps and Nick's work hours to sort through every file and paper in the house, as well folders on the computer, in an attempt to discover any of my husband's misdeeds. What shopping could no longer fill, snooping could.

While Nick never left his work email open again, leaving me to constantly wonder if he was still romantically conversing with the secretary from San Bernardino, he did leave quite the paper trail of his past relationships. I found an eight-by-ten headshot of a woman with blonde hair whose name I'd never heard before. He also had notes from (and about) various women he had relationships with. Among the stash, I found photo albums from his previous marriage, pics of his children, and one photo that made me do a double take—a sweet shot of him and his ex-wife relaxing in bed, her right hand buried in his thick black hair. It wasn't the photo that made me look twice; it was the bedspread in the photo—a pastel floral pattern that looked like it had come out of a 1980s JCPenney catalog. The same bedspread that was currently resting atop our marital bed ten feet above me.

One of the things that stayed with me, long after Nick was out of my life, was the gut-twisting feeling of a partner who held on so tightly to their past. It reminds me of a saying my Mom once told me, "You can't park a new car in a garage if the old car is still parked there."

22

Annalise's First Birthday

Eliza

February 2005

It was late February, and I was sweating. Annalise crawled around on the floor while I frantically ran from one end of the room to another, hanging streamers, placing cups and ice on the tables, organizing the food station, and taping down wanton paper tablecloths. I'd been running for hours at this point, from bathing and dressing Annalise, to grabbing a six-minute shower of my own, to picking up the catered order of Persian food that would feed roughly fifty invited guests.

"Honey, you're gonna get dirty!" I chastised, worrying about keeping my one-year-old daughter's pink and white outfit pristine. I made a mental note to search for her discarded hair bow before the guests arrived.

Annalise squealed and ripped a portion of the tablecloth from one of the tables.

"Seriously, child?" I said, scooping her up off of the floor and placing her onto a blanket surrounded with toys. "Stay here for five minutes. Just five minutes." I gave her button nose a light tap and turned my attention to the torn tablecloth.

Unfortunately, babies have no concept of time or of party décor, and she quickly transitioned from quiet and happy to screaming and mad.

Something flew by my ear and landed with a crash. Bits of plastic scattered as the toy hit the concrete floor.

I could feel the anxiety rising in my throat, closing my airway. I picked Annalise up from the floor. She was angry and having none of my nonsense, which she made evident by the high-caliber screams in my ear and the forceful jerking against my chest.

"Cooperate with Mommy. Come on," I said, shushing her softly as I rocked her. "It's your birthday. Annalise, Annalise's turning one today. Annalise, Annalise only wants to play." I singsonged as I rocked and held her tightly.

She stopped screaming and looked at me. Her bottom lip stuck out, stubbornly resisting my attempts to make her smile.

"Mad at Mommy?" I asked, holding up her chubby hand to give it a kiss. "Mommy's horrible, right? Just doesn't love you."

Her eyes furrowed, and then she laughed.

"Oh yeah?" I laughed with her. "You like mean Mommy?"

She cuddled her head into my shoulder and relaxed. I looked at the clock. In thirty minutes, the first guests would arrive, and I still had so much to do.

"Where is your daddy?" I whispered into the top of her head.

Nick was late, leaving me to tend to party decorations and the baby. Plus, he was meant to bring the birthday cake. It made me nervous that I hadn't heard from him since he left earlier that morning to attend a special session of office hours on a Saturday.

We'd had an argument about it as he was grabbing his wallet and car keys that morning.

"Why today? Can't you postpone them? I mean, it's our daughter's birthday!" I'd said angrily.

"I can't postpone. Otherwise, your mother will fire me," he spat back. It was his usual response to my questioning anything having to do with his erratic work schedule. Ironically, my mother was no longer his supervisor. Her promotion meant she was associate dean in charge of the students, while the faculty reported to another associate dean. He almost never mentioned his actual supervisor, however, always preferring to direct his hostility toward my mother.

Nick and my mother had managed to put aside their differences, at least in public. It was no secret that there had been a rough patch in the beginning. My mom hadn't taken it well when she found out I was pregnant with Nick's child, especially since he was nearly twenty years my senior and I was still in college. The fact that we'd initially kept our relationship a secret had only made it worse.

"There's no way my mom won't understand. This is her grandchild's first birthday. And you never have office hours on Saturday. Why today? Why all of a sudden?"

His face grew dark. "Eliza. I have to go. I'll be at the party in time."

"But you're leaving me to take care of Annalise and put everything together on my own."

"I'll be there with the cake. If you don't want to do it alone, just wait for me. I'll help you put things together."

"But you won't be there until a half hour before everyone is supposed to get there! It's not enough time."

He shot a laugh in my face. "It won't take long to blow up balloons and put tablecloths on tables. That will take ten minutes."

I walked with a now sleeping Annalise outside of the park clubhouse and turned toward the parking lot. Five minutes later, Nick drove into the lot, driving the white Mercedes that had been my Christmas present just two months before.

He sat in the car for another five minutes, finishing a phone call. When he saw me standing and staring, he got out of the car and busied himself with the Costco sheet cake and a case of Kirkland water bottles.

"Hey. How is it going?" Nick asked as he approached me, stealing a glance at Annalise.

"Well, I managed to get most of the decorations up and the food set up, but the birthday girl had a meltdown, so I couldn't finish it up entirely. I still need a portion of the tablecloth to be repaired where she ripped it."

"Show me. I'll do it." He walked into the clubhouse and moved the meticulously set-up food station to one side in order to plop the cake down.

"Oh, um. Can you put the cake on that other table? With the drinks?"

"Why? It's fine here."

"Because then people can get to the food without having the cake in the way."

"It's dessert. It should go by the food, Eliza."

"Yes, but they'll eat first. Then we will light the candles on the cake and sing."

"You really want me to move the cake?"

"Yeah. Can you please?"

He scooped up the cake and gingerly set it down on the drink table.

Right at that moment, a group of his friends walked into the clubhouse. Nick's mood instantly changed. He hugged them and spoke in Farsi. They greeted me warmly and asked where they should put the gifts. Nick answered them and motioned to the table that I'd designated for birthday presents.

A few times over the next hour, our guests came over to remark how wonderful it must be to have a husband who took the time to put the entire birthday celebration together. Nick had mentioned that he was the one who hung the streamers, blew up the balloons, picked up the food, and brought the cake. I said nothing. What could I say? After all, this day was about our daughter. If Nick wanted to make the day about him, then that was his issue.

Annalise didn't need any encouragement to be the center of attention. And so it was that on her first birthday, with fifty people crammed into a clubhouse, my magical little girl decided to take her first real steps. She's a born performer, that one.

23

Hydrocephalus

Eliza
March 2005

At Annalise's one-year checkup, her pediatrician tells us that Annalise's head circumference has grown exponentially from her six-month visit. It is the first time that we hear the words *hydrocephalus* and *brain injury*. Our sweet little girl, who just a week ago began walking, is now facing a horrific crisis, resulting from hydrocephalus or an excess of water on the brain.

Annalise's pediatrician refers us to a neurologist. I attend the appointment with Annalise and my mom. The neurologist provides no answers, instead using most of the visit to make inappropriate comments about my age and physical appearance. My mother and I leave the office disgusted but with a referral to a neurosurgeon in Los Angeles who is the expert in the field of pediatric neurology.

Nick and I take Annalise to Los Angeles to meet with the specialist. He reviews Annalise's CAT scan and sends us for an MRI, which Annalise has to be sedated for. A week later, we visit him a second time, where he tells us that Annalise does in fact have hydrocephalus. He urges us to schedule a brain surgery for her as soon as possible. If we delay, the fluid in Annalise's brain will build up to the point where it will either cause major brain damage or death.

I cry the entire time. I'm not sure and feel pressured into making this decision so quickly. I tell Nick that we should get a second opinion. The doctor once again urges us to proceed, telling us how quickly his schedule fills up. Nick makes the ultimate decision to schedule the surgery with this doctor and says that if we decide not to go through with it, we can just cancel. He is insistent that we schedule the appointment before the doctor is booked. In tears and fighting against the pit in my stomach, I agree with my husband.

Nick and I attempt to get a second opinion from the head of neurology at another children's hospital. A few emails are sent from both Nick and I to a Dr. Glasgow at one of the other children's hospitals. We are told that because of Nick's high income, we are unable to be seen at the hospital without paying for the entire course of care ourselves, which could equal hundreds of thousands of dollars. Also, because we are insured through our HMO, we are forced to see HMO doctors. Dr. Glasgow sends us an email telling us how highly respected and experienced Dr. Henry is. It is Dr. Glasgow's advice that due to the restrictions of our HMO plan; we entrust our daughter's care to Dr. Henry.

We visit Dr. Henry a second time, asking him as many questions as we can. Notably, I ask him what the risk of something going wrong is. He tells me, very matter-of-factly, that there is less than 1 percent chance of anything going wrong, for the following reasons: He is the top surgeon for the job, having performed thousands of these procedures. He has years of experience with endoscopic surgery. The endoscopic procedure is a quick surgery. Annalise will be out of the hospital and on her way home good as new within three days tops.

On the morning of Annalise's surgery, she is in high spirits, smiling and giggling and running around the hospital waiting area, even though it is five o'clock. Everyone in the waiting area assumes the surgery is for Nick or for me. They are shocked when we tell them it is for our extremely exuberant little girl. More than one person remarks, "But she looks so healthy!"

The anesthesiologist is late. The nurses give Annalise a little bit of Tylenol to calm her down, to prepare for the insertion of the IV into her arm, so she can receive the anesthesia to knock her out. After four hours of waiting, Annalise is put under, and her tiny body is wheeled through the double doors that lead to the operating room. I stand and watch as a team of people in green scrubs take my baby away. I pray to God that she returns to me healthy and happy. A sudden chill runs through me, and

I hug my arms to my chest. Nick grabs my shoulder and leads me to the waiting area.

My mom, stepfather, Nick, and I sit in a row of metal chairs in the too crowded waiting area. "How long is the surgery?" my mom asks.

"It's supposed to be quick, forty-five minutes or so," I say. I didn't want to talk much. I just sit and pray, wringing my hands together, imagining them shaving off Annalise's beautiful, sun-kissed baby curls. I try not to cry when I imagine them taking the knife to her skull. I bite my lip, willing away the tears that won't dry. Forty-five minutes pass, then an hour, then two. What is taking them so long? My eyes remain glued to the double doors that separate the waiting area from the surgical corridor.

Finally, after what seems like forever, two doctors finally walk through them. I immediately recognize the older of the two men as Dr. Henry, the surgeon who operated on Annalise. There is another doctor with him, whom I have never met. I run toward them. "How is she?" I ask, my entire body shaking. My heart is beating furiously in my chest.

"She's fine, in recovery," Dr. Henry says.

"Can we see her?" I ask. I'm smiling, relieved that my little girl has made it through the surgery.

"She needs just a few minutes to let the anesthesia wear off, but then yes, you can see her." Dr. Henry smiles, but his eyes look tired.

I ask him again, "So, everything went OK? She's OK now?"

He looks back at the other doctor, the one I didn't know, then back at me. "She's just perfect. Everything went textbook."

He tells us that he needs to begin his rounds to check on a few of his other patients, promising to check on Annalise that evening before he leaves, adding, "I'll be around to check on her a bit later."

The fluorescent lighting in the waiting room casts shadows on their faces. While Dr. Henry speaks to me, his eye contact keeps shifting from my face to the other doctor, who is wearing a badge identifying himself as Dr. Lin. When Dr. Henry turns to look at Dr. Lin, so do I. In the back of my mind, something feels off. Dr. Henry attempts to assure me that everything went according to our highest hopes, complete with a warm and weary smile that causes the elder doctor's eyes to crinkle. Dr. Lin, on the other hand, is staring at the floor and doesn't utter a single word, give a muffled "mmhmm," or even a head nod. Nothing.

24

Morphine

Eliza
May 2005

A mother's hope can cloud a woman's intuition. I thank them profusely for bringing her out of the surgery safely. Feeling a rush of relief in hearing that Annalise has made it out of surgery safely, I stand and sob as I watch the doctors walk away. Dr. Henry walks ahead of Dr. Lin, his body rigid as they make their retreat.

My mom envelops me in a hug. "She's all right, honey. It's all going to be all right." I sob openly against her neck, releasing a month of pent-up emotions all over her shirt.

About an hour later, a nurse comes to get us in the waiting room and takes us to the recovery room to see Annalise. She is still sleeping, and her head is wrapped in a bandage. Her tiny arms and legs are limp. I ask the nurse if she's woken up at all.

"Oh no," says the nurse. "She won't wake up for a while. They just gave her morphine."

I'm shocked. Dr. Henry told me that she'd be waking soon, and yet they'd given her morphine?

The nurse brusquely explains the reason to me. "She's just had brain surgery. She needs her rest to recover."

It sounds reasonable enough that she'd need sleep after brain surgery, so I don't force the issue. After we sit with her for less than an hour in the recovery room, the nurse ushers us out so that Annalise can be taken up to the PICU, pediatric intensive care unit. I am told that I can't go with her and am told to wait outside of the locked doors of the PICU until it is cleared for me to gain entry. I am told the reason for this is that they don't want parents in the way while they are preparing the room.

When I'm finally granted entry into the PICU, I'm shocked. It is one large, open room, with only a few closed-off areas for patients with extreme illnesses. Annalise's "room" is just a small space that they'd made up for her in the corner. I'm confused. If she needs to rest, like the nurse just told me downstairs, then why are we being placed in the corner of this extremely noisy and crowded room? There is no way that Annalise will get any rest here, with bright lights overhead, multiple beeping noises from the medical equipment, and screaming and crying coming from the other patients inhabiting this claustrophobic space. I ask one of the nurses if this was where Annalise is expected to stay for the duration of her hospitalization. She raises an eyebrow at me and mutters sarcastically, "Yup, this is it."

I sit on the corner of Annalise's bed and hold her tiny fist. I brush my fingers down her leg and touch her cheek. It feels warm and clammy. I tell her, "Mommy's here, honey. I'm right here with you." I kiss her forehead and cheeks. She makes no signs of waking, no movement in response to my touch or sounds of my voice.

When the doctor finally arrives to see Annalise, I've made the gruesome discovery that they give all of the kids in the PICU morphine in order to keep them calm and asleep. The second a child would wake up; they would give them another shot of morphine through their IV. The nurses continue to pump Annalise full of morphine for three days straight, until I protest. I want her to wake up so that I can assess how she's doing. She remains groggy after waking. Her body is limp, but she opens her eyes. I cuddle her in my lap and kiss her tiny head.

Dr. Henry waits three days to finally visit Annalise. It is the first time that I've seen him since we talked in the hospital waiting room after Annalise's surgery.

Dr. Henry walks to the left side of Annalise's bed and removes a silver tool with a spiked wheel on the end. He grazes the wheel along the bottom of Annalise's left foot, then down the length of her left arm. She doesn't respond to this. I think how strange it is that he'd do that and ask him, "Is something the matter? What is that for?"

He just smiles and says, "Nothing's the matter. Just doing my checkup." He leaves quickly, saying again how many patients he needs to see, and we don't see him again for another three days.

After the sixth day in the hospital, I am getting more anxious. Annalise isn't responding to any touch on the left side of her body. She doesn't even realize if you are standing on her left side. Multiple times during the day, I'd walk over to Annalise's left side and talk to her, call her name. Annalise would search all around on her right side, looking for the source of my voice, and would start to cry when she couldn't find me. When I walk to her right side, her reaction is one of surprise, as if I'd popped out of nowhere, when in fact all I'd done was walk from her left side to her right. I'd pick up her left hand, checking for any motion. If I let her hand go, it would do a dead drop onto the white hospital sheet.

One day, while attempting to get her to laugh, I notice that her smile has also changed. The right side of her face lifts into a grin as usual, but her left side remains neutral. Her hand, arm, leg, foot, eyes, mouth—nothing on the left side is in motion. An image of my grandfather pops into my head. He'd had a stroke early on in his life, and his left arm had hung lifeless by his side. He had never recovered use of his arm.

I bring up my concerns to Dr. Henry and to any other nurse or attending doctor who will listen. An MRI is scheduled, and Dr. Henry informs us that they discovered a small patch of blood resting over the area of the incision, as well as a small amount of air, causing a bubble to rest on her brain. He tells me that this is without a doubt the reason for the left-side paralysis and that once these things are reabsorbed, she will be all better again. I once again feel immense relief that this is only a passing thing and thank God that Annalise will not suffer through a lifetime of paralysis.

25

Someone Tells the Truth

Eliza

On the day we are to be discharged from the hospital, a physical therapist on the hospital staff comes to see Annalise. She is young, with auburn hair. She smiles at me and touches Annalise's cheek gently. She chats with me about exercises to use on Annalise at home and hands me a sheet of paper with illustrations on how to properly execute the exercises with her.

I look at her, confused. "How long do we need to do this? Just until the blood bubble is absorbed?"

"What do you mean, blood bubble?" she asks, looking at me as if I am crazy.

"You know, the blood bubble. Or maybe it was an air bubble. They weren't sure which one it was." I give a light chuckle, which I often do when I'm feeling nervous about something.

"There is no bubble," she says.

"No—there is," I insist. "Once it is reabsorbed back into the bloodstream, she'll be OK," I say knowingly, stroking Annalise's hair with my thumb.

The therapist stands. "I'm sorry, that's not ..." Her voice trails off, and she looks toward the exit. Her voice lowers, and it's almost a whisper. "They didn't tell you, did they?"

Her reaction causes the wheels in my tired brain to churn. "Tell me what?"

She turns to leave, and I grab her hand. She looks scared, panicked. Surely she is thinking about her job security and what can of worms she just opened.

"Please." I hold her hand in mine. I must look scary. No bath in days, my hair a frizzy red mess, no makeup, dark circles under my eyes, lack of sleep from staying for days in a chair that didn't recline next to my baby's bed in the intensive care unit.

"Please. You have to tell me," I plead again.

"I'm so sorry." She closes her eyes tightly before opening them again. "She'll need therapy for a long time."

"How long exactly?" I say, my hand still clasping hers.

"Mrs. Reza, she'll need therapy services for life."

My head begins to pound, growing stronger until I can feel my heartbeat pulsing in my brain.

"Why does she ..." I trail off.

"She's paralyzed. I'm so sorry. They should have told you."

It is the first time I heard those words associated with Annalise. "She's paralyzed."

My head feels like a hot-air balloon. I let go of her hand, or she pulls away—I don't remember. But I do know it was the last time I ever saw her. The photocopied slip of white paper with stretches that we were to perform at home floats to the floor.

In a few hours, we are meant to be released from the hospital.

I sit there with tears streaming down my face, holding Annalise in my lap. No one dares to come near me, everyone knowing that I now know the truth.

Nick is at work but coming to get us in a few hours when he is done. I want to call him but have no idea how to speak the truth of what I've just been told over the phone.

When Nick finally shows up, I try to explain to him what I learned. He doesn't believe it. Honestly, I am finding it hard to believe myself. This was supposed to be temporary, this paralysis that stole the function of our daughter's entire left side. And now it is here to stay, a constant part of our lives.

We sit in silence. Nick holds a completely still Annalise against his chest as we wait for the wheelchair transport to take us downstairs.

The bed starts to shake, and the lights in the PICU move back and forth and cast an eerie spotlight on the room and its inhabitants. Someone down the hallway screams. It is a Southern California earthquake.

When the motion settles, I laugh at the irony. Our entire world is shaken. Literally.

Nick turns to me, careful to not disturb Annalise, and says "Eliza, something is wrong."

I look at him and say, "You think?"

He says again, "Eliza, really. Something is wrong with her." His normally tanned face has gone pale.

I jump off the bed and kneel down toward Annalise's tiny face. Her breathing is shallow. Her head is jerking, and only the whites of her eyes are visible.

My college roommate had epilepsy. I recognize immediately that Annalise is having a seizure.

I dart to the nurses' station, where a single nurse sits. She is on the phone.

"Excuse me. Miss! Miss!" I say urgently, trying to get her attention.

She mutters something to the party on the other line and without looking at me says, "Yes?"

"My daughter. Something is wrong!" I am panicking.

She sighs deeply, telling the person on the phone that she will have to call them back. She is exasperated that I am bothering her. "I'll be right there, ma'am. I'm the only one here right now and can't leave the nurses' station."

"But she's having a seizure!" I am screaming now.

She spins off the chair and runs to Annalise's side.

In what seems like mere seconds, we are surrounded. Nurses, doctors, specialists, our elusive neurosurgeon, Dr. Henry. And security.

I am yelling, frantic, hysterical. "What is going on! What is happening! Someone tell me something!"

"Ma'am, I'm gonna need you to calm down." The large security guard takes my arm in a tight grip.

"Don't touch me." I practically snarl at him. He is easily three times my size, but my concern isn't about his size; it's about my daughter.

"Ma'am, I'm not going to ask you again." His voice and the grip he has on my arm are growing stronger.

"Are you serious? My child is seizing, is paralyzed! How do you want me to react? What if this was your kid? Get your hands off of me!"

A large woman with orange hair approaches me, stepping in between the heated exchange I am having with the security guard.

"Honey. Settle down. Take a seat," she says gently.

"Don't tell me to settle down!" I scream.

"Honey, they're doing what they can to help your daughter. Your yelling won't help her." She stares into my eyes and motions for me to sit in a chair close to Annalise's bed.

I open my mouth to once again protest, but the sight of Annalise forces it shut. I reluctantly sit on the edge of the chair.

"Is she going to die?" I ask her as I begin to cry. Thick tears stream down my face.

"Look. There is a team of doctors here. They're doing everything they can," she says.

I look up. There are easily ten doctors in the room, conferring with one another. Arms crossed, silent conversations going on, one examining Annalise's eyes with a light.

"They have to save her." I am having trouble breathing, trying to catch enough breath to get the words out. "She's my only one. She's my only baby. Please!"

At that moment, a nurse approaches me. It's the same one who was on the phone before. She is carrying a clipboard with a paper she needs me to sign. "We have to readmit her," she states matter-of-factly.

Without a word, I run the pen sloppily along the paper, unsure that I've even signed in the right place. The orange-haired woman rubs my back as I do so.

"Can you not touch me please?" I hiss, not even bothering to look at her. The feeling of compassion from any one of these people sickens me. They've done this to her, and now they want to provide comfort?

I rise and quickly walk over to where Dr. Henry is standing engrossed in a quiet conversation with another doctor in a lab coat. "What is going on? I want the truth." I glare at him, a mixture of hatred and need fueling me.

"We're giving her some medicine to stop the seizure," he says.

"And then?"

"We will keep her for a few days for observation."

"Then what? Why is she having a seizure?"

He pauses, staring only at Annalise, never looking at me. "I'm not sure."

"You're not sure?" I throw my hands in the air. "Well, that's just great."

The doctor who was standing with him pats him on the back and leaves.

"We will do everything we can," Dr. Henry says. I'm trying to read his emotions, but he is stone-faced.

"She's my only child. My baby. My whole world is that kid." My eyes well up and overflow with tears. "Please. Fix this."

He purses his lips and with a furrowed brow says, "I know."

I walk over to Annalise, who is now sleeping on the bed, her small body pumped full of anticonvulsant. I get into bed with her and hold her. A nurse starts to tell me that I can't be in bed with her, and Dr. Henry stops her.

I search the room for Nick and find him sitting in a chair in the corner. He is stunned, motionless. His eyes, practically unblinking, are fixed on Annalise.

"Nick," I say, trying to get his attention.

He looks up at me, his eyes dark and watery.

"Do something," I say.

His lip quivers, and he closes his eyes, causing them to overflow with tears. I lie there and hold Annalise in stunned silence. It is the first time I can remember ever seeing him cry.

I begin to cry again too and fix my gaze on Annalise. They've given her another dose of IV fluids to force the seizures to stop, and the intensity of the dosing has put her to sleep. Her once tan face is now pale, highlighting the petal pink of her cheeks. The doctors seem to dissipate all at once, leaving our family alone to assess the damage.

Nick stands and walks over to the side of Annalise's bed. He kisses her on the top of her head and tries to hug her, careful to not disturb her or the

IV tubing that hangs from her arm. I wrap my arms loosely around them both, with one arm above Annalise's head and one around her waist. My forehead drops to rest on the bed, and I begin to plead with God—not a prayer, more of an intense begging.

Dear God, please. Please save her. Save Annalise. I need her in my life, God. Please don't take her from me. Please. Save her. You have to know, God, please know how much she means to me. I love her so much. Please. Save her. Please God, hear me, I'm sorry for all of the things that I've done to make You angry, to make me unworthy, and I am unworthy, but please. Please. Please. Save my baby. Please.

The sobs come long and hard. I can't feel God, can't hear Him. At that moment, I am certain that He doesn't want to hear me. A thought pops into my head. *She's suffering because of me. Because I'm a horrible person, because I've been far from God. He can't hear me because he doesn't remember ever knowing me.*

God, please. Don't do this to her because of me.

26

Anger, Tears, Resentment, Worry, Pleading with God, and Therapy

Eliza
Post–Brain Surgery #1—2005

The first two months after we bring Annalise home from the hospital pass by in a blur. For the first time, I feel what debilitating depression is like. Multiple times a day, I open the door for a therapist of some sort—physical, occupational, nutritional. We have had supervisors from county child welfare agencies and social workers visiting us to make sure we are taking care of Annalise properly.

I am angry all the time. The fact that we now have social workers in our home scrutinizing every inch of our lives is turning my anger into something much darker.

"So, you're here to judge if I'm an unfit mother?" I ask Rick, the supervisor for the regional center.

Rick smiles, but it is too tight of a smile and strikes me as incredibly fake. "No, Mrs. Reza. We're just here to observe and chat."

"Funny, seeing as I'm not the one who paralyzed her. Maybe you should go have a chat with the doctors who did this." This statement barely escapes my lips before I burst into tears. I cry all the time now. I don't want to. I would much rather allow the dark anger to engulf me in flames, or at least every judgmental stranger I have to allow into my home.

Rick stands there, motionless and quiet. He doesn't offer a caring hand or a tissue. He simply waits until my outburst is over, and then he proceeds with his questioning.

"And Annalise, she was walking before this happened, you said?" The pen in his hand is poised on a form, ready to record my answers.

"On her first birthday. She wanted an audience." I look over at Annalise, who is screaming at the physical therapist's attempt to get her to focus on her paralyzed left hand.

"Come on, Annalise. Just hold the ball," the therapist says to her.

"If she could *just* hold the ball, you wouldn't be here," I say.

Rick and the therapist exchange glances. I close my eyes, sigh deeply, and apologize.

"I'm sorry," I say. "This is very hard." I look at the floor and then back to Annalise, who has been placed in a cross-legged position by her therapist. "The last thing this family needs is more stress, and with you here, strangers in our home every single day, it's not what I envisioned motherhood to be like, not what I wanted for my daughter."

"And we want Annalise to get to as normal a place as possible, which is why we're here," Rick says, a genuine look of concern on his face. "I can't imagine what you're going through, but we need to work together to get Annalise set up for these services. To help her."

One day at a time. This phrase pops into my head, and I can almost see the words floating through the room.

Then I say them out loud, "One day at a time."

"Exactly. That's the best way to go about this. These first months will be crucial for Annalise's development," Rick says. "And the first step is getting services. Let's focus on that, and then everything else will fall into place."

I look over at Annalise's therapist, who nods in agreement. "And you're not alone. We're here to help."

"I hate asking for help," I say quietly.

"Well, you need to get over that," the therapist says with a laugh.

It will take me much longer than expected to get over that. Nearly fifteen years will pass before a second failed marriage will cause me to stop and ask for help—from my mom, from friends, from God. And when I finally ask for help, to my surprise, it comes in droves. My anxiety eases, my health improves, and my relationship with the Almighty becomes much more defined. It dawns on me that the helpful voice that I have heard in the difficult moments was none other than the Holy Spirit Himself. He'd been there the entire time, even when I was cursing His name. He never left but instead prompted me to return to Him and waited for me to follow His instructions.

27

A Visit to Dr. Henry

Eliza
July 2005

Two months after Annalise's initial brain injury due to surgery, we are asked to return to the neurosurgeon's office to face the doctors for the first time since her hospitalization. This has provided the hospital with enough time to formulate a plan to cover themselves, which they thinly disguised as a plan for Annalise's care. I'm not buying it. These two months have been a period of intense emotions for me, as our lives have been completely flipped upside down. My understanding over what happened hasn't grown, but my anger has.

Being back at the hospital sends me into a pit of dark emotions. I can't help but think of how my little girl came running into the hospital waiting area the last time we were here. Only now I'm having to carry her because she isn't able to walk due to the left-sided paralysis that these doctors caused. I don't even feel the urge to cry. Instead of fighting back tears, I'm fighting back the urge to scream and rip people's heads off.

We check in and find seats in the waiting area. Annalise has a bit of a runny nose, and I send Nick to the counter to grab a tissue. When he comes back, his demeanor has changed.

"What happened?" I ask as I wipe Annalise's nose.

"I saw Dr. Lin." His eyes are fixed on the door ahead of us.

My eyes fly to the check-in window and scan the area for any sign of the younger doctor who performed the surgery with Dr. Henry. He pulled another disappearing act, and as such, there was no trace of him.

"Did he see you?" I ask Nick, who nods his reply.

"Well, did he say anything?" I ask.

"Not to me," Nick says. "He was talking to a nurse about his vacation plans for the Bahamas."

"Oh, how incredibly *wonderful for him*," I say, the anger I'm feeling causing a sharp increase in the volume of my voice. "How *awesome* that he's able to just move on and go to the beach while we have a paralyzed baby."

The waiting room door opens, and a woman in a dark suit appears. She introduces herself as the hospital administrator and shows us to a small room off to the side of the waiting area. I never noticed this room before, but it becomes clear to me that they want to seclude us from the rest of the families who are there to see the neurosurgeons today.

I make a comment about this. "You have us here in this room so we don't cause a scene?"

The administrator looks taken aback and then laughs. "No, of course not. We just thought this would be more comfortable." As she says this, she looks at Annalise.

I wasn't about to let anything slide today for the sake of *comfort*. "Oh, right. She's not comfortable at all these days."

"I'm sorry to hear that," the administrator replies.

"Are you?" I ask. "Because it was your doctors who did this, who made her this *uncomfortable*."

She tries to turn her attention to Nick, who I suppose she assumes will be the more reasonable of the two of us. She attempts small talk, and her comments about the weather annoy me. She's a part of this organization, and I can't help but feel anger toward her. I maintain a steely gaze on her until the door opens and Dr. Henry appears.

"Mr. and Mrs. Reza, how are you?" he asks casually and with a smile.

"You're kidding, right?" I practically spit at him.

He takes a deep breath and looks at the administrator, who takes that as her cue to start the meeting officially.

"We're here to discuss options for Annalise," she begins. "After looking at Annalise's history and now understanding that she still has fluid buildup in her brain, we think the best course of action would be a shunt placement." She pauses and looks once again at Nick.

"Hold on," I say. "What are you talking about?"

Nick quietly answers, "They mean another surgery."

I let out a loud laugh. "No way are you *ever* touching my child again." I say this directly to Dr. Henry.

He looks over at Annalise and then down at the table.

"Mrs. Reza, I understand your frustration," the administrator begins before I cut her off.

"You understand?" I say with a forced laugh. "You understand absolutely nothing. *Nothing!*" I look at Annalise, who is now sitting in Nick's lap with her head against his chest. She's awake but looking at me with a quiet intensity.

"Of course." The administrator begins again. "We simply want to discuss the options so that we're doing what's best for Annalise."

"What's best for ... wow, lady. Listen to me. I will only say this one more time, and I want to make sure you both understand me." I look from the administrator to Dr. Henry. "You. Will. *Never.* Touch. My child. Again. *Ever.*"

Silence fills the room, to the point that the only sounds are the A/C blowing air through the ceiling vents and the buzzing of fluorescent lights.

I sit there staring at them. I feel as if I haven't blinked in minutes.

The administrator breaks the silence. "We understand, Mrs. Reza, but we do hope that you will get help for Annalise."

"Here's what's going to happen," I say. "You will sign whatever releases need to be signed so that Annalise can leave this hospital system and go to a hospital of my choosing."

The administrator glances at Dr. Henry, who simply nods his head.

"We can do that," she says. "Give me just a few minutes so I can gather the necessary paperwork and put the referral into the system for you to go see a specialist at another hospital. Did you have a doctor in mind?"

I nod. "Yes. Dr. Glasgow."

Dr. Henry speaks up once more. "He's terrific and a good friend of mine."

"Well, I won't hold that against him," I say coldly. "By the way, Dr. Henry, where is Dr. Lin? I assumed he'd also be here."

"Oh, uhm. He's not here today," he replies.

"Oh really?" I say, my voice rising an octave. "So funny, because my husband saw him when we were checking in."

Dr. Henry smiles tightly. "Oh, yeah. He was, uh, just on his way out."

I return his tight smile and look at Nick. "Probably has to go see the travel agent about that Bahamas trip."

"What's that?" Dr. Henry asks.

"Oh, his Bahamas trip, it sounds *so fun*. He couldn't help but brag about it to the nurses while we were checking in. It's *so nice* that he can just move on with his life. How wonderful for him. And what about you, Dr. Henry? Any amazing vacation plans coming up?"

Dr. Henry shakes his head. "Uh, no. Nothing planned right now."

I make a tsk sound. "Oh, well, that's too bad. Considering all of the therapy and now what seems like another brain surgery, I doubt we'll be taking any vacations either."

Dr. Henry smiles his tight smile again. "Well, I'm hoping for the best. Annalise will be in good hands with Dr. Glasgow."

"Let's hope so," I reply.

The administrator comes back in, and Dr. Henry excuses himself, saying he needs to go see other patients.

Once we have the referrals in hand and the necessary paperwork signed, we leave his office for the last time.

Within a few days, we have another surgery date set. In two months, Annalise will undergo her second brain surgery.

28

Annalise Walks Again

Eliza
August 2005

Annalise is now eighteen months old and has started walking again. The walking is something I hadn't expected to return so soon. We'd been told by various medical professionals that she may never fully regain the use of her left hand or leg. I remained hopeful, but the image of my little girl confined to a wheelchair for the rest of her life was incredibly hard to bear.

Both Nick and I are at different stages of the grief-processing cycle; while he is stuck in denial, I am planted firmly in anger. When we sit down with each other to try to work through what has happened, Nick shakes his head and quietly says, "I just can't believe it. This can't be happening." Meanwhile, my response is to spurt angry obscenities and curses on both of the doctors who harmed our baby girl.

None of it is fair. Our hearing that Annalise may never walk or use her left hand again is something that neither Nick nor I are able to deal with. Regardless of our lack of faith, Annalise is a different story. She shows us early on who she is—and more importantly who God says she is.

I've gotten used to carrying Annalise around with me everywhere. She screams if I put her down and walk where she can't see me. As such, it is less stressful (at least on my eardrums) to bring her along with me. Unfortunately, this makes certain household chores impossible. One afternoon, while Nick is at work, I decide to do a load of laundry. Our laundry room is located down the hall from the master bedroom. I put Annalise down on the floor of our room, grab the basket, and walk down the hallway. I begin to tell Annalise exactly what I am doing in the hopes that she will understand and not scream.

"Mommy's here, Annalise," I say as I sort the clothes into the washer. "Mommy's right here. Don't worry, baby. I'm here, OK?"

I put the soap into the washer and crank the dial to start the cycle. I breathe a sigh of relief as it appears that my consoling Annalise from down the hallway is working. She isn't screaming at me to come back and pick her up. I walk out of the laundry room and make a left toward the master bedroom. To my utter surprise, I find Annalise in the hallway. Even more amazing, she's standing! My jaw drops as I see her little cherub face staring back at me.

"How did you get here?" I ask her with an exuberant giggle.

She replies with a laugh.

My instinct is to swoop her up into my arms, but I want to see this miracle for myself, so I take a step back. Annalise looks at me and seems to understand what I want from her. She uses her left hand to hold on to the wall for support and takes a step forward. A laugh gets stuck in my throat as tears start to well in my eyes.

"That's it, Annalise! Come on, baby. Walk to Mommy," I encourage her.

With each step back that I take, Annalise takes a step forward. This continues until we reach the end of the hallway, at which point I sweep her up in a victorious hug and hold her tightly.

"I am so proud of you! Oh, my brave, beautiful, determined girl!" I say as I smother her head with kisses. "You are amazing!"

She wriggles in my arms, wanting to be let down. This girl has no time for affection from her mom. She wants to go! I carefully put her down, and holding her left hand for stability, we walk the length of the hallway in the opposite direction. We repeat this five times, back and forth, back and forth, until she finally plops down and lays her head on the carpet.

"Tired?" I ask. Her little brown eyes just look at me.

I lift her up and carry her to our bedroom, placing her gently into her crib. I put her pacifier in her mouth and stroke the top of her head until her eyes begin to close. She's worn herself out, but I am elated. My baby girl is walking!

Once I know that she is finally in a deep sleep, I fall to my knees beside her crib and utter a tearful and thankful prayer.

"Oh, God. Thank You for this. Thank You so much for this." Tears stream down my face. "You let my baby walk again. You did this for her, Father. Thank You, God. Thank You."

I sit and pray like this next to Annalise's crib until she wakes from her nap. Her body stirs, and her eyes flutter open.

She would normally cry, signaling to me that she was awake. But today, she simply finds my eyes and stares back at me. I'm not sure if it is because I am already there, or because I am crying, or because I am staring at her, but she stares quietly at me for a couple of minutes, just taking in the sight of her crazy mommy crying at the side of her crib.

When Nick arrives home that evening, I tell him what happened that day. I wanted to keep it a surprise so that he could experience the miracle for himself. Annalise does not disappoint. His hand flies to cover his mouth as he watches Annalise brace herself against the wall as she walks toward him. She is tired, and her little legs are still weak from not walking for a few months, but she is determined.

The second she reaches him at the end of the hallway, he scoops her up and excitedly praises her. "Oh, Boosie, baby Boosie!" he says, using the pet name that in Farsi means *kiss* or *baby kiss*. "You did it! Oh, thank God!"

29

Another Brain Surgery

Eliza
September 2005

The miracle of Annalise walking was bittersweet as we prepared ourselves for yet another surgery. This time she would be treated at another well-known children's hospital, by Dr. Glasgow.

The drive up to the hospital was a quiet one. I said a prayer over our family and over Annalise before we left the driveway of our home. I asked God to keep Annalise safe, to guide the surgeon's hands, to protect her brain and her body from harm. I also asked God to allow Annalise to be able to walk after this surgery. My prayers were all tearful ones these days, and once I said the prayer out loud and Nick had directed the car toward the freeway, my prayers went from spoken to silent. The car was totally quiet as we drove; the radio was off, and even Annalise was quiet. It seemed as if we were all in our own little worlds of thought.

Once we approach our exit, Nick and I look at each other. It is the same exit that we took just three months earlier, when we entrusted Annalise into the hands of two other neurosurgeons.

Nick is the one to break the silence. "If only she'd been able to go here first."

My mouth purses, and I nod. I'm trying to remain strong and trust that the outcome of this surgery will be vastly different from the one before.

After we met Dr. Henry for the first time, we left his office with a surgery date scheduled. I convinced Nick that we needed to get a second opinion. Nick reached out to one of his colleague's wives who worked for a doctor's office, and after asking around, she'd given us the name of a doctor who had a great reputation in the field of pediatric neurosurgery. The doctor's name was Dr. Glasgow, and he was at a well-known children's hospital.

We'd called and chatted with Dr. Glasgow, but because our insurance was through an HMO, he was unable to diagnose or do a deep dive into Annalise's records because it would not be covered by insurance. I voiced my opinion about this hypocrisy during our consultation, saying it seemed unfair that we were unable to get a true second opinion based on us *having insurance*, while other families who had no insurance at all were welcomed with open arms.

The realization of this infuriated me even more now, considering that we were now going to see the same doctor we had attempted to take Annalise to in the first place. All because of insurance. Because we had insurance elsewhere, we'd been refused. If we had no insurance at all, Annalise would have been seen by Dr. Glasgow with no problem at all. It was unfair how broken this system was.

This time around, we were not turned away. Word had obviously gotten out about us, and we were treated with kid gloves upon check-in. This was the first time I experienced just how much of an anomaly we were. Every nurse, doctor, and admin that we met had heard about what had happened to Annalise while under the care of Drs. Henry and Lin, but they'd only gotten the bulleted point version.

- Annalise, age fifteen months, had an endoscopic procedure done with Drs. Henry and Lin.
- Endoscope had made hole in brain. Endoscope track can be seen on MRI.
- Annalise developed left-sided paralysis and seizure disorder following initial surgery.
- Referred here by HMO hospital (due to mother's refusal of any further care at HMO hospital).

This was the rundown they'd all gotten. However, what they wanted to know was what really happened. My answer was always the same, "I wish I knew."

We had been lied to so much and had so many secrets kept from us about what really happened. The truth about that won't come out until years later when Dr. Henry will finally admit under oath that it was Dr. Lin who pushed his way through Annalise's brain with an endoscope, having entered the brain from the wrong entry point, and he had continued to bear through her fifteen-month-old brain even as Annalise began to bleed out. This is why she's paralyzed and why she has seizures.

Dr. Lin intentionally disregarded the fact that Annalise had begun to bleed out as he forced his way through her brain with the endoscope, against the urging of the much senior and more experienced Dr. Henry, who had encouraged him to reverse the endoscope. Dr. Lin did not listen and left a permanent and damaging hole in Annalise's brain. I wonder if he had his amazing beach vacation on his mind instead.

The next few hours are spent in the hospital waiting area while Annalise once again goes under the knife. I pray with Nick that the doctor's hands will be guided by the Great Physician, believing that God will bring her through. I plead with God for Annalise to come out of this surgery complete and able to see, walk, talk, and recover completely.

Three hours after Annalise is wheeled into the operating room, she is wheeled into recovery. Nick and I are able to visit her briefly before she is transferred upstairs to the pediatric intensive care unit, or PICU. I practically run to Annalise's side. She is still sleeping, a steady morphine drip keeping her out of pain and in dreamland until she is settled in the PICU.

At one point, I ask the nurse in the recovery room about the morphine. "How long will she be on morphine?"

Her answer surprises me. "She will only get morphine until her current IV runs out. Then she'll be switched over to Tylenol, supplemented with Codeine only if and when she truly needs it."

Tylenol. Regular, plain old Tylenol. The difference in treatment astonishes me. I was shamed after Annalise's last surgery, told that I was a bad mother who wanted her child to be in pain because I asked for the morphine to be stopped. And now they are relying on Tylenol?

Dr. Glasgow comes to check on Annalise about thirty minutes after she's been settled into the PICU. Not days later but almost immediately. He tells us that the procedure went extremely well. Annalise won't require a shunt (a device implanted into the ventricles of the brain to allow spinal fluid to be transferred from the brain to the spine), and that while he also performed an endoscopic (laser) treatment, he went in from the correct position, making what appeared to be a smaller right ventricle opening a tad larger to allow the fluid to flow more easily. It truly was a textbook procedure, and if Annalise's intracranial fluid pressure (ICP) remained regulated, she would be able to go home in about three days.

Three days later, Annalise is prepped for discharge to return home. The only incident that we encounter during her hospitalization is when a junior nurse attempts to remove Annalise's ICP tube. Essentially, this small white tube is hooked into Annalise's skull and sends a report of how much pressure, due to cerebrospinal fluid, exists. As the nurse removes it, the tube becomes a bit stuck, so the junior nurse calls for backup from another well-seasoned RN. As the junior nurse pulls on the tubing, it immediately dislodges, sending cerebrospinal fluid flying directly into the face of the senior RN. Everyone's mouths hang open in shock, including the mouth of the senior RN.

I gag. I've spent my fair share of time in hospitals, but my stomach has never gotten strong enough to be able to endure that. The senior RN quickly and quietly removes herself from the situation and rushes out of the room.

I wonder if she's ever forgotten that or if it was just another day at the office for a PICU RN. Also, thank God for the wonderful nurses who don't panic when they get a splash of brain fluid in their mouths but instead immediately excuse themselves to go (I presume) vomit. Nurses. Thank you so very much.

30

Guided by God's Hand

Anna

1971

After the period in our life that we refer to as the cat attack, life gets back to what we call normal for us. But it seems like our life usually experiences what we call the seasons of quiet before the storm. One day, I catch a glimpse of myself in a department store mirror and gasp. Why haven't I paid attention to the way I look? Staring back at me is this extremely thin, gaunt-looking woman with sunken cheeks. This reflection staring back at me is that of a woman who appears years older than me. There are huge, dark circles under my eyes. What is going on? Recently, I began experiencing chest pains and found that it hurts to breathe. I am coughing a lot as well.

I must just be tired, I think, but an uneasy feeling resides within me. Anyone who knows me can attest to how unlikely I am to go to the doctor except for yearly checkups. So, I know it must be God who directs my footsteps that day to go to our community clinic for a checkup. After a brief examination, the doctor tells me I need to check into the local hospital for tests. He tells me not to worry. Yet he looks at me with concern and adds that he doesn't want to frighten me, but my symptoms could be nothing or very serious. I am instructed to check into the hospital immediately. Not to worry but ...

My in-laws tell me to send for my mother in Massachusetts immediately to watch the children. My mother gets on a bus and comes right away when contacted. I was surprised that she did not hesitate to come when I needed her. Even in all this, God was doing a healing in more areas than just my physical healing.

The next days are a whirlwind from them first ruling out lung cancer to placing me in isolation with a rare lung infection. The doctor informs me that if they had not caught this when they did, I would have died. I am placed on medication, and after two weeks in isolation, I go home. I am given instructions that I must never allow myself to get overtired or exhausted because it could be fatal to my health.

Overtired or exhausted—I am not about to live like that! I have two children to care for. No! I do not believe that is the way God intended me to live. That medication keeps me tired all the time; I have no energy. So, one day, I decide to throw the medication away. After that, I start regaining my energy. This brush with being sick is like giving me a booster shot to ramp up my life. What is that saying? When life gets tough, the tough get going.

Even in this situation, I believe God has His hand on my life. Up to this point, I am truly just existing. I love my children. Their welfare is especially important to me. I keep our home spotless. I fix them healthy, nutritious meals. I play with them and take them to the park or on walks each day. But until my illness, I must admit that while I love my children, there is a part of me that is afraid to love them too much. I have convinced myself that if I hold back from loving them with all my heart, then God will not take them from me.

If I had to choose one adjective to describe my life at this point, the word would be lonely. Lying in that hospital bed in the isolation ward with an infectious lung disease becomes a wake-up call for me. I become acutely aware of the only thing to live for—my two children. I must begin fixing me. I cannot live the way I am living anymore. And I desperately want to live again. I want to live a life that is more than just going through the motions of existing.

A month after my release from the hospital, my little family returns to church. It is during this time that I accept Jesus as my Lord and Savior. There is no one more surprised than I am to find myself at the altar, asking

Jesus into my heart. My life is about to change in so many ways, and I am amazed at the journey life will take me on once again. I always believed in God, but once I gave my heart to Jesus, something different begins to happen that changes me. I went from just having a knowledge of God to beginning a relationship with the Lord.

> For God so loved the world that he gave his one and only Son, that whosoever believes shall not perish but have eternal life. (John 3:16 NIV)

Anyone reading about me throwing my lung medicine away might wonder why I would do something so foolish. I can only say that my Lord had already begun the healing in my heart, mind, soul, and body, knowing what was to come. I so believe the healing took place that Sunday at the altar when I accepted Jesus as my Lord and Savior. The proof came when I had my next medical checkup, and the x-rays showed my lungs to be completely healed. Where the scarring had previously been, due to the lung infection, it was now scar-free! I will never forget the doctor staring at the x-ray of my lungs for the longest time. I will never forget as he stared at me in amazement and said, "I can't explain it, but your lungs are somehow healed."

31

Nick Grows Distant

Eliza

September 2005

Taking Annalise home after only three days in the hospital, following her second brain surgery, felt like a miracle. There were no earthquakes, no seizures, no new devastations. Finally, we were able to go home and try to rebuild our life according to what I started calling *our new normal.*

Annalise continued therapy, which, because of her age of eighteen months, was focused around play. Anything other than that, and she would cry and scream at the top of her lungs until the forty-five minutes of torture was over, after which she would snuggle into my neck, sucking on her pacifier while glaring at her therapists.

"I'm so glad that for once I'm not the bad guy," I would joke, squeezing Annalise closer to me.

If there was one constant during this time, it was Annalise and I. We were together constantly. While I had returned to school, most of my time was spent with Annalise (and a tribe of therapists who were in and out of our home on a daily basis). Nick remained at Crusader University, Los Angeles, as a full-time professor, was faculty advisor for an on-campus club, had a part-time job at a city college in Long Beach, and monitored the computer lab at another college campus on Sundays.

While Nick had always been busy, it now seemed as if he was spending more and more time either at office hours or working. I was still hurting (and suspicious) over the email I had discovered in my sixth month of pregnancy from a secretary who claimed she had been giving sexual favors to my husband. Because of this, Annalise and I would go with Nick on Sunday to his computer lab job, waiting with him for four hours while he worked.

This became part of our routine. On Sunday, we would all hop into the car for the drive to the Norco campus and wait for Nick to be done with work. On the drive back home, we would stop by Costco to get groceries for the week.

It was rare that Nick and I would fight, but the toll of our new normal had begun to rip at the seams of our already shaky relationship. We were still intimate with each other on rare occasions, but the truth was that we were both exhausted. Being with Annalise all day long was difficult, especially now that she was trying to relearn how to walk for the third time in her young life. The surgery had derailed her previous progress since she had to take it easy for a while, and when it was time to get back on her feet, she was finding it difficult to regain her balance. This meant she was frustrated and irritable because I was not carrying her around the house with me, in the hopes that she would get so fed up that she'd stand and walk like she'd done after her first surgery.

When Nick would come home at the end of the day, I was either in bed or on my way to bed and not in the mood. It didn't seem to matter to Nick that I wasn't fired up about sex. Neither of us had initiated sex in months, and in my opinion, Nick seemed relieved to just crawl into bed beside me and go straight to sleep.

One Sunday afternoon in mid-September, three months after Annalise's second surgery, we were standing in a very crowded checkout line at Costco. We spent the day with Nick in the computer lab, and Annalise screamed for most of the four hours. To keep the peace and quiet that was the norm for a college lab, I put Annalise in her stroller and walked around the campus. It was extremely hot outside, and we were both irritated by the time Nick closed up the lab and got us into the air-conditioned car. Although Costco was cool, thanks to industrial-sized

A/C vents, it was still crowded and loud. Annalise began to scream as we waited in line, and while I tried in vain to soothe her, Nick grew impatient.

Costco on a Sunday is a madhouse to begin with, but on this particular day, it was even more so. People had begun to abandon their carts, filled to the brim with produce, underwear, and other goods found in the aisles of the big-box warehouse store.

Nick saw this as an opportunity. He looked around and saw a container of fresh pineapple that had been abandoned on an endcap. It wasn't sealed, and there was no way to know just how long it had been there or what had been done to it prior to being left behind. He popped open the top, grabbed a slice of pineapple, and put it into Annalise's mouth. She stopped screaming as she began to chew the fruit.

I did what I feel a lot of mothers would have done in this situation. I grabbed the pineapple from Annalise and looked at Nick in disbelief. This prompted Annalise to begin wailing once more.

"What are you doing?" I said. "You have no idea where that's been!"

He glared at me, and without saying a word, he popped another piece into her mouth.

"Nick, stop it! That's not ours, and you have no idea how long it's been out here or if someone did something." I once again dug the fruit from Annalise's mouth.

He grabbed my wrist and warned, "Don't tell me what to feed my baby."

I was stunned. He'd never grabbed me in that way. It was dark and a bit frightening. I looked to the side of Nick and noticed a woman who appeared to be in her late fifties staring at us. She shook her head.

My face was hot with embarrassment. "Nick, please. Don't give that to her," I said, lifting Annalise out of the shopping cart.

"Give her to me," he said, his hand still holding the container of pineapple.

"No, you're going to give her that pineapple," I said, rocking Annalise to try to quiet her. "Come on, be reasonable. You have no idea where that's been."

"It's been right there," he said, pointing to the endcap. "Someone just left it there. It's fine." He reached for Annalise. "Give me my baby."

"Put the pineapple down first," I said.

"No."

I glanced once more at the woman to the side of Nick. She was watching us intensely. When she noticed me looking at her, she shook her head once again and said, "I wouldn't give that baby something I just found lying around either."

Nick heard her comment and spun around. He glared at the woman, who did not shrink back from him. Instead, she returned his gaze, clenching her jaw and narrowing her eyes.

I put my hand on his shoulder. "Nick, let's just pay for this stuff and go." It took a few seconds, but he finally turned around to face me once again. I handed Annalise to him. "Listen, why don't you take her to the car. I'll finish up here, and we can go home. OK?"

Annalise was no longer crying. She nuzzled her head into his shoulder and looked back at me.

"See? She's OK now. Just wanted her daddy." I smiled at him. "Just take her to the car. I'll meet you. Please?"

He walked out of Costco, with Annalise still nuzzled into his shoulder. When he was out of earshot, the woman he'd nearly had a confrontation with said, "I hope he doesn't hit you, honey."

I shook my head vehemently and answered, "He would never. He's just tired."

"Mmhmm" was her only reply.

My only focus was getting out of Costco as quickly as possible. I paid for the groceries and didn't look back at the woman again.

Even though the rest of that Sunday evening passed without incident, Nick begins having more outbursts that previously were of character for him. I write it off as stress—over Annalise, over his job, over our marriage, over his kids, over his ex-wife, over his extended family. The insults about my mother are now being hurled on a daily basis. He frequently makes comments about how my mother is trying to ruin his life, how she's been in his class auditing him, how she's poisoned the entire faculty against him.

To be honest, I don't know what to believe. I know that my mom was angry about our relationship in the beginning and that she'd wanted something else for my life. Once Annalise was in the picture, all of that anger had been left behind, and she was now the picture of a loving grandma. She adored her granddaughter, and regardless of what Nick was saying about her, I knew in my heart that my mom would never do anything that would intentionally hurt Annalise. I tried to reason with Nick, but he had grown so bitter and paranoid about not only my mother but about other faculty at the university; there was nothing I could say to ease his mind.

He was saying horrible things about professors I had known for years, who I knew to be kind people. Yet my husband was sure they were all out to get him, and he would tell me things that made it seem as if there was an undercover spy ring running the university.

"Thanks to your mom and Piruz, backstabbers, I have no schedule. And oh, very strange that right after we spend a weekend with your mom, Maziar comes in and grabs my two class sections. I guess your mom got what she always wanted," he says one afternoon as he is coming into the house and I am getting ready to leave for my evening classes.

"Nick, come on. We've been through this over and over again. I don't think my mom is trying to do anything to you. First of all, she wouldn't risk her career just to take some classes away from you. And second, I've been hearing some things about how you really spend your time on campus," I say, pulling on a hoodie and grabbing my backpack.

"What does that mean?" he barks.

"It means that I've heard about how you have closed-door appointments with certain students." I glare at him, searching his face for any sign of deceit.

"Another lie your mother has been telling!" he yells, waving his hands in the air and nearly hitting my face.

"Don't lie, please. This whole thing has to stop." I motion to the computer next to the couch. "This nonsense has been going on since I was pregnant."

"What are you talking about?" he asks.

"You're kidding." I nearly laugh. "The secretary, the secret meetings? The reason why Annalise and I go with you to Norco on Sundays?" My voice raises an octave. "This has to stop, or you need to let us go!"

"I'm not a cheater! Those women your mom says I have, they're there for Jack, not me!" Jack is another professor Nick shares an office with. He is a notorious philanderer, and there were often rumors of his dalliances with students.

146

"Jack," I say, with obvious disbelief in my voice.

"Yes, Jack. It's his affairs, not mine. I would never do anything to hurt you or Annalise. You are both my world." He reaches out to grab my hand. I withdraw from his grasp and grip my backpack straps instead.

"How can I believe you?" I question, searching his face for scraps of honesty.

"Stop listening to your mother. She and Piruz are out to get me. They want us to be destroyed. They want to destroy our family. They—"

"Nick, stop! My mom is our family. She is Annalise's grandmother. If you really believe that she's out to get you, to ruin you, then maybe we need to sit down with her and ask her."

"Yeah right. She will lie. That's what she does best."

I throw my hands in the air and motion to the door. "I have to go, or I'll be late for school. Can you please make sure Annalise has a bath and just …" I trail off. I was about to tell him to just relax on the conspiracy theories, but I am too frustrated to say the words I am thinking. Instead, I say, "I'll just see you later."

The stress in the house gets worse as the weeks go by. The level of discord in our marriage is now palpable to not only us but everyone who walks through our front door. Annalise's therapists begin asking me if everything is all right with Nick and me. In truth, the only reason our marriage is still intact is because I am busy. Between Annalise's therapy and doctor appointments and trying to finish school, our time together is measured, and the conversations mostly revolve around our schedules.

32

Annalise's New School

Eliza
October 2005

Our caseworker for Harbor Regional Center, Rick Ocho, says that in addition to starting therapy, he wants Annalise to begin preschool. There are only two programs near our home, and of those, only one provides both speech and language therapy in addition to educational learning—Tracy Infant Center.

Annalise will attend the center five half days a week. While there, she will engage in play therapy with other children, attend group speech therapy, and sit in a preschool environment for three of the five half days.

The first day she attends Tracy, Annalise is not thrilled. Nick and I both drop her off that first morning, and I can't tell you who is more nervous, Annalise or her parents. I look down at the white terrazzo flooring as we walk. It is dingy, obviously worn from years of stampeding preschoolers.

Annalise is comfortably seated on my hip, taking in her new surroundings. She doesn't appear nervous at all. I silently pray that she will enjoy this school, that it will be safe, and that she will make some new friends.

When we reach the doorway to her new classroom, Nick enters first. He greets Annalise's teacher and then gestures toward Annalise as if he is introducing the next Miss America. I give him an odd look, and Annalise, noticing that the attention has been turned toward her, buries her face in my shoulder.

"She's a bit shy," I offer. "Once we leave, I think she'll come around."

"Of course. Should we let Mom and Dad go?" the teacher asks Annalise, giving me a wink.

Annalise does not appreciate the sentiment. "No!" she screams in my ear, holding my neck tightly with one arm.

"Come on, baby. It's time to go make new friends," I say, giving her a tight hug. "Don't you want to make new friends?"

"No!" she screams again.

Nick steps toward me and lifts Annalise from my grasp. "Come on, Boosie. You'll be fine." He manages to remove Annalise from around my neck, but she's regained a firm grasp on my hair.

"Ouch! Annalise, let go," I say, attempting to disentangle my long hair from between her tightly gripped fist.

"Nooooo!"

I grab my hair as close to the ends as I can, to prevent her from ripping it from my head. "Annalise! Let. Go," I say firmly.

She hesitates for a moment and then releases my hair.

"Thank you," I say to her.

"Mmpphh," she grunts in reply.

The teacher, who has been silently watching this battle of wills, finally says, "Don't worry, Mom and Dad. Once you are on your way, she will be just fine. I see it every day."

"Well, call us, would you? If she needs us or if you want us to come and get her," I instruct.

"Of course. But she will be fine," the teacher says soothingly.

"Say bye-bye, Mommy," Nick says as he put Annalise down onto the floor.

Annalise immediately begins to cry, a passionate and loud wail that resembles an injured animal.

Nick takes me by the shoulder and turns me toward the door. "Byebye, Annalise. Mommy and Daddy will see you later."

I turn once more to look at her. She is now screaming in protest, and my legs threaten to turn to jelly. The sounds emanating from this small child are breaking my heart.

"Nick, I can't. I have to go back," I say as we head toward the main entrance.

"Just keep walking. She'll be fine. Just keep walking," he responds.

We pick her up a few hours later. I expect to find out that Annalise has cried the entire time and be told that there is no way she will be able to return due to her heartbreaking emotional outburst. What we find, however, is that Annalise was fine. According to the teacher, Annalise cried for a few minutes after we left, and then she settled down. She hadn't made any new friends but had instead followed her teacher around like a little shadow. She said a few words, preferring to grunt her approval or disapproval. Finally, she became attached to one of the Little Tykes Cozy Coupes in the play yard. This is where we found her upon pickup, sitting inside it, pressing on the airhorn as if she'd never thrown a tantrum or attempted to give her mother a bald spot.

33

Mommy's Mad, Daddy's Sad

Eliza
2005

Annalise's two brain surgeries are behind us. I'm focusing on trying to absorb as much information as possible about how to help Annalise recover from the muscle weakness caused by the brain injury.

Our family life isn't at all what I imagined it would be. The days of worrying over my mother-in-law giving me cleaning supplies and having that be my greatest point of frustration are over. I want to go back to what was—or rather thinking about what should be. But life is more complicated now.

I'm angry. I wish for all sorts of terrible things to happen to the doctors and their families. I want them to suffer as much as we are or more. I want their suffering to be so great that it drives them to the point of no return from their darkness. Darkness. It started as a small thing really. Like a spot you see after you stare at the sun and then blink. Just a small bit of darkness. But now, after hearing Dr. Lin talking about his vacation plans to a pretty nurse; after meeting with Dr. Henry and knowing that he tried to get us to have another surgery with him, just so he could cover up his mistake; after seeing Annalise running in a hospital corridor and then not moving an entire side of her body—I'm angry. Darkly so.

Nick is not angry. Not really. He's irritated. He doesn't spew hatred or wish ills upon the doctors like I do. Instead, he acts as if he has an annoying mosquito bite. Fidgety and unsettled. He stays that way for hours, and then he walks to the couch, lies down, and falls asleep. It has gotten to the point where he isn't sleeping in our bed anymore. He tries to, but every night it's the same routine. He follows me to the bedroom, carrying Annalise up the single flight of stairs. He lies down and kisses me and then her. He sometimes falls asleep, but mostly he just stares into the darkness as he waits for me to drift off. When he's sure I'm asleep, he rises slowly and walks down the hall to Annalise's room or back downstairs, where he stays all night. The couch has become the only place where he seems to get any sleep at all, and only for a few hours during the day.

Annalise wants to play with him, to be held by him. But he's reserved with her now, withdrawn. I've tried to talk to him about it, but he just can't seem to get the words out without falling apart. He just says, "I'm sad. I am so sad."

I'm worried about him, but I can only handle so much. It's sad what happened to Annalise, and I understand that he's sad. I'm sad too. There just isn't time to fall apart now. Now is the time to act, when she's young. Her brain is pliable now; that's what all of the specialists say. We have to act. Maybe my anger keeps me going, and I can't be in that pit of sadness that Nick seems to be focused on. My focus needs to be on Annalise, on her recovery. She needs both of us, but I can't wait for Nick to break out of this funk he's in.

34

We Fight Back

Eliza
Early 2006

In addition to dealing with marital issues, new addresses, and schools, working full-time, and raising Annalise, we are coming up on an important deadline. In California, there is a one-year statute of limitations to bring a medical malpractice lawsuit. In other words, we are racing against the clock to find out what really happened to Annalise in that operating room with Dr. Henry and Dr. Lin. The thought has crossed my mind that perhaps they didn't tell us what really happened to cause Annalise's paralysis and seizures, not only because they wanted to cover their own butts but because they wanted to stall long enough so that we were so preoccupied with obtaining care for Annalise that our time limit to file a lawsuit would be reached.

Suing a major HMO is scary. They have lawyers that all seem to wear a version of the same suit, black jacket and pants or skirt with a white button-down collared shirt. Never smiling, just intimidating. Meeting with these lawyers made me constantly question the presence of their souls. They're mean, unflinching in their lack of emotion, and cold. I'm fairly certain that eternity holds a special place for HMO lawyers, and God help you if you ever end up in front of them while still a resident of Earth.

We are fighting for restitution for Annalise. As she is so young, we have to estimate what her life might be like as she enters into adolescence and adulthood. Scenarios that have become nightmares we now have to face head-on. Will Annalise be able to ride a bike? Will she attend typical classes? Will she be able to drive? To work? Can she take care of herself? Will she be able to one day live on her own? All of these questions and more we need to answer in order for the judge in our case to adequately pass down a judgment that will affect the rest of her life.

Specialists are brought in by both sides. Our side's experts testified that Annalise will not recover completely and will need substantial medical care as the years pass. The HMO panel of experts argued that children similar to Annalise grow up perfectly normal, living lives not unlike our own, having children, careers, and prospects. While I want to believe the side of the HMO, I have to prepare for the worst. The worst-case scenario means that we need to make sure that Annalise will be provided for, no matter what.

Even though I am only in my late twenties, the reality is that I will get older. The possibility that Annalise will need someone to take care of her when I am gone becomes my focus. It keeps me awake at night. I have nightmares about dying and leaving her without anyone who can care for her needs. What if she became homeless one day, just one of the countless numbers of disabled individuals living on the streets. What then?

35

Lonely but Determined

Anna
1972–1986

I truly wish I could say that after I accept Jesus as my Savior, my marriage is miraculously restored. It takes two people who are willing to work at restoring the relationship. We continue to live together for the sake of the children. We are like two ships passing in the night. Each night, I set the dinner table for the four of us. I proceed to tell the children to wait for an hour to see if their father can make it home from "work" to have dinner with us. During the week, he never comes home for dinner. He never calls to say he is going to be late.

No one in our extended families, neighbors, or church families is aware of what is transpiring in our lives. On Sundays, we appear to be the perfect family who attends church and has lunch after church with family. To all who know us, we epitomize the perfect family. The lies and secrets of my past have followed me into adulthood and taken on a new form. First, my mother, and now, my husband never ceases to remind me of the saying, "Oh, what a dangerous web we weave when first we practice to deceive."

After my illness, I go back to work to earn enough money to get another family car. The lack of a second family car keeps the children and me unable to venture far from the house. We live several miles from town, and I feel trapped with no way to do something as simple as go grocery shopping. I miss having the freedom I once enjoyed in my teens. Besides, I grew tired of always sitting at home, waiting for someone who was never there. I enjoyed working and mostly being around people again.

Then after working for a few years at various companies in accounting departments, my life is about to take another turn. I have some errands to do when suddenly I find myself at the local community college. The most remarkable thing about that is I never intended to stop there. I have no plans to attend college. I am a mother of two young children with a job. I need my job to pay for a car I recently purchased to commute to work. What am I doing?

It is as if an invisible hand is guiding me as I park my car and walk up the pathway to a specific building. Let me emphasize that I have no idea what I am doing or where I am going. I know nothing about college. My parents never went to college; they never even finished high school. My mother had an eighth-grade education, and my adopted father had a third-grade education. No one in my family had ever gone to college. I did not have the slightest idea about how to go about attending college. I had never thought about getting a college education.

As I walk into that building and down the hallway, I find myself standing in front of a window, asking about going to college. Before I know it, I am taking entrance tests. Never in my wildest dreams did I believe that one day I would not only attend college there but one day return to teach there. And even more amazing is the journey that led to me earning not only my bachelor's and master's degrees but a doctorate. God certainly works in ways that may seem impossible to us but are possible with God. I genuinely believe with all my heart that when I accepted Jesus as my Lord and Savior, He laid out a path that He meant for me to take all along.

However, I am getting ahead, so as usual, I need to backtrack and tell the whole story. God is still working on me in the patience department.

Interestingly, there is opposition to my attending college from my extended family members. "Can't you wait until your children are grown before doing this? Are you now making education your god?"

The evil one knows the plans God has in store for us and will do whatever he can to thwart our destiny. Thankfully, I knew in my heart that God directed my footsteps from the very moment I first arrived on the campus to begin that journey.

I decide I want to major in business and begin on that path. One day, a counselor on campus asks me if I ever considered going into education. I tell him, "No way am I going to be a teacher. I am too shy to talk in front of people. I don't want to be a teacher. I want to work in an office as an accountant." Besides, I could work by myself and not have to put up with people being around me all day. That statement now brings a laugh from everyone who knows me!

"If you become an educator, you could be off three months a year and spend more time with your children," the counselor said as he gave me that encouraging smile.

He did make a good point. A three-month summer break each year would certainly save on childcare expenses. But pursuing a profession as a teacher, that really wasn't for me.

He saw my hesitation and added, "Think about this. You could major in business education, which would give you the best of both worlds. You could decide to use your degree to work in business or teach. You would have an option and nothing to lose."

That comment did make sense. I liked the idea of not putting all my eggs in one basket. My life had been chaotic enough; I did not want to take any more risks.

"OK, no harm in taking that route," I replied.

But as for that three months off—I went into teaching but usually worked every summer.

I am determined to stay on track and complete my bachelor's degree within the allotted four years I have given myself. The money for school comes from the funds I try to set aside while also working full-time. I supplement those funds with student loans. The quicker I finish my degree, the better for everyone. Everything is going along quite smoothly. I look back and am still amazed at how I attended school, worked full-time, and almost single-handedly cared for my children. Only God ...

But as my life goes, I am almost through my first two years of college when I encounter another trial. I undergo a gallbladder operation. I try to put off the surgery, but the pain is almost unbearable. It is during this time that the company I work for decides to scale back. I am a likely candidate for a layoff since they know I likely will quit to finish my degree. That saying "out of sight, out of mind" comes into play: I am laid off when I am on sick leave. Here I am with no job, in the middle of a semester of schoolwork and recovering from surgery. But again, I stand amazed at how God works everything out, and I complete my first two years of college on time. My husband even enrolls in school, and we find ourselves taking a course together. But even on campus, we always seem to go our separate ways—partly due to his work schedule, partly due to the separate lives we lead.

Those who know us often joke that watching my husband and me together is like observing a biplane and jet trying to fly in formation. "Poor guy struggles to keep up with the jet!" Their comments take me by surprise because since my firstborn's death, I feel like my life has changed me from the girl I used to be growing up.

Even during my stay in the hospital, I believe God is working in more ways than I can ever imagine. There is a nurse who often sits in my room after his shift is over. I often awaken to find him sitting here. He refers to himself as my guardian angel. I recognize him as one of the students on the campus. He is in the nursing program and studying to earn his nursing degree. Later, much later, I learn that he appoints himself to watch over me. He feels a sense of moral responsibility due to some knowledge he has. A few years later, he shares with me that one of my nurses (also a student on campus) is having an affair with my husband.

"I never thought any harm would come to you, but morally, I felt responsible for you," this nurse shares. I see him at a grocery store, and we begin talking about our lives. I thank him for being such a kind person who made my hospital stay more tolerable and safer. I leave the store and say a silent prayer to my Lord for his protection.

Life speeds up, and I finish the next two years of college. I accept my first teaching job in a small northern Arkansas town. This new job requires me to relocate. The move means the children and I will live alone for a while. I am practically alone most of the time, so this adjustment does not faze me. My husband stays behind to work in his current job and finish college. The plan is for him to join us in one year. He continues to live in our house while I relocate and live in an apartment with the children until the house is sold.

That first year is full of surprises. I have been on birth control since my son's surprise birth. But surprise, I discover I am pregnant once again. I do not know why I should be surprised. Nothing I do is ever easy. I am learning my new job and preparing once again to welcome a new baby into the world. My two older children, ages nine and seven, are now both in school, and this means finding a new babysitter to care for my expected newborn. I am in many respects a single mom with a husband who visits us on the weekends.

During my pregnancy, the calls begin coming in from a woman my husband is seeing. In the past, he kept his indiscretions under wraps from me, but this time it is different. Here I am in a new job, expecting another child, and he is ... This time I confront him about the calls. All those years of indifference are changing me. I know enough about what is happening. I tell him I do not need someone like him disrupting my life anymore. He realizes I am serious and ready to end this marriage immediately. After our talk, he asks me to forgive him and promises to be faithful. My mother's words come back to haunt me, "You make your bed; you lie in it." Never once do I share with my family or his what is going on.

Eventually, my husband finishes his degree and joins us in our new town. He finds a job, and soon the late hours begin again. My family is now complete with the addition of a beautiful little girl. She is mischievous and feisty. She holds her own in a family with an older sister, ten years her senior, and a brother, eight years older than she is. From a noticeably young age, she doesn't hesitate to say what is on her mind. While her older sister is a tomboy who loves to play soldier and build forts, the baby of the family is a little princess. She loves to dress up in the frilliest dresses and wear a tiara on her head.

Life reverts to being lonely. I throw myself into my teaching job. The satisfaction of teaching others is incredibly fulfilling. It is during this time that I decide to begin work on my master's degree. My days and evenings are filled with work, attending college to earn my master's degree, and spending time with my children. My busy life keeps me from thinking about the loneliness that looms over my relationship with my husband. His promise to be faithful is forgotten.

This hectic lifestyle goes on for five years. I complete my master's degree and am ready to take on a new challenge. I find myself applying for a teaching job at the college where I began my postsecondary education. I never dream that I will one day be teaching alongside the college teachers who once taught me. Once again, God is directing my footsteps to the place it all began.

Back we move to the very area where we once lived. We settle in a lovely home, and I am beyond excited to be teaching alongside those who were my former instructors. My life is busy. Part of that busyness is to deflect that my marriage is so lonely. Appearances are so deceiving regarding our family life. Our friends, extended family, and church family see us as one happy family who has it all. We attend church every Sunday—the one day we spend any time together as a family. The rest of the week, we live very separate lives. We fill our lives with the things that bring us a false sense of satisfaction. Mine is work and the children. Things go on this way until life rears its ugly head once more.

Life throws another curveball my way in the next few years. I am living with constant abdominal pain. I begin losing a pound a day and soon look like a walking skeleton. My clothes hang off my body. My first fear is that the prior lung disease returned, but it is a disease called endometriosis. The disease is spreading rapidly and even growing up my spine.

I begin to look so bad that the college president comes to me and asks me what is wrong. "Everyone is worried about you. Are you ill?"

It is his comment that leads me to admit that I cannot keep putting off what is happening. I have been diagnosed with stage 4 endometriosis, which is spreading and causing severe pain and almost daily blood loss. I need to get an operation, but the semester is only half-over. I do not have the resources to take off from work until summer. I am the sole supporter for the family at the time. My husband took over his grandmother's business after she died. The business is not doing well financially. We live mostly on my income, and money is very tight. I am afraid to go through another period like the previous summer.

The summer before, my husband became bored working for his grandmother's business. He decided to take an advertising sales job for an oil company. The job was straight commission based and required him to relocate to Nevada and surrounding states for a few months. The responsibility for our new house payments and all bills were my responsibility until he earned some commission. On top of that, our former house had not yet sold, and I needed to make those house payments as well. Things that summer got really tough. There was one week when some unexpected expenses came up that needed to be paid. There was no food in the house except for a bag of flour. My children lived on flour gravy biscuits made with water. There wasn't even any milk in the house. I did not eat for three days so there would be enough flour to last until payday.

My credit cards are maxed out. My husband is making charges on the cards for his living and travel expenses. There is no money left in the bank account. We are broke. I work a full-time job as a professional educator, and we have no food to eat. I cry as I think about my mother and her abuse of money. I am far worse a person because I do not even have the means to provide my children with the essentials, such as food.

That week teaches me a lesson that has stayed with me my whole life. There is not a day that goes by that I do not stop to thank God for my daily bread and His provisions in times of little, enough, and plenty.

So, facing another time of scarcity is scary. But I need to have the surgery and waiting is endangering my health. I talk to my husband and tell him that the surgery cannot wait. I tell him that he needs to either take over some of the bills or take on a part-time job for a few weeks until I am able to return to work. The doctor says I will require six weeks of bedrest. Once I am well, I can assume the role of major breadwinner again until the business expands.

His next words set in motion a course of action I vowed not to take. "That is your problem," he coldly responds and walks away.

My problem! This situation is about our kids, the family. After everything that has happened in our lives together, after all the hurt and the pain—he does not care. Those words are springboard to make some changes in my life. I know what I need to do.

I undergo the surgery and spend the next six weeks recovering at home. While I lie there in bed recovering and taking care of the children, I am consumed with one goal I need to accomplish. As soon as I am able to leave the house and drive a car, I head straight for an attorney to file for divorce. After all these years, I am now convinced our life together is not going to change. My doctors comment to me many times, "It is not what you are eating that is causing all these stomach issues you are experiencing but what is eating you."

They are right! I keep trying to be the strong one. My pride keeps me in bondage. This is no different from growing up pretending that my mother could not hurt me. I continue to build a wall around me that no one else is going to penetrate. Why do I keep letting others hurt me? I need to stop this pattern of abuse. I have been hurt enough.

After nearly twenty-one years of marriage, my life as a single mom is truly just that. No more pretenses. Or so I believe. Of course, families quickly take sides as to who is to blame for the breakup of our little family.

Immediately after the divorce, my now ex-husband begins showing up every night at dinnertime. He says he wants to spend time with me and the kids. He begins sending me flowers and cards at work on a regular basis. Suddenly, he starts becoming the man and father he has never been. This really confuses our youngest daughter, who starts crying every time her father leaves each evening. What should be a transition for us becomes confusing. He shares that he has begun attending a new church close to us and is seeing a psychologist who is helping him work through his issues.

For the next three months, our disjointed family life seems to be on the right track for the very first time. Then my ex-husband asks me if I would consider us getting a marriage license and starting our life over again. After much insistence on his part, I agree to go to the courthouse with him and get our license. "One step at a time," I tell myself on the way there. I inform him that I will meet him there. To be honest, I do not think we will go through with getting the license. He is notorious for not keeping his commitments to me. I doubt he will meet me at the courthouse. But to my surprise, he does show up—and on time. We obtain the license and prepare to leave when the clerk informs us the judge is ready to meet with us.

Judge? Why does the judge want to meet with us? The next steps happen before I truly realize what is truly taking place. The judge greets us, smiles, and begins the ceremony. Yes, ceremony! We remarry. I walk out of the courthouse in a daze. Everything is happening too fast. What is happening to the one-step-at-a-time plan?

We exit the courthouse and turn to look at each other. Silence. Then my new, no longer ex-husband shrugs his shoulders and mutters, "Well, I better get back to work." And with that said, he practically runs down the stairs as he dashes to his car. I stand there in a daze as I watch him drive away.

That evening, my new husband moves back home as if nothing happened. He is quieter than usual that evening, as am I. The next few days, we keep the same quiet, uneasy feeling when we are around each other. Finally, that weekend, he blurts out that he really does not want to be married to me again. He has second thoughts about what we have done. What have we done? I am sick as I realize I have once again become a victim of his tactics.

He began going to another church during our divorce and feels that maybe we can go there for a while. He has joined this new singles group at the church. He said he enjoys this group and thinks we should take part. Singles group? And that church is way leftfield of what I am used to attending. But frankly I am embarrassed about going back to the church we always attended as a family. So I decide to give his new church a try. Again, as I look back, I stand amazed at how God takes my broken life and heals my broken heart, mind, and soul. God is about to raise me out of the ashes to a new life. While all this is going on, I am about to find peace beyond anything I could ever imagine possible. Even in the midst of our greatest heartaches, God is there to meet us right where we are.

36

Marcello and Milan

Eliza
Winter 2006

I haven't felt sexy to Nick recently, instead feeling as if I am the thing in his life that makes him the most miserable. My attraction to him has waned. This is due to several factors but is also driven by the fact that I have rekindled conversations with an old boyfriend. The old boyfriend, Marcello, makes me feel sexy and desired. After months of chatting, we make a plan to see each other in Milan, where Marcello lives. I lie to Nick, telling him I am going to meet a girlfriend of mine in Germany.

My best friend, Monet, drives me to the airport along with Annalise. We go for lunch beforehand, and I get Annalise a balloon. For the first time, I feel horrible guilt. Even Monet thinks I am meeting a girlfriend in Germany. Annalise cries at the airport, her little hand clutching the red balloon. I kiss her nose, eyes, mouth, and cheeks. I kiss her hands. I kiss her left hand for a long time. I smell her hair—the floral shampoo that I used on her when we took a shower together in the morning. I hug her and then hug her again. I tell her, "Mommy will be back really soon, honey."

Monet exclaims, "Go! Enjoy yourself!"

I pause, wanting to tell her the truth.

There is meant to be a stop in Frankfurt with a continuation onto Milan. However, the weather isn't cooperating, and all flights into Milan have been cancelled. I call Marcello. He tells me to get a night train ticket that will take me from Frankfurt into Milan, and he'll pick me up at the train station in the morning.

I can't get my luggage from the airport and make the train in time, so with just a pashmina to protect me from the cold, I buy a ticket and board the train to Milan. I attempt to sleep but can't. The all-night ride includes a scenic thoroughfare through snowy Switzerland, two passport checks, a two-hour delay so that the tracks can be defrosted, and finally, the arrival at the train station in Milan.

Although it has been nearly fifteen years since I've seen Marcello (I was sixteen when we first met), I recognize him right away. He is there on the platform, his hair gray at the sides, holding a stuffed teddy bear for me as a gift. I stop to look at him for a minute before he notices me. I run into his arms, and we embrace for a long time.

My clothes are disheveled, the bottom of my pants soaking wet from the slush and snow, and my hair and makeup are a mess. But it doesn't matter. Marcello takes me shopping for a few items of clothing, things to hold me over until my luggage arrives from Frankfurt. He refuses to let me pay. He holds my hand in the stores, kisses me on the escalator, and after we make our final purchases, he brings me to his apartment. I take a much-needed hot shower, and Marcello asks me to please go to sleep. I comply but only after we spend some intimate time with each other. It is phenomenal, and I fall asleep shortly afterward. For the first time in a year, I sleep without waking up multiple times.

I spend the next four days with Marcello in Milan. We spend lots of intimate time together multiple times a day, he cooks for me, we explore the city, I meet his friends and his son, and I watch his band practice. It is like living in a fantasy.

The morning I have to return home is met with sadness and exaltation. I am sad to leave Milan, to leave Marcello. I am exuberant to see Annalise again. I speak on the phone with Annalise a couple of times, very briefly, and I just want so badly to see her baby face, to kiss and hug her.

37

Nick Knows

Eliza

The night I get home, Nick wakes me from my dreams.

"I need to talk to you." His voice cracks in the stillness.

I open my eyes, blinking them rapidly to focus on the extreme darkness of the bedroom. "Right now?" I ask, rubbing my eyes and feeling the clumps of dried mascara as they stick against the tips of my cheekbones.

"Yes, now." He lifts the covers from my body.

I carefully extract myself from beneath the tiny fists of our little girl and follow him through the corridor to the stairwell. The top stairs creak as we make our way down to the lower level of the house. I feel a chill as we enter the kitchen and cringe at the sight of the countertops cluttered with hardly used appliances.

"Did you have a nice trip?"

His words sound tight, and he nods as he speaks. He always nods or shakes his head when preparing an argument. The gray shading he normally has under his eyes, a nod to his Iranian heritage, is now purplish black.

I know immediately what this will be about. He knows.

"It was ... okay."

My head suddenly clears, not only from the effects of the deep sleep but from the effects of the past three years of marriage to this man, of the happenstances that occurred when our daughter underwent brain surgery at fifteen months of age, leaving her paralyzed on the entire left side of her body. I don't cry. I don't feel the urge to do that. I just want it to be done.

"I want you to tell me the truth. You've been lying to me for months, and I want to know what exactly happened in Europe."

I have no intention of holding back. I open my mouth to speak, but he interrupts me like he always does.

"And I want you to know that I know *everything*." He glares at me, his eyes holding a fury that is only slightly masked by the sadness that clouds his face.

I inhale deeply. "Can you sit down?" I pull out one of the heavy chairs that sit at the breakfast table and motion for him to take it. I remain standing.

"Did you even go to Frankfurt?" he asks.

So, he doesn't know everything. He only knows the highlights. I know I have to tell him what really happened. There is no point in lying about this anymore. To be honest, it is a relief to stop lying.

"I did. I flew into Frankfurt just like I told you."

"But then had a connection into Italy?" Nick asks. His voice is so calm it scares me.

"I did, but it was cancelled because of snow. I would've been stuck in Germany but decided to take an overnight train to Milan," I answer, knowing the entire truth will come out tonight.

"Did *he* meet you in Milan?" he asks, emphasizing what he really wants to know.

"He did," I answer softly.

"Was this your plan all along? It had nothing to do with you needing time on your own; it was just about seeing this guy?" He rapidly fires the questions at me, the tone of his voice beginning to rise.

"Not entirely." I take a deep breath, not quite knowing what Nick's full reaction to my cheating will be. "I mean, I did need time away, but …

yes, I wanted to see him." I spit out the words, needing them to be said. Needing the truth to be freed.

"How long? What about his wife? He's married. You're married! You abandoned your daughter to run off and be with this man!" His anger rose with each statement.

In my head, I imagine ripping a Band-Aid, knowing this is what needs to be done. I need to not hesitate and rip the Band-Aid. My voice just above monotone, I tick off answers to each one. "I saw him for four days. He's not married. And I would hardly call going away for a week abandoning Annalise. I always knew I'd come back."

"He is married! I know! I saw the emails!" He points to the desktop that sits perched near the couch. The house is so cluttered that in order to use the computer, I have to sit on the couch with the keyboard in my lap, mouse on a cushion. It is a messy, packrat's dream of a house, and I hate it.

The clutter makes it impossible to have a clear mind, and I am constantly policing my baby to ensure that a stack of thick textbooks or a shelf doesn't come tumbling down on her as she attempts to crawl through the house. The fact that this is the home he bought with his ex-wife, where he planted roots with her and lived in the past life he made with her make it a daily nightmare. I have never felt as if this home was mine. Even the floral bedding is a blast from his past, something that was popular in the mid-eighties, and I feel betrayed by the sight of it. I despise this bedding, ever since I spotted it in a picture found in his file cabinet—a sweet shot of him relaxing on top of the comforter with his ex-wife, her right hand buried in his thick black hair.

"If you know everything, Nick. Why do you need me to tell you?" I ask.

"I want to hear you say it!" He is so close to my face that I feel the heat of his breath on my forehead.

"Fine. I cheated. I slept with him. I spent four days with him, in his house." I'm not sure what I was expecting him to say or do at this point.

"Is he better than me?" He asks, the question posed so sincerely that I immediately take a step back.

"That's what you want to know? Of all the things, *that's* what's on your mind?" I search his face for something that I'm not sure I'll actually find. Something resembling anything besides possessiveness. Something resembling love.

After many more weeks of thought and discussion, Nick and I decide to try another go at making our family work. We slide very slowly back into the roles of husband and wife and try to put on a brave face for Annalise, but the resolve lasts only for a brief period.

I tell Nick that living in a home where he made a life with his ex-wife isn't working for me, that we need a place of our own. We decide to move to Belmont Shores and find the cutest little beach house to rent. I'm hoping that the move will signify a new start for us, and I'm looking forward to spending more time together as a family.

38

Marketing Motorhomes

Eliza
February 2006

Since Nick has been trying to sell the Cerritos house, and our move to the beach has left us with additional house expenses, I told Nick that I would like to get a job to help out. He agreed, and shortly after I began searching, I landed the role of marketing associate for a small motorhome manufacturer. The pay is reasonable, but the drive is a bit of a killer at fifty miles each way. I have to be at work at eight in the morning, which means leaving the house by seven at the latest. The drive doesn't really phase me, however. I'm excited to gain the experience and am happy living at the beach. My paycheck is enough to cover the monthly rent and utilities for the beach rental, which in my mind is a small price to pay for the serenity of being in a place that is entirely ours.

My first day at the new job is on Annalise's second birthday. I am introduced to several people who work at the manufacturing facility, from salespeople to line workers to engineers. I am shown my office, which consists of a desk on the left side of the small room. Next to my desk is a very cluttered desk that belongs to someone by the name of Christopher who goes by his preferred name of "Grifter."

"Grifter?" I ask Jerry, the HR manager who is in charge of showing me around.

"Yes, that's what everyone calls him. Even his dad," Jerry replies.

"Who's his dad?" I ask, unsure as to why this man's father would matter in this discussion.

"His father is Jeremiah, the CEO and founder." Jerry looks at me. "You'll be sort of looking out for him."

"Looking out for him?" I survey Grifter's desk, taking in the empty chip wrappers and soda cans that littered its surface. "What do you mean? Looking out for him—how?"

Jerry looks embarrassed. "Yeah, his old man wants someone to keep an eye on him. Keep him in line, make sure he comes to work, stuff like that."

"Is he my boss?" I wonder aloud. "Aren't I here to write ads and marketing materials?"

"You're actually his boss," Jerry answers. "And yes, you're here to do the marketing writing and such."

The *and such* part of the gig would end up being one of the worst jobs of my career. Grifter was consistently late, if he bothered to show up at all. And when he did show for work, he would most likely disappear by lunchtime. This did not go unnoticed by his father, my boss, Jeremiah.

Jeremiah was a small-statured man who smoked cigars in the office, spoke offensively to everyone, and flaunted his family money (he was heir to a large fortune, left to him by his father, who'd paved the way for Jeremiah by starting his own company). He would frequently make blatant sexual passes at me, and on more than one occasion, he attempted to make my personal life the butt of his jokes. He called both my husband and my daughter foul names and didn't care that this was not only morally wrong but could have legal ramifications as well.

My employment lasted approximately eight months and came to an end when Jeremiah came storming into my office shortly after lunch and, finding Grifter's desk empty, began hurling loud and threatening insults at me. He blamed me for Grifter's inability to work, for his growing drug problem, for his lack of motivation. When I told him that I didn't think I should be responsible for babysitting his grown son, he grew incensed and yelled, "That's exactly what we hired you for! You think we hired you because of your experience or your brains? More like lack of brains! Go and find him and bring him back here—or don't come back!"

I called Nick from the parking lot after I stormed out of work. I explained to him that I didn't want to go back and told him about this latest turn of events. I'd had altercations with Jeremiah and Grifter before, but today's episode was the last straw. I expected sympathy. What I got was a stern lecture. Nick said three words before hanging up the phone.

"You can't quit."

I sat in the car, the phone heavy in my hand. I knew what he meant. I needed this job to pay our bills, to pay the mortgage on the beach house. Without my job, we would have no choice but to move back to his house in Cerritos—back to the ghosts and memories of his past. Back to the stifling feeling of sleeping in a bed that had been bought with and for another woman.

I felt my chest tightening, and my breathing was shallow. I thought it was a heart attack. I drove to the nearest emergency room, and after explaining the events to the doctor on call, it was decided that I was suffering from a panic attack. I'd been through the paralyzing of my child, watched her undergo two brain surgeries, caught my husband cheating, had my own affair, and yet it was another man who would cause so much stress that I would have my very first panic attack. Congratulations, Jeremiah. You're the absolute worst.

39

Beach Days and a Gateway

Eliza

After the Jeremiah and Grifter debacle, all I want is a regular corporate job that will not present any hidden job requirements like babysitting the CEO's son. I pray to God, "Please, just let me find a good job with no drama."

Nick is upset that I quit my job. He has become increasingly anxious over our living situation at the beach. I have enough money in my savings to take care of the rent and bills for a couple of months, and while I'm looking for a new job, I am relishing being back home with Annalise.

Every day, Annalise and I take walks up and down the nearby promenade. As we walk, we look inside the shops, and Annalise waves hello to every dog she passes. There is a small inlet attached to the beach, named Mothers Beach, and as you can probably guess from the name, this is where all of the stroller moms congregate. The water is calm on Mothers Beach, and I have learned that my baby is part mermaid. Annalise loves to splash, giggling as the water spatters her face. The only time she cries is when I take her out of the water. We have spent so much time in the sun that Annalise has developed the cutest diaper tan. Being part Iranian, she tans easily, like her dad. She's the most adorable little beach baby and being in the cool ocean water is so inviting during California's hot summer days.

While Annalise and I are having great days at the beach, Nick seems miserable. Every evening when he returns home, I expect him to immediately say one of two things. Either he hates that there is no parking close by our home, as our small garage is filled with boxes yet to be unpacked, or he despises the beach traffic leading to our home. Either way, the message is clear. Nick hates living at the beach. Now that my job with Jeremiah is done, the frequency of these complaints has increased to the point that I dread his arrival home. This fact makes me sad, since I want to share with him the stories of new discoveries I've made with Annalise or tell him all about how much she loves the water. But he is always in a terrible mood when he gets home, so instead of telling him anything, I just retreat into a television show, typically with a glass of wine.

The wine is a new thing. I have never been much of a drinker up to this point. Even in high school or college, when all of my friends were partying on the weekend and drinking until they couldn't stand, I just didn't. In fact, I was typically the designated driver, the one entrusted with the keys at the end of the night. Lately though, I am finding that I not only want the glass or two of wine at the end of the night, but I need it. It seems to be the only thing that takes the edge off when Nick begins his verbal diatribe about how much he hates this home that I happen to love.

There's a threatening feeling attached to Nick's constant negative ranting. He constantly reminds me that we still own the home in Cerritos, his home. I felt so trapped there, surrounded by clutter and his past. At the beach house, I feel free. Fresh air streams in through open windows daily. The living room lets in the most brilliant sunlight thanks to large windows. My time with Annalise at Mothers Beach is my favorite thing in the world. I'm happy. Annalise is happy. Nick is unhappy.

After two months of searching for the right opportunity, I finally get a bite that is promising. Gateway, a large computer company headquartered twenty minutes away in Irvine, wants to interview me for the position of web content writer. I'm elated, and Nick seems excited as well. I have a total of three rounds of interviews, all of which go well. I get a call from the human resources representative that I've been dealing with about an hour after my last interview, and she tells me that they'd love to have me as part of their team. On the outside, I'm playing it cool, but on the inside, I'm jumping up and down. This is the real deal. I'll be part of an actual web team, full of creative people, and the pay is great. After I hang up the phone and see the offer letter come through my email, I fall to my knees in the living room. The sunlight is warm on my face, and I begin giving thanks to God.

"Dear God, thank You, thank You, thank You. You made this happen. You heard my prayers, and You made this happen. Thank You for taking care of us. Thank You for giving me this chance."

When Nick gets home that night, I tell him the great news.

"So, I got a letter today," I begin, barely able to hold my excitement.

Nick is going through the mail I've left for him on the table. He isn't really listening to me. "Mmhmm."

"Uhm, so this letter." I put my hand on his arm. "Nick, listen."

He jerks his head from the mail. "I'm sorry. I'm listening. A letter?"

My smile is a mile wide. "I got the job!"

He looks at me for a moment. "Gateway?"

I nod my head enthusiastically. "Yes! I got the call this afternoon. They want me to start in a couple of weeks. I just have to get a drug test, and they are doing a background check. But it's mine! Isn't it awesome?"

"Yeah, Boos. That's great news. I'm so proud of you." He pulls me in for a hug, my face getting squished into his shoulder.

"You are?" I ask, my voice muffled by the hug.

"Boos, of course. I knew you'd get it," he says and pulls away. "Two weeks? They won't let you start sooner?"

"Well, they have to do a background check, and I need to go for a drug test," I explain again.

His brow furrows. "And that takes two weeks?"

My heart sinks a bit. I expected Nick's excitement to last a little while longer than this. "Yeah, I guess so," I say.

"Can you tell them that you'd rather start in a week?" he asks.

"Not sure that's something I can just tell them, Nick."

"The worst they can do is say no."

I shake my head. "I don't want to start my employment with them that way. It's just another two weeks. I'd rather just wait it out, get everything done, make sure we have day care for Annalise."

"Whatever you want then," he says, shrugging his shoulders. "I don't see what the point of not telling them you'd rather start sooner, but whatever you want to do."

"Hey, why don't you go check in on Annalise?" I say, changing the subject. My excitement about my new job is fading with this conversation, and I just don't want to talk about it anymore. I can tell he's becoming more agitated, and frankly, so am I. As he walks into Annalise's room, I grab a glass from the cupboard, uncork a bottle of wine sitting on the counter, and pour a glass.

40

Annalise and I Make a Move

Eliza
October 2006

Nick is growing increasingly annoyed with living at the beach. The only time he seems to enjoy it is when his older daughter visits. During these times, he is joyful, fun, and even playful. He hoists Annalise onto his shoulders and trots like a pony. The action makes Annalise laugh, and I stop them to take a picture to capture the moment. The sun will be setting soon, and Nick has planned to make dinner for everyone. His daughter won't stay the night, but she does stay late. The evening is fun, and the two sisters are obviously enamored with each other. It makes me smile to know that Annalise has a sister who loves her.

Once his daughter leaves and it's just us in the house again, Nick begins to push the issue of moving back to the Cerritos house. I refuse.

"I'm happy here," I explain. "Annalise's happy here. Can't you see that we're both thriving?"

He waves his hand, dismissing me. "And I'm not happy here. Can't you see that?"

"I just don't understand what the problem is. Why are you unhappy? We have the beach right down the street," I say, motioning to the large living room window. "I take Annalise to the beach all the time, and she loves it. Haven't you seen her cute little diaper tan? I clean the house every weekend. This place feels like our home," I say, listing off reasons to stay, hoping it will sway him to agree. Maybe he hasn't realized just how much Annalise and I are loving it here. I consider this and smile at him, reaching out to grab his hand.

"It isn't our home. It's a rental. We own our home." His face is serious, and his eyes are dark. "We will not stay here. It's time to stop messing around, now. We are moving back home."

His words stun me, and I take a step backward. "No," I say quietly.

"What was that?" he asks. I can't tell if he really didn't hear me or if he just wants me to repeat the word.

I take a deep breath and clear my throat. "I said no." I look at him, forcing my gaze to remain steady with his. "I'm not, and Annalise is not moving back there." I refuse to use the words "back home."

He scoffs. "And what? You're going to stay here? Take my baby from me?"

I shake my head. "What are you talking about?"

He waves his hand toward Annalise's room, where she is currently sleeping. The day at the beach and playing with her older sister have worn her out. I'm thankful that she's not awake to see her parents arguing.

"You want to use my baby against me? Fine. Take her. You might as well go back to Italy now too." He spits the words out so fast that they run together.

My mouth drops. "Why are you saying this?" I ask.

"Go ahead. Just take Annalise. Go be with that Italian scum."

"Hold on a second." I raise both hands in defense. "You're talking about something that's not happening. This isn't even about that."

He blinks his eyes a few times and attempts to backpedal the conversation. "You hurt me. I can't live here anymore. We are moving. That's my final word."

"Then move." The words come out fast but sure. For a split second, I can't recall if I actually spoke the words aloud or if I just thought them.

"What do you mean, just move?" he asks.

I swallow hard. "I mean I'm not coming. You can go. But I'm staying here."

He stares at me for a second, then storms toward our bedroom and slams the door so hard the windows shake. My body jerks at the sound of it. I pause for a moment, listening for Annalise. I hear nothing, not even the sound of crickets from outside. It's as if the entire world has gone on pause, waiting to see what his next move will be.

The next afternoon, I find out what Nick's next move is. I get a call from our landlady, who tells me that Nick has emailed her to tell her of our impending move out.

"It's so sad. I know how much you love the house," she says.

"I do love it! And, uhm, actually, I'm not the one who wants to move out," I say.

There is silence on the line for a moment. "You know, I wanted to ask you about that but didn't want to assume the worst," she says. "The way that Nick worded the email, it said that *he* would be moving out. You know, instead of *us*. I made a remark to my husband about it, and he told me to call you. So, I have to ask, is everything OK? Did he tell you that he was going to give notice?"

"Uh, not really. Nick isn't happy here, and he still has his house in Cerritos," I say. "But the important thing is I really want to stay in the house with Annalise."

"Oh, I see. Well, that is possible," she says, her voice low, as if she's trying to speak and not be overheard. "The only thing is you'll have to go through a credit check, and I'll need another deposit."

"What? But why? We're already in the house, and I'm the one who has been paying the rent this entire time." Paying another deposit seems unreasonable, and I simply won't have the extra funds for that.

"I know," she says. "I wish there was something I could do."

"Couldn't you apply the security deposit back to my new solo account?" I ask.

"We would need it in advance to hold the listing. This house, as you know, will go fast."

I do know. Nick and I had asked for an application as they were putting the sign out on the lawn. The only reason we got it was because we had the fortune of timing.

"Listen, I hope you get everything worked out with your husband. I think it's pretty low that he'd give notice to vacate without even telling you."

"Yeah, that is sort of a shock." My mind is racing as I try to figure out what to do next.

"I'm going to email you a copy of the letter. I think you deserve to know what kind of man you're married to."

When Nick gets home that night, his mood is lighter than usual. He doesn't complain about traffic, or parking, or my mother. In fact, he seems to be in amazing spirits, with a grin on his face. I stare at him with disgust.

"You seem cheerful," I say. "Almost as if you have an amazing secret you're keeping." I am sitting at the kitchen table, watching him as he practically dances around the kitchen.

"Hmm, maybe."

"You know, Nick, maybe you should have told the landlady to keep your amazing secret too." I watch as realization creeps over his face.

"Oh, she called you?" he asks.

I nod, saying nothing.

"Good. Now you know the gig is up. Time to go back to reality." He hums gleefully.

"Actually, I won't be going with you. I already told you that I wouldn't."

"We have already had this discussion, Eliza. I'm tired of the games."

"It's not a game, Nick. I'm not going to Cerritos." My tone is even and calm. I remain seated at the table.

"And where do you think you're going? To your mom's?"

"No. I found a place in Yorba Linda. A townhouse. It's in a good school district, close to my mom so I can rely on her for help when I need it, and I won't ask you for your help." After reading the letter Nick sent to the landlady and seeing his reaction to pulling Annalise and me out of a home we adore, I am starting to better understand the type of mental games he is playing. I know that I will not be moving back to the Cerritos house, but my alternative plan will be a hard sell to Nick.

He stops smiling and approaches the table. He pulls out a chair and sits. "For how long?"

"I don't know. We can try it for six months, see where we are after that." I take his hand. "I know you've been unhappy, and I'm sorry for that. I also know that you need a break. Work has obviously been stressing you out, and the issues with your colleagues and classes have taken a toll. The last thing you need is more stress at home." I take a steady breath, ready to drive this home.

He studies my face, but I can see that I am telling him just what he wants to hear. "We just take a little break. You can see Annalise whenever you want, take her to dinner, whatever. Then in a few months, we reevaluate. For now, you go and be happy again. See your friends. Be free."

"But we stay married, and I get to see you and Annalise?" he asks.

I nod. "Mmhmm. You can see Annalise anytime."

"And you. Every week, for dinner," he says. "Every Sunday, we go to Costco. I help you guys get groceries, then we do family dinner."

In my head, I know that this arrangement won't last. But I nod my head and say, "Sounds good."

"I want to see this place you got. I need to make sure it's right for you," he says.

"We can go tomorrow. No problem," I say, knowing that if he's agreeing to see the townhouse, he's already on board with the plan.

A few days after Annalise and I move to the townhouse and Nick moves back to his house in Cerritos, he calls me. I'm at work and in the middle of completing a project, but he tells me that it's urgent. I tell him to hold on for a moment and walk out the back door to continue the call.

"Nick, what's wrong? Is it Annalise?" I ask, my head beginning to race through every potential disaster that could have happened to our daughter.

"I just got off the phone with our landlady at the beach house," he says. He's speaking fast and sounds out of breath. "She is threatening to keep all of our security deposit because she's saying the place isn't clean."

I take a deep breath. "OK. And why isn't the place clean?"

Nick's voice immediately becomes stronger. "I've had too much on my plate with Cerritos house and you. I can't do it all!"

"OK, but our agreement was that I would clean the bathrooms, kitchen, and floors, and you would make sure that the rest of the house was clean," I say. "What exactly is she saying wasn't cleaned?"

"She's also demanding an extra hundred and ten dollars for the two extra days of the month, because she says it's in the contract."

"Nick. What is she saying needs to be cleaned?" I repeat.

"Everything!"

"It can't be everything. I'm going to call her," I say.

"No! I already talked to her. This is horrible. And now she just wants more money. I'm not paying it."

"Nick, I never asked you to pay it. I'll pay it." I'm trying to keep my voice even and calm. I know that if I say anything in anger, it will blow up in my face.

"This is total BS, Eliza. We should have never moved to that beach house. It caused all kinds of issues, and now my family is broken."

I go silent. I know that when he gets this way, there is no amount of arguing that will result in reason.

After a few seconds of silence, Nick asks, "Eliza, are you still there?"

I tell him I am but that I have to get back to work. Once I hang up, I immediately dial our landlady's number. She picks up on the second ring.

"Hi, Eliza," she says. "I was wondering when you'd call."

"Hi," I say with a stilted laugh. "Can you please let me know what's going on?"

"Sure. When I showed up at our agreed time for the inspection, Nick was still mopping the floors, and the unit was not ready for inspection. It was still a mess. The baseboards were filthy, the living room walls were dirty, the master bedroom walls were dirty."

"I'm so sorry," I say. "I'll go over there tonight after I pick up my daughter and make sure everything is clean. Can you give me until tomorrow morning?"

"That's fine. Also, because it's the second of the month, there is an additional fee for the two extra days, equaling a hundred and ten dollars."

"It's not a problem. I will give you a check," I tell her.

"Thanks, Eliza," she says. "This is really none of my business, but your husband told me that the only reason you guys rented from us was because you cheated on him and he was only trying to make you happy."

My stomach drops. Not only was Nick making a scene with the landlady over the move out, but now he was telling her extremely personal things about us! And conveniently leaving out his own infidelity?

"That's uh … I'm not sure what to say." I groaned into the phone.

"He said you never cleaned. That you were just there to meet more men and hang out with other divorcees."

Nick hated our upstairs neighbor, who happened to be divorced. He didn't like that she and I had become friends. She also knew how much

I adored the beach house and had witnessed me cleaning it every single Saturday. I told the landlady that if she really wanted to know the truth about my cleaning habits, to ask the tenant upstairs. As to the other accusations, I apologized for her being dragged into what was an obviously personal matter. I ended the call saying that I wished to stay on good terms with her and that I would make sure that all matters with the beach house were resolved by the next morning.

I never mentioned the call to Nick. I knew that if pressed, he would explode, and I didn't have the energy to deal with that.

Our agreed-upon Sunday Costco arrangement worked out for exactly one afternoon, starting the day after we moved into the Yorba Linda townhouse. After that, for weeks Nick would call on Sunday morning, asking when he should stop by for family time. Every week, I'd tell him that I was feeling under the weather, had menstrual cramps, or had already been grocery shopping but that he was welcome to come by and take Annalise out for dinner.

41

Threats, Tears, Anger, Fear

Eliza
October 2006

At the start of our separation, things seem to be going OK. Nick isn't necessarily happy about the sudden change of plans with his intended Sunday visits, but we have been civil about it. Nick keeps Annalise from Thursday night to Sunday morning, and I keep Annalise from Sunday morning to Thursday night. The split is fair, and this way we aren't jostling Annalise around too much. The worst arguments we get in seem to be over clothes, as I pack clothes for Annalise to go to Nick's house, but instead of returning them, he just keeps them. This is an annoying habit but manageable and something we are able to talk through for the most part.

At some point, there is a distinct shift that occurs. Nick once again becomes irritable and upset with me. He sends me emails with the day of the week and the time as the subject line. The body of the email seems to be a rambling stream of Nick's consciousness.

From: Nick Reza
To: Eliza Reza

Subject: wed 4:30 pm

hi Eliza,

i had no internet for few days and finishing up grades and you don't like to get phone call from me i just want my family back you make your points nobody ignores you.

i picked up Annalise fri and brought her back on sunday to your mom. I think you should give a little consideration to our contract we had with each other. I tried very hard to sell this house but the market went down i do appreciate all the things you are doing for our daughter and proud of you like i always have been.

Annalise needs both of us and she would be the happiest kid in earth i promise.

this was your choice and begging you to give us another chance. I cannot write like my writer wife just call me talk to me for few minutes can i see you both for ½ hour tonight or tomorrow night?

thanks
Nick

I repeatedly decline his offers to get back together, and his erratic behavior only gets worse. Nick calls me constantly when he has Annalise. Most of the time, I answer, worried that something has happened with Annalise. Nick explains that the reason for the frequent calls is that Annalise really wants to talk to me. When it keeps happening and increases in frequency, I begin to get terse with him. Eventually, the calls begin coming in every hour, on the hour, sometimes up until three in the morning.

One Saturday afternoon, after I'm settled in on the couch, content to spend the day watching old movies on AMC, I get a call from a friend of mine who says there is a small get-together happening on one of his friend's yachts in Newport Beach and that I should come. I groan a bit, saying that I really want to stay home.

He replies, "How often do you get to go out on a yacht?"

Realizing that the answer is *never*, I get myself together and head to the beach.

Annalise is with Nick for the weekend, and after he calls once and I speak with Annalise, I feel assured that she is safe and that if anything critical happens, he can just leave me a voice mail while I am out on the boat.

At 3:30 p.m., I decline a call from Nick because I am busy chatting and having drinks with friends on board the boat. Since he can't get a hold of me, he calls my mother. When my mother doesn't answer her phone, he calls my stepfather, Dustin. Nick tells Dustin he is not feeling well and that he can't get a hold of me. He then says that he needs someone to drive to his house in Cerritos and bring him to the emergency room in Anaheim Hills, which is thirty minutes from his house but less than ten minutes from mine. Nick explains to Dustin that he can't find the car keys for either of the two cars he owns and that he's dehydrated. When my mother and Dustin drive to the house, they find Nick waiting with Annalise. They also note that while Nick is complaining of dehydration, he isn't drinking any water, Gatorade, or anything else to help combat the issue.

Later on, when I finally check my phone, I notice that I have one missed call from Nick and three missed calls from my mother. I immediately dial Nick's phone and am sent straight to voice mail. I then call my mom, who picks up on the third ring.

"Mom? What's happening? Is everything OK?" I ask her, my voice frantic.

She explains to me what happened, about Nick's call, dehydration, and the drive to the ER.

"I have Annalise," she says. "She's in bed, and it's fine if you want to let her stay with us tonight. She's been through enough today, I think."

I sigh. "Of course. She can stay. Thank you for taking care of her."

"It's no problem," she says.

"I'm so sorry, Mom. So sorry."

"Eliza, it's fine. You were out having fun for once. I'm actually glad he couldn't reach you. It gave me a chance to see what you've been talking about. He's really acting strange," she says.

"I know. I have no idea what's in his head these days. It's like he's just gone crazy." I promise to get Annalise the following morning and hang up.

The next day, before I head over to pick up Annalise, I call Nick. This time, he answers on the first ring.

"Yes?" he answers tersely.

"Nick, what is going on?" I question.

"I had to go to the emergency room." His voice is low and sounds as if I've woken him.

"Yes, I heard that much. What was wrong with you though?"

"I had a heart attack," he says nonchalantly.

"You had a what?"

"Heart attack. Brought on by stress and dehydration."

I pause. In my mind, I am thinking, *What in the world?* Instead, I say, "Uh, OK. What hospital are you in?"

"I'm at home," he says.

"Home?" I scrunch my face. "What do you mean home? If you had a heart attack, you should be in the hospital."

"No, because this is my third time in the ER this month."

"Third time? When were the other two times? Nick, what is going on, really?"

At this point, he becomes irate. His silent, barely awake voice turns harsh. "You wouldn't know because you don't answer your phone. If you would just listen to me and stop this stuff with keeping our family apart, I wouldn't have heart attacks."

My head begins to reel. "Nick, I'm going to let you get some rest. You obviously need it."

"I need my family, Eliza! You don't know how hard it's been for me without you both. I need my family! This is killing me."

"Nick, I have to go. Annalise's at my mom's house, and I am late picking her up." I cradle the phone, not knowing what else to say or think. I hear a click, and the line goes dead. Nick hung up.

42

Seizures Start Again

Eliza

Annalise had gotten into the habit of sleeping in my bed with me. She would crawl up right next to me, drape her leg and arm over my body, and awake screaming if I dared to get up to go to the bathroom in the middle of the night. I quickly learned to limit my nightly water intake, unless I wanted to lie there for hours thinking about my full bladder.

We'd just gotten into the throes of potty training, and I'd gotten Annalise a little portable toilet that I insisted stay in the downstairs bathroom but which Annalise insisted be placed in the middle of the floor in the kitchen. Every night as I was making dinner, Annalise would be seated pants-free on the tiny plastic commode, keeping me company while I cooked.

One evening after we'd finished our evening routine of cooking and toileting; we made our way upstairs and headed to bed. Annalise was restless. She'd been cranky all evening, at one point even picking up her toilet and tossing it in my direction after I'd tried to get her to sit at our dining table to eat. Upon hitting the sheets, she'd normally calm down relatively quickly, but this evening she was restless, tossing and turning and throwing her arm and leg around in a fit. Shortly after eleven, she finally settled down, and I fell into an exhausted sleep. I couldn't have been asleep more than an hour when I was startled awake by the sound of Annalise moaning and throwing up. I jumped up, narrowly escaping the waterfall of vomit, and ran to get a towel from the adjoining bathroom. The trip to the bathroom took fifteen seconds, tops. However, when I returned, Annalise was lying on her side with her eyes rolled into the back of her head, her small body stiff, with her breath coming in short and shallow bursts.

In college, my freshman year roommate had been a girl named Griselda. We'd made an instant connection, talking about our room decorations, our classes, and our families. She was friendly, with kind eyes and a gorgeous smile, and I felt safe and comfortable with her from the start. The day we moved into our apartment, there was a swarm of bees that I narrowly escaped as I trudged my suitcases up the single flight of stairs to our second-floor apartment door. Griselda, whom I nicknamed "Griz," was in the living room, unpacking some tchotchkes that would go in our shared common room. I made my way into our bedroom and began the laborious task of unpacking and making up my twin bed with the linens that my mom and I had bought at Target. I heard a sound coming from the living room, which sounded as if Griz was being attacked by one of the bees I'd seen outside.

"Griz, you OK?" I yelled. "Did a bee get in?"

She didn't reply except to continue making strange sounds. I dropped the bedding and went into the living room to try to assist with the bees.

Only it wasn't a bee. Griz was on the living room floor, in the throes of a seizure.

I ran to her and turned her head to the side, which is what I remembered being taught at one point in some history class or TV show. It was a tidbit of knowledge that I'm not sure where I learned, but I plucked it out of the ether to assist in this situation.

"Griz, you're OK. It is going to be OK," I said to her as gently as I could. "I'm going to call 911, OK? Just lie here. I'm coming right back."

As I stood to get the phone, Griz, through the attack of the seizure, managed to shakily say, "No ... don't ... 911. No."

I protested. "Griz—"

"No!" she said again, this time more forcefully.

"OK, OK. I won't. I'm right here." I sat with her head in my lap, stroking her hair to soothe her.

It took a few moments, but Griz came out of the seizure. She sat up and looked into my obviously startled face.

I didn't speak. I wasn't sure what to say. I just stared at her, wondering if she was in fact OK.

She finger brushed and smoothed out her hair and stared back at me. Then she gave a nervous laugh, which I returned. "I'm really sorry. I wanted to tell you today, but … well … surprise."

"It's OK," I said. "But what exactly happened? I mean, I feel like we should take you to the doctor."

"No, please don't," she said, grabbing my arm. "If you do that, my parents will worry and make me come home. Please."

I searched her deep brown eyes for any sign of distress, but all I found were the pleading eyes of a girl who wanted a normal college experience, mixed with embarrassment. She told me about her history of seizures and that she'd meant to tell me later on today, when we'd gotten a chance to know each other better. When she finished telling me all that she felt she needed to, I smiled and embraced her in a firm hug.

Seeing Annalise lying stiffly on the bed, with her eyes jutted up into her skull, I realized immediately what this was. A seizure. Only this time, I called 911 immediately.

43

One Week of Every Month Lost

Eliza
Fall 2006

It had been a good year between Annalise's seizures, so I thought they were just a fluke or something that would only occur sporadically. She'd been seen by neurologists in the ER, and I'd scheduled a visit for her with a well-respected neurologist at UC Irvine. We'd been given the green light to continue on with our daily lives, so that is what we did.

Every morning, I'd take Annalise to therapy at seven o'clock and wait for her forty-five-minute session to be over so that I could take her to day care. From there, I'd hop on the freeway to my job at Gateway computers in Irvine, where I worked as a web content writer. I was the only female on the team, and while this wasn't a huge deal to me at the time, looking back, I realize just how little they were able to comprehend the struggles of being a parent, much less a single mom to a toddler with special needs.

A month following Annalise's seizure, we'd settled back into a routine at home. Annalise had been kept for observation in the hospital following her seizure and then was sent home when the emergency medicine they administered seemed to be keeping the seizures as bay. Tonight, I'd prepared a dinner of grilled chicken and mac 'n' cheese. We headed up to bed around nine and fell quickly asleep. Annalise was being extra sweet this particular evening, thanking me for her favorite dinner and lovingly snuggling up to me as we drifted off.

Around midnight, Annalise made the smallest of noises, and my eyes flew open upon hearing them. I switched on the light and saw that Annalise was once again having a seizure. I grabbed my phone to dial 911. Only my phone was unresponsive, instead giving me a frozen screen. I pushed Annalise onto her side and propped pillows against her back so she wouldn't roll over in case she vomited. I ran down the stairs and sprinted to my next-door neighbor's house. I rang the doorbell and knocked frantically. The door flung open, and my neighbor stood there with a look that was murderous.

I yelled, "Help! Call 911! Annalise's having a seizure, and my phone isn't working!" He stood there, frozen, trying to figure it all out. "Please—911!" He sprang into action, and his wife followed me as I sprinted back into my house.

I ran back up the stairs to where Annalise lay on her side, still seizing. "Mommy's here, Annalise. Mommy's here." I choked back tears and kissed her on her forehead multiple times. In the distance, I could hear the sound of both the ambulance and the fire truck, which was typical for this type of call.

Within a few minutes, the sound of frantic chatter and EMTs sprinting up the stairs of our house could be heard. I turned my head toward my bedroom door as two large firemen filled the frame. I quickly explained the situation, that I had given the recommended Diastat, an emergency medicine that had been prescribed to us in case she ever seized again, but that it wasn't working. After a quick check of her vitals and download of her medical history, which I nervously stumbled through, the EMTs loaded her onto a gurney and into the waiting ambulance that had backed into our driveway. I asked my neighbor to lock the front door and jumped into the back of the ambulance with Annalise. It took approximately three minutes for the ambulance to get to the closest ER. By the time we made it there, Annalise had been seizing for close to thirty minutes.

Immediately upon our arrival, a doctor was in our room assessing the situation, a nurse had started an IV, and Annalise was being pumped full of Lorazepam. It took several milligrams of the anticonvulsant drug to pull her out of the seizure. It was the first time that I heard the term for the type of seizures she was having, *focal status epilepticus.* Annalise was admitted to the hospital, this time for monitoring, so that they could once more attempt to figure out what was causing the seizures.

There was just one catch. The ER that was closest to our home was the same hospital network as the hospital that had damaged Annalise in the first place. I refused to let them admit her, telling everyone I could about what that hospital network and its doctors had done to my baby girl. I had vowed to never allow them to cut into her again, and so, after hours of arguing and keeping my foot down, they airlifted us to a children's hospital thirty miles away.

It was the first helicopter ride for both Annalise and me, although she was so drugged that she slept through the entire ride. I stared at her beautiful cherub face, sleeping so peacefully ten thousand feet above the morning commuter traffic in Los Angeles. The sun peeked out through the buildings, forcing me to squint. The contrast of the situation wasn't lost on me, this peaceful moment in the daylight attempting to eclipse the nightmare of the evening before. I grazed Annalise's cheek with my fingertips.

The EMT who was riding with us and monitoring Annalise's vitals on the way broke the silence. "She's a gorgeous child."

I couldn't pry my gaze from Annalise but smiled at the comment. "She is." The words caused my voice to crack, and the strength that I'd been holding on to cracked as well.

We said little else for the duration of the flight, although he did make a brief announcement when the helipad for the hospital came into view. Atop the hospital, I could see two nurses waiting to greet us upon landing.

When the propeller blades quieted and the doors were opened, I whispered to Annalise, "You just had your first helicopter ride."

The EMT heard me and smiled. "I think you're entitled to a do-over for this one."

Once we were inside the hospital, the flurry of doctors and nurses started up again—getting Annalise admitted, answering questions about insurance, giving my spiel about her medical history. "No, she wasn't born paralyzed." "No, she didn't have seizures prior to her first brain surgery." "Yes, prior to surgery, she'd hit all of her milestones." "Yes, it is horrible about what happened during that first surgery."

One thing has remained exactly the same in the fourteen years that I've been telling doctors her medical history—the reaction when I get to the part about the endoscope putting a hole in Annalise's brain, leaving my fifteen-month-old baby paralyzed. The doctor's expression will include a lifting of the brows in surprise, a pursing of the lips, an audible sound, be it a sigh, an "Eesh," or "Wow," the pen will stop writing for a moment, and they'll look up at me for validation.

What they see in me has changed, however. I went from being overcome with grief in my twenties, to incredibly angry in my thirties, to matter-of-fact in my forties. It's the evolution of how my faith has grown. And while I still feel pangs of sadness and anger for what happened to my daughter, I can now profess that God loves us now, loved us then, and has always carried us through.

44

That Preschool Life

Eliza
November 2006

From:
Rick Ocho
To:
Eliza Reza
Nov 14, 2006 at 7:25 PM

Hi Eliza,

I was saddened to hear that you and Nick have separated. Eliza, I am writing to you requesting that I meet with you and Nick to discuss and that I may receive your input regarding planning for Annalise, her Transition to the public school district, and physical/occupational therapy services. The meeting would be during the time when Annalise is receiving her occupational therapy. Wendy usually meets with Annalise in Cerritos to provide therapy on Thursdays at around 12:30. I recognize that you are working and very busy with this, however, I would like to include you in this meeting and receive your valuable input. The meeting would last approximately 90 minutes. Please let me know if you would be available.

Most Sincerely,
Rick Ocho

Annalise started a new preschool in our new school district. Her teacher seemed the tiniest bit brusque, but maybe it was just my perception of the situation. I took Annalise in to take a look at the school, and her teacher, Ms. G, asked me about Annalise's dad. When I explained that we were separated but that he was still in Annalise's life, she gave me a disapproving look.

Every day, Ms. G sends out an email detailing what the kids did at school—things like singing songs, finger painting with shaving cream, and, of course, snack time. I'm also waiting on Annalise's very first IEP, which is short for individualized education plan. The purpose of the IEP is to develop educational goals that Annalise will work toward during the year. For example, Annalise will string together three- to four-word sentences by the end of the year, and Annalise will learn how to walk on uneven pavement when on the playground.

Annalise is the one person I spend most of my time outside of work with, and I feel like I understand her just fine. But following the IEP meeting, it begins to dawn on me that Annalise might have a learning delay. It's hard for me to understand this at first. Annalise is my only child, so I don't have a point of reference for how a typical three-year-old should speak or behave.

I am trying to remember examples of three- to four-word sentences I'm sure I've heard her speak. "Mommy, come here." That's a three-word sentence, although when Annalise says it, it's more like, "Mommy! Cahm'ere." OK, that one might be stretching it. But what about when she asks for a drink? "I want joooose!" That's three words for sure. I'll just tell her to add *please* to her requests. Then it'll be "I want joooose, please." That is four words. Mission accomplished. But if I ask her to say "Mommy" before the ask, well then she'll be a genius, blowing everyone away with her five-word sentences.

I think I'm starting to understand why Ms. G makes strange faces at me.

45

Only God—Come, Holy Spirit

Anna
1986–1989

Never, ever could I have believed what is about to happen my first month of attending our new church. God truly put blinders on me the first couple of times I attended the church. I do not know much about Pentecostals and their worship services. All I know is that there is something different happening in these worship services. I feel my heart soar with the music, and my heart is touched by the sermons. I make friends quickly with so many in the church. I feel welcome and accepted. Despite what is still going on at home, I feel a renewed hunger for peace in my heart, mind, and soul. God is about to meet me in a most amazing way that will transform my life. I am about to discover what happens when we truly let go and let God into our lives. I believed I was saved and had accepted Jesus years before, but I was soon to discover God was not done with me yet.

After about a month of attending the church, a lady in the church comes over to me during the altar call. I do not know her and do not recall ever talking to her. She tells me she felt led by the Holy Spirit to pray with me. She asks me to go to the altar with her to pray. I really do not want to go to the front of the church. I notice several people at the altar praying with their hands raised. I pray, but I never raise my hands to pray. That hand-raising process seems strange and foreign to me.

"Will you come with me?" she asks softly.

I hesitate again. What is so important about dragging me down to the altar to pray? I look at her, searching in my mind for some way to gently refuse going to the altar. No words come out of my mouth. Suddenly, as if a hand is gently guiding me, I find myself following her to the altar at the front of the church. I am not sure if I go with her so I will not cause a scene or … I want to tell her that I once went down to the front of the altar at another church when I accepted Jesus as my Lord and Savior. But no words come out of my mouth.

"Raise your hands and ask the Holy Spirit to fill you," she says softly.

Again, I hesitate as I wonder what I have gotten myself into, but I go ahead and raise my hands. I close my eyes. I am thinking that the sooner we get this over with, the sooner I can return to my seat. I feel her hands on my shoulders and hear her praying. For a moment, I wonder why she thinks it necessary to place her hands on me to pray for me.

"God, help me!" I say softly more as an utterance than a prayer. "God, help me!" The words just burst forth out of my mouth, louder this time.

The next thing I know, I feel what sounds like a mighty, rushing wind sweep over me. I feel this incredible sensation wash over me, almost like being wrapped in a cocoon of love and protection. This sensation continues to wash over me, like every burden I have is being lifted from me. In my spirit, I suddenly feel like a white dove soaring over the congregation. I hear this heavenly voice in a strange language near me. Then I realize that voice is coming from me.

Afterward, I learn that I received the gift of the Holy Spirit with the evidence of speaking in tongues. Several in the church, including the pastor and worship pastor, who witnessed my gift of receiving the Holy Spirit, remark later to me how I appeared to be floating. A few weeks later, I follow the Lord by being baptized again. I truly feel like I am alive again. I begin reading my Bible with a new hunger for God's Word.

The next three years lead to my going back to school to work on my doctorate. I do have to say that during this time, my husband is there to help with the kids as I work and attend school. He seems more focused on building his business. We settle into a quiet period in which we are more at peace with each other. We still have this chasm that exists between us, and we are still two individuals traveling in separate directions.

I come to realize part of our problem is we are not the people we once were when we first met. He is a dreamer who has grandiose plans and dreams but never grasps how to bring them to fruition. I believe anything can be accomplished if I do it, and that requires action. In a strange way, his dreaming has been the inspiration that a poor child from the wrong side of the tracks needed to believe she could be an achiever.

After being remarried for three years, my husband files for divorce the second time around. After rededicating my life to God, I made the decision to stay in the marriage and make it work. I believe my husband sensed that and knew the break would only happen if he took the final step. We divorce in March. I receive my doctoral degree that May. Life settles down to being truly a single mom again. But this time, I start sensing that I am not about to settle into a nice, quiet life. One day, I am in the backyard doing some yardwork. Abruptly, I stop and take a deep breath. I feel so content, so at peace as I look around at my surroundings. Suddenly, a still, small voice seems to speak to me and says, "Don't get too comfortable. This is just a stopping place."

Oh, no! What is about to happen? My spirit quickens as I remember one evening at church a few weeks earlier. I feel compelled to go to the altar and pray. Now that I am finished with my doctorate, I want to totally focus on what God's will is for my life and my family. I pray, asking God to direct the next steps in my life. My prayer begins, "God, I want to do whatever You want me to do. Go wherever You want me to go, except LA." I stop praying and let out a little gasp. *LA? Why did I say LA? Los Angeles? Why pray something like that?*

God, surely you do not want me to move somewhere. Surely, you do not want me to change jobs or cart my youngest daughter to a place like California. I have no desire to go to California. Never been there and do not really want to go there. Boy, I am really having a desperate one-sided argument with God, who does not respond to anything I am saying.

The next summer, I find myself planning to take my first vacation alone, outside the United States. This is a huge step for me for two reasons: This vacation is completely outside my comfort zone without my children or husband. This trip is the first time I venture outside the US either alone or with anyone else. I am about to take a trip that will forever alter my life and hit me with the biggest surprise of my life.

I try to convince myself of all the reasons I should not go on such a trip. I schedule a trip, cancel the trip, reschedule the trip, cancel the trip. It takes me a few additional weeks to finally settle on a solid vacation plan. My oldest daughter, who is now married, and my ex-husband say they will look after my youngest daughter if something comes up during her stay at Bible camp. My son has a summer job and will spend time with his father while I am away. So, all barriers and excuses are eliminated. All except for my hesitation and fear. I take a deep breath and finalize my travel plans.

I need this time away to think some things through about my life. Since my divorce, my mother begins dropping hints about coming to live with me. We have come to a place where we have a good relationship. Not a perfect one but a good one. I have made plans to visit her in Massachusetts after my vacation. I have never entirely given up on her telling me about my biological father. Why does she feel the need to keep it such a big secret?

As for her living with me, it would not work. I am absolutely obsessed with cleanliness when it comes to my home and even polish the light bulbs. I think I get some of those tendencies from my maternal grandmother.

46

Divorce Lawyers

Eliza
2007

After being separated for over a year, I decide that it is time to get on with obtaining a divorce. I want to believe that Nick and I can divorce peacefully, but I have no clue how to begin, so I consult and eventually hire an attorney. This does not bode well with Nick. He becomes extremely agitated when I tell him that I've obtained a divorce lawyer.

"What are you trying to do to me? Kill me?" he asks me one night over the phone.

"Nick, I just want to make this as seamless and painless as possible. All I'm hiring the lawyer to do is file the papers correctly and ensure that there is adequate child support for Annalise. I am sorry that this is upsetting. It's upsetting to all of us."

"I want our family back together. Eliza, please just consider it. We don't need to do this; we can be together under the same roof with Annalise."

The thought of living with Nick again and being in his house in Cerritos makes me cringe. "Nick, we tried that. It doesn't work. We don't work," I say.

He screams into the phone and hangs up.

Summer is turning into the season of lawyers. Aside from my divorce attorney, we also have Annalise's case against the HMO.

It isn't an easy task. We have already undergone a full year of depositions, expert testimonies from both sides, and discovery. Experts have been called in, including the doctors involved in the case, as well as Nick and me. Our depositions are never scheduled on the same day, but I am aware of the dates that Nick is called to provide his statements under oath. One such afternoon, I get a call from our malpractice lawyer, who tells me that Nick left the deposition suddenly due to a medical issue.

"I'm just calling to make sure Nick is all right," she says. Her voice is professional yet laced with concern. "When he left, I asked him to make sure to give me a call so that we could reschedule, but I haven't heard back from him yet."

"I honestly have no idea. I didn't even know anything was wrong." I hadn't heard from Nick that day and hadn't expected to since I had Annalise. He usually only called me if he was watching her. "What happened during the depo? Did he not finish?" I ask.

"No. We had to cut it short. He started coughing and then asked for a short break. So, we took a ten-minute break, and he came back and said that he couldn't continue because he had taken all of these pills and couldn't concentrate."

My jaw drops open. "You have to be kidding me." I let out a sigh. Didn't he get that this was all for Annalise? He could blow this entire case acting this way! "I don't even know what to say. What happens now? Can we reschedule the deposition?"

"Yes, we can. But I wanted to ask you candidly, is Nick doing drugs that you know of?"

Her question throws me off. I haven't really noticed anything like that, but his behavior has been erratic over the last month or so. "I don't think so?" My answer comes out more questioning than I anticipate. "But honestly, I don't know. I hope not."

"It's just, his eyes were kind of strange today. It looked as if something was off with him."

"Strange, how?" I ask.

"Just off. I know you guys are separated, but you might consider checking on him. Make sure he's OK."

"Sure, of course," I say.

I immediately call Nick. He picks up on the first ring.

"Yeah?" he answers.

"Nick? Are you OK?" I ask.

"Yeah. No. I don't know." His voice sounds tired, as if I've woken him from a nap.

"What happened today?"

"Oh nothing. I just came home and laid down for a bit."

I shake my head. Was he really not going to say anything about the fact that he walked out of a deposition in our daughter's case against the HMO? "Uh, Nick, I just got a call from our lawyer. She said you had to leave the deposition early today. What happened? Be honest with me."

"I just couldn't do it today. I took this medication, and it made me really tired."

"What medication?" I ask.

"Just my blood pressure medication."

"Haven't you been taking that forever? Why all of a sudden would it have this effect on you? Are you sure you didn't take anything else?"

"What are you saying? Like I've been taking drugs?"

"Well, I don't know. This seems a bit unlike you to not go through with the deposition. You know how important this is for Annalise, right?"

"My entire life is Annalise. Of course I know it's important. I just couldn't do it today, all right? Did you really want to check on me, or did you just want to rub it in my face that I couldn't go through with it today?"

"Nick, come on. Of course, I'm concerned. That's why I'm calling," I say, exasperated. "You're sure you're OK? Do you need anything?"

"I just need some rest."

"OK. Rest. We can talk more tomorrow, OK?"

47

A Call from Janie

Eliza

I don't hear from Nick until a few days later. He calls to let me know that he won't be able to take Annalise for the weekend as planned. I tell him that is fine but that Annalise will be disappointed to not see her dad. This has become a habit of his, and I assume that he is purposefully not seeing her because it is his way of making sure I am staying home with her instead of going out with friends or on dates.

When he calls me a few hours later and says that he is near my house and asks if he can take Annalise for the weekend, I am confused by his sudden change of heart but agree to the ask. I put a bag together for him, consisting of Annalise's medicines and clothing, and make sure Annalise is ready to go when he arrives at our house.

Nick appears to be in good spirits when I open the door. Annalise toddles toward him and squeals at the sight of him, which causes him to smile broadly. He steps inside the door and sweeps her into his arms, kissing her repeatedly while she giggles in reply.

"Aww, she missed her daddy," I say, warmed at the sight of them so happy together.

"Not as much as I missed her," he answers as he buries his face in her soft curls.

"Well, she's all packed. I gave her a quick bath too, so you can just put her right into her pajamas when she's ready for bed," I say. "Probably no later than nine, OK?"

"Sure. She'll be fine."

I nod, looking at his eyes to see if I notice anything odd about them. I haven't forgotten what our malpractice lawyer said about him leaving the deposition early, or how he's been napping in the middle of the afternoon after taking his medication.

"You sure that you're OK?" I ask. "I mean, have you had anymore, um, issues with your medicine?"

He answers me but keeps his attention on Annalise. "No, it's been fine. Just a strange thing happened with them, I guess."

"But you're good?" I ask again.

"Yes. Eliza, I'm fine. I can take care of my baby." With that, he grabs her bag from me and turns to leave. "Listen, don't worry. I'm not going down that easily."

"I don't know what that means, but please just be safe, OK?"

He looks back at me. "I'm still the lion, OK?"

Nick has said this to me since the early days of our courtship. He always referred to himself as the lion, but it has been a while since I've heard him say it.

"Sure. Just, please. Be careful." I lean in and kiss Annalise on her forehead. She lets me kiss her but is eager to leave. Now that her dad is here and holding her, she is all about him.

I say a final goodbye to them and watch as he puts her in the car seat and drives out of sight.

The weekend passed, and I had only one phone call with Nick, which I initiated. I felt peaceful about the way this visit had gone. He hadn't called me in a panic and hadn't put a screaming Annalise on the phone. When he returned her to my house on Sunday evening, we said a brief and amicable goodbye. It seemed as if any drama we experienced in the past had run its course.

Around the middle of July, I received voice mails from Nick's daughter and from his ex-wife. Since I was in a meeting, I didn't see that they had called for about an hour. When I finally looked at my phone and saw both of their names appear, my initial reaction was that something had happened with Annalise. But Annalise was at day care, so it didn't make sense that they would be calling me about her. I stepped outside to listen to the voice mails.

I listened to the one from his daughter first.

"Hey, Eliza, I just wanted to call and let you know that things with my dad are not good. He's talking about suicide, and we're not sure what to do. But we wanted to call you because we're worried about Annalise. He's not really watching her when she's here, and he just lets her wander around the house, and it's not really safe for her to be there with him on the weekends or anytime soon, because he's just not doing well. We are headed over there tonight to talk to him and see if he needs to go to the hospital. But for right now, just give me a call if you have any questions or anything."

I held the phone against my ear long after the voice mail ended, completely in shock. What was she talking about? Suicide? Nick? There was no way. I mean, this was crazy. And what did she mean that Annalise wasn't safe with him? He was her dad, and no matter how upset he might get with me, I knew that he adored his daughter and would never hurt her.

I listened to the voice mail from his ex-wife next.

"Hey, Eliza, I hate to tell you, but I have more bad news. My son came home today and found Nick in the garage with a rope up over the rafters, and it seemed as if he was trying to hang himself. My son called me and asked me what he should do, and I told him to call the police. The police came, and they placed Nick in the car and took him to a hospital in Cerritos. Nick, of course, is trying to get out, but since the police brought him there, they have to keep him for a mandatory hold. So, he's in the hospital for three days so they can figure it out. Anyway, Nick is trying to call people and offer them money to get him out. I wanted to call you to ask you to please not allow him to give you any money to get him out. He needs to stay there, so they can evaluate him. If you want to call him, you can, but please don't get him out."

Not believing what I just heard, I plop down on the curb. *What in the world is happening?* I sit there until the door opens and a coworker who I rarely talk to walks out. She is leaving for the day and seems surprised to find me sitting on the curb.

"Did you lock yourself out?" she asks, reaching for the badge attached to the waistband of her suit. "I can badge you back in." She holds up her badge and gestures toward the door.

"No, it's fine. Thank you. I have mine. I was just ... sitting here, thinking." I give her a faint smile.

She cocks her head and studies me briefly. "You OK?"

"Yeah, I uh ..." Not sure what to say, I reply, "I needed some air."

"Totally get it. That place gets a bit stifling sometimes," she says, gesturing toward the building. "Well, hope you get to leave here soon. Go home, get some rest. You look a bit tired."

I nod and let out a sarcastic half laugh.

"Yeah. Thanks. Well, see ya," I say.

"See ya," she says.

When I get back to my desk, I Google the name of the hospital and make a note of it. It is close to five, and I have to leave to get Annalise. The drive to her day care takes thirty minutes, and as I drive, I call the hospital. A woman picks up, and I tell her that I am trying to call my husband who was brought in earlier that day. She brusquely tells me that she cannot verify any information regarding patients, nor can she tell me if he is even there. When I try to explain again that I am his wife and am just concerned, she tells me that if he is there, he can contact me after the mandatory hold is completed.

The mandatory hold is seventy-two hours, which is this Saturday. I realize that if the suicide attempt is true, and if he is released, he can legally call me and request to take Annalise for the weekend. I don't want him to take Annalise right now, as I'm not sure what his mental state is. Not knowing what my legal rights are, I call my divorce lawyer and explain what transpired.

"Eliza, I think what we need to do is file an emergency ex parte so that you and Annalise are both protected. If Nick was pulled in on a fifty-one-fifty, you need to make sure that you are looking out for the best interests of your daughter," he says.

"What's that? A fifty-one-fifty?" I ask.

"It's threatening suicide resulting in a mandatory and enforced three-day hold for psychological evaluation."

"I cannot even believe this is happening," I say.

"Just breathe and let me handle this," he says, his tone assured and steady. It makes me wonder how many of these types of situations he's handled in the past.

"I don't want to punish Nick. This seems so sudden."

"Eliza, you have no idea what sort of mental state he's really in. If he's threatening suicide enough to force his son to call the police on his own father, you can't take the chance. This isn't about the divorce now. It's about protecting Annalise."

Within two days, an emergency declaration is filed with the court and validated by a judge. The declaration means that Nick cannot take Annalise without a verified and mutually agreed-upon chaperone. In other words, Nick can only see Annalise under supervised visitation with a person that I've agreed is reliable and trustworthy. The declaration is signed and cemented with the court before Nick is released from his temporary hold. The judge agrees that supervised visitation is necessary, especially given Annalise's special needs. The order will remain in effect until Nick undergoes a complete psychological evaluation.

On Saturday, Nick is released from the hospital, and I am on edge waiting for his call. Only Nick doesn't call. In fact, no one seems to know where he is. On Monday evening, I finally get a call from his ex-wife. She says that he convinced the psychiatrist at the hospital that everything had been blown out of proportion. He placed the blame on his children for overreacting and on me for hiring lawyers. He said that everyone in his life was out to get him. The psychiatrist for some reason agreed with Nick that he had no intention to harm himself. Nick was released and immediately flew to Seattle, where his mother, father, and sister live.

This news is dumbfounding. His behavior has been erratic for weeks, he was forced into a psychiatric ward by police, and now he has flown out of state without anyone knowing beforehand. His ex-wife also tells me that Nick knew about the emergency supervised visitation ruling from the judge and that his reaction was not a happy one.

"He was spouting all kinds of obscenities about you," she tells me. "I'd just be careful. He's not here now, but who knows when he'll return."

I have no idea if his intention is to harm himself, Annalise, or me. I do know that I can't take any chances, so I call a man I have been dating for a few months and ask if we can stay with him for a while. Thankfully, he agrees. It isn't ideal, but at least it is an address that Nick is unaware of. I've been extremely secretive about my relationship with this man, not telling Nick much of anything about him. I am thankful for my discretion now, since it is our best option to ensure our safety.

My divorce lawyer manages to track Nick down at his sister's house. He calls him to let him know that while we do have an order for child custody in place, it is ultimately so he will get the help he needs so that he can see his daughter again. I have no ill will toward Nick; I just need to ensure that Annalise will be safe. Nick agrees with my lawyer on the phone and then goes silent for another week.

When we finally hear from him again, it is through his own divorce lawyer, who he hired while in Seattle. I completely understand and tell Nick that perhaps this is the best thing for us. If we allow the professionals to deal with the icky parts of the custody and visitation issues, then we can focus on being the best parents we can be for our daughter.

48

Erratic Behavior

Eliza
August 2007

Nick and I fall into a routine of coparenting that is workable. We have our fair share of strain because of the court-enforced visitation, which is in effect until Nick undergoes a formal psychiatric evaluation. But we are managing our relationship the best we can for the sake of our daughter. Annalise has been exhibiting some troublesome behavior. Every time she returns home from spending time with her dad, she acts out in violence. She spits, kicks, and hits, and it's always directed at me. I have tried to speak with Nick in an effort to understand why she is upset when he returns her to me, but his answer is always a version of the same sentiment. She is acting out because she wants her family back together.

"Nick, she's three years old. All she needs to understand is that both of her parents love her," I say to him one evening after he brings her back home. "She needs to see that we're good, civil, friendly."

"She needs her parents together in the same house, Eliza," Nick says. "She needs us together. Don't you see that?"

"Nick." I close my eyes for a moment, trying to get my thoughts together while keeping my voice steady. "We have talked about this. You and I do not work well under the same roof." My gaze shifts to Nick's car in the driveway. His friend Paul, who has become the official chaperone for supervised visitations, is sitting in the driver's seat. He doesn't look at me and instead looks busy with a paper in his hand. I'm sure that these times are hard for him as well. It can't be a very comfortable situation to be in, and I wonder how much more Paul knows about Nick's state of mind that he hasn't shared with me or anyone else.

Nick stares at me, his dark eyes narrowing. "And you wouldn't even do that for Annalise? We can try again. Don't do it for me. Do it for your daughter, our daughter. Doesn't she mean that much to you?"

"Nick ..." His name comes out more like a sigh.

"And can't you cancel these slimeball lawyers? How much more of my money do you want to spend on this? Why can't we just stop all of this?" With every question he fires at me, his tone grows louder.

I feel the sudden urge to step back. I could remind him that I have been spending my own money on my lawyer, that I have been the one taking on the payments for Annalise's day care and all of her medical bills. But I stop myself. Something in the way he is staring at me combined with the tone in his voice frightens me. "Nick. I'm staying here, in this house, for our daughter," I say, looking at him with as much compassion as I can muster. "We fought all the time when we lived together. We didn't trust each other. Don't you think that affected her as well?"

"You don't understand, Eliza. I need you. I'm not well." Tears fill his eyes. I glance behind me into the house, to make sure that Annalise is out of earshot. She is busy removing all of the plastic Tupperware from the cupboard in the kitchen and is seemingly paying no attention to us. I know that if she looks up, even for a moment, she will come running back toward the open front door.

"Nick, you need to get help. I can't fix whatever is going on with you right now. And putting Annalise in the middle of this, whatever this is, is not fair to her." I reach my hand out and lightly place it on his shoulder. "We care about you. But we can't live together. That wouldn't help any one of us. Please. I don't know what's going on, but you need to go talk to a doctor. Get some help, please. Annalise needs you to be healthy."

Nick nods and looks down at the ground. "Can I give her one more kiss and a hug?" he asks.

I nod and call Annalise's name. She looks up, runs toward the open door, and flings herself into her dad's arms. He squeezes her tightly and gives her a long kiss on her cheek. "Daddy loves you, baby Boosie," he says, the words muttered into her soft pink cheek before he gently places her back down on the ground. "Be good for your mom."

"We'll see you next weekend?" I ask.

"I'll call you," he says as he turns to leave.

I pick Annalise up, and we both watch as the car reverses out of our driveway. We don't go back into the house until the red taillights disappear from view.

The week before Labor Day, Nick emails me to ask if he can take Annalise to San Jose for the holiday weekend. Since he is still under a court order for supervised visitation, I reply to ask him who will be going with him.

From: Nick Reza
To: Eliza Reza
Sent: Sunday, August 26, 2007 11:45 PM
Subject: re: Labor Day weekend

hi Eliza.
i was thinking of taking Annalise to san jose this coming weekend sat-mon
i need to buy her ticket.
let me know .
Nick

From: Eliza Reza
To: Nick Reza
Sent: Monday, August 27, 2007 12:39 AM
Subject: re: Labor Day weekend

I'll call you tomorrow and we can discuss this.

Thanks,
Eliza

Since my reply was after midnight, we didn't speak until the next morning. The conversation with Nick was confusing. He mentioned several times that he wasn't sure who would be going with him to San Jose. When I asked about his travel plans, he couldn't decide whether or not he would be flying or driving. His voice was low, and he sounded nervous. When I asked him to provide the details of the trip in an email, he became irritated and hung up on me. Since we hadn't agreed on the plans for him to take our daughter to Northern California, I was utterly confused and more than a little irritated when I opened an email from him acting as if we'd hashed all of the plans out.

From: Nick Reza
To: Eliza Reza
Sent: Tuesday, August 28, 2007 11:04 AM
Subject: re: Labor Day weekend

as per our discussion over the phone can you please bring Annalise to my house on fri morning.
one of my sons and i will bring her to you on monday evening.

From: Eliza Reza
To: Nick Reza
Sent: Tuesday, August 28, 2007 8:17 PM
Subject: Re: Labor Day weekend

I need more details Nick.

How are you going to San Jose? Are you flying, driving? Who will be travelling with you? Which son? What time will Annalise be home on Monday?

From: Nick Reza
To: Eliza Reza
Sent: Tuesday, August 28, 2007 11:38 PM
Subject: Re: Labor Day weekend

i already told you my son and his girlfriend will going along and we'll probably be driving at this time ? what time you prefer to have her Monday?

From: Eliza Reza
To: Nick Reza
Sent: Tuesday, August 28, 2007 11:56 PM
Subject: Re: Labor Day weekend

If your son and his girlfriend are driving with you then that's fine with me. I get home from work around 6 pm, and Annalise has school early the next morning, so if you could drop her no later than that, I'd appreciate it.

You know that I have to work on Friday, so I'll have to drive her early in the morning to your house, probably around 7 or 7:30 am.

Also, do you have any clothes for her to take? She's a size 6 or 6x. Otherwise, I'll have to pack her a bag. But, if I do that, I'll need the clothes back so I can wash them for her to wear to school.

Eliza

From: Nick Reza
To: Eliza Reza
Sent: Wednesday, August 29, 2007 12:09 AM
Subject: Re: Labor Day weekend

that's fine i need the clothes . i'll do my best to get to your
house by 6 pm on mon.

From: Eliza Reza
To: Nick Reza
Sent: Wednesday, August 29, 2007 2:05 PM
Subject: Re: Labor Day weekend

Please try to get her back to my home by 6 pm.

She starts school the next morning, and also has therapy
on Wednesday and Thursday mornings. I do not want her
to be exhausted for these events in her life.

Also, you did not clarify if your son would be driving with
you. When I went to Hawaii with Annalise you had a full
itinerary. I expect the same.

Plus, I would like to get a phone call from Annalise one
day while she's gone please.

Thanks,
Eliza

Nick does not reply to any more emails that day. Instead, I get a phone
call from him the next afternoon.

"Eliza, can you drop Annalise off at my house by two o'clock?" Nick
asks. There are no niceties or greetings. The moment I pick up and say
hello, he launches into his reason for calling.

"Nick, hold on a sec. I just want to clarify a few things." My mind
begins to race. I want him to have time with Annalise, but he's been

hospitalized for attempted suicide. If he couldn't give me clear answers now, what would happen when he had Annalise hundreds of miles away?

"We already talked about everything."

"Will your son be with you and Annalise the entire trip?" I ask.

Nick sighs. "Yes. He will be driving up with me, along with his girlfriend."

"And he'll be with you and Annalise the entire time?" I know enough about Nick to know that he always looks for the loophole in a discussion. If I don't phrase the question exactly right, he'll give an answer that suits his immediate needs. His need right now is getting Annalise. But as her mother, I need to make sure that she will be safe.

"He will be there most of the time," Nick says. "It's enough. I want my daughter."

The back of my neck starts to tingle upon hearing the urgency in his voice. "I understand that you want to spend time with Annalise. I want that too." I know my next words will have to be phrased carefully. "Are you staying in a hotel?"

"We'll be at my cousin's house. It's big enough for us all to stay there, and Annalise will have lots of family around her."

That is a relief to hear. Even if Nick's son won't be there the entire time, there will be other family members around, most of whom I've met. Based on our past trips when Nick and I were still together, there would be several people around at all times. Nick and Annalise will be the center of attention, and they will notice if Nick seems out of sorts.

"That sounds fine, Nick. I'm sure Annalise will have a great time with everyone around her," I say. "I'll drop her by your house tomorrow at 7:00 a.m."

"OK, that sounds good." Nick pauses and adds, "What about the court order?"

"That's why I'm asking about who will be with you," I say.

"But do we need to submit something to the court?"

"I'll send an email to you and include the details we decided on, and I'll cc my lawyer on it, so there is no confusion. Does that sound OK?"

"Yes, that makes sense," he says.

"I'll do it when I get home from work tonight, since I really shouldn't be sending personal emails from my work computer."

"That's fine. Tonight then. Thank you, Eliza."

"Sure. Thanks for talking to me about this."

We hang up, and I feel good about our agreement of the travel plan. Once I get home after work, I type out a quick email to Nick and cc my lawyer.

> From: Eliza Reza
> To: Nick Reza
> Cc: Eliza's Divorce Lawyer
> Sent: Thursday, August 30, 2007 6:36 PM
> Subject: Annalise - San Jose Weekend
>
> Hello Nick,
>
> I am allowing you, in good faith, to take Annalise this weekend to San Jose, with the understanding that you will be travelling with your son. I understand that although your son will not be with you the entire time of the trip, you will be around and staying with other family members whom I know personally.
>
> I only ask that you remain with the family members when Annalise is in your care, and do not attempt to leave with her by yourself.
>
> I will drop Annalise off at your home at the designated time between 7–7:30 am, and understand that you will have her brought back to my home on Monday evening around 6 pm
>
> As understood from our conversation, I have cc'd my lawyer regarding this visitation.
>
> Thanks,
> Eliza

I step away from the computer and busy myself with getting dinner ready and on the table. Annalise climbs up and down on the couch while I call out for her to be careful. After dinner, I give Annalise a bath and wash her hair. I talk to her about the trip she will be taking with her dad. Annalise seems excited to see him, even though I know she doesn't quite understand what *driving to San Jose* means. What is important to her is that she will be seeing Daddy tomorrow.

Once Annalise is tucked into bed, I creep downstairs and open my computer to make sure that my lawyer has not yet emailed back any instructions about Nick and Annalise's weekend trip. My lawyer has not sent an email, but I notice that I have two unread messages from Nick.

From: Nick Reza
To: Eliza Reza
Sent: Thursday, August 30, 2007 6:53 PM
Subject: Annalise - San Jose Weekend

just forget about it and you keep her entire weekend.

From: Nick Reza
To: Eliza Reza
Sent: Thursday, August 30, 2007 9:09 PM
Subject: Annalise - San Jose Weekend

the way things are going it seems like you and your
attorney want me to disobey the court order.
i cannot do that or go to jail. since i cannot guarantee that
i will not be alone with Annalise up north
i cnnot take her this weekend.

I read the emails from Nick a couple of times. He replied directly to me and took my lawyer off of the email chain. Had my lawyer emailed Nick after I'd sent the initial message? I don't see any other emails regarding the trip from my lawyer or Nick's lawyer. How has Nick taken what we discussed earlier in the day and turned it into this? I decide to call him and speak with him directly about what happened.

When he answers the phone, Nick sounds tired. I glance at the time on the computer screen. It is after nine, but I know Nick typically stays up till at least midnight.

"Hey. What's going on? I thought you and I agreed that I would send an email about the plans and include my lawyer so we wouldn't have issues with the court order. Did you get another email or a call or something?"

"You just want me to get arrested," Nick says. He sounds drunk, which is odd because Nick rarely drinks any alcohol aside from the occasional beer with dinner.

"That's not true," I say.

"It is. You know I just want to see Annalise, and you're keeping her from me."

"Nick, come on. Annalise's all packed for tomorrow. She wants to see you. I want you to see each other. Don't do this, please."

Nick laughs. "I know what you're trying to do."

"Which is what, exactly?" I ask.

"You're trying to get me to take Annalise so you can have me arrested. I talked to my lawyer."

"That's ridiculous, Nick. Your lawyer told you I was trying to trick you?"

"Yes. You want me to violate the court order."

"That makes no sense. My lawyer will even write your lawyer a letter stating as much. No one is trying to get you arrested."

I open a new email and type out a message to my lawyer while still on the phone with Nick. What he is saying makes no sense, and I am hoping that we can clear things up before everything gets blown out of proportion.

From: Eliza Reza
To: Eliza's Divorce Lawyer
Sent: Thursday, August 30, 2007 9:20 PM
Subject: Annalise - San Jose Weekend

On the phone with Nick now. He says that his attorney said that we are trying to get him to violate a court order. I told him that you were willing to talk to his lawyer and even write a letter and he still insists that I am trying to get him arrested.

Eliza

Nick continues his ranting as I type. "You only want me to sink deeper into this pit. You just want me to be alone."

I don't respond to his accusations, which he takes as a positive affirmation. "So, you're not denying it then!"

I stop typing. "Yes, I'm denying it. I was just sending an email, because this is so crazy, and I'm trying to work this all out. I have no idea why you're acting like this all of a sudden. What happened to the conversation we had this morning?"

"This medicine makes me feel like you're attacking me," Nick says, his tone suddenly changing from angry to sad.

"Can you stop taking it then? Can't you see that this is kind of crazy?" I say. "All I want is for our daughter to be happy and safe."

"That's all I want for her too." Nick begins to cry. "You don't even know how much I love her. She's my entire life."

"I understand that. Really, I do." I glance at my computer screen again. My lawyer replied to my email, stating that he would give Nick's lawyer a call in the morning. "Nick, listen please. My lawyer and your lawyer will talk in the morning and will clear this all up. Can you try to get some rest in the meantime? I'm worried about you."

"It doesn't matter what these slime lawyers decide." His voice has changed again, and the anger is palpable. "You have nothing to lose, but I have everything to lose. Just kiss her for me since you denied my visitation."

I lean back in my chair and rub my eyes. The sheer insanity of this exchange is exhausting. "Nick, I'm not denying anything. I want you to be able to spend time with Annalise. She wants that. We packed her bag tonight. She's ready to come see you."

"You enjoy time with her this weekend. I can't take her. Your attorney won't let me, and you want me arrested," he says before abruptly hanging up.

I sit there, holding the phone in my hand. My head is reeling over the absurdity of the conversation. Nick's tone flip-flopped several times during our short conversation, going from angry to sad and back to being angry again. He acted as if I was out to get him and included his own lawyer in the accusations as well.

While I sit, I attempt to process everything that has taken place over the course of the past few weeks. All I end up with are more questions.

What about the medication he's on? He said that it made him feel as if I was out to get him. If the medication was making his behavior erratic, he should tell his doctor. As far as I know, the only medication he's on is for blood pressure. It is the only medicine I've ever seen him take. Has he been prescribed something else after his suicide attempt? Is he on some sort of antidepressant? What about the psychiatric evaluation he was supposed to get? Has that happened yet?

I want to know what's happening but know that I won't get any clarification from Nick, at least not tonight.

The next morning, I call my lawyer and update him on the conversation I had with Nick the night before. I also ask him to seek an update on Nick's psychiatric evaluation. Once Nick completes the evaluation, if everything is cleared, he won't have to worry about supervised visitations with Annalise. Plus, I really am worried about him. He hasn't sounded like himself for a while now, and it is obvious that Nick's paranoia has begun to take over for his reasoning.

My lawyer assures me that he will mention it to Nick's lawyer to see if the psychiatric evaluation can be done soon.

49

A New Address, Again

Eliza

October 2007

My mom has relocated to Georgia after being offered a new great new position with a university there. I am upset about it, though I'll never tell her. I know her career means a lot to her, and this is a great opportunity. She's going to be in a leadership role at Gem University, and I'm just so proud of her.

On the plus side, her departure opens up a new opportunity for Annalise and me. She and my stepfather had the house on the market, but because of the dip in real estate, they were unable to let it go for anything but a ridiculously low price. I asked if I could rent it from them, and they agreed. I'm excited. It's a nice home with a fenced pool. Annalise, who I've discovered is part mermaid, will love swimming in it when summer rolls around again.

Moving from Yorba Linda isn't that far, about fifteen minutes, but it means a new school district. Ms. G shows about as much emotion over this news as Spock from *Star Trek* would. She sends me an email telling me, "Good Luck. You can pick up Annalise's Diastat in the front office."

Annalise finishes her Yorba Linda preschool on Tuesday and begins her Anaheim Hills preschool on Wednesday. Annalise's new teacher is a young and energetic man named Mr. Dean. He has a great spirit about him, and I'm instantly impressed when he crouches down so he can talk to her at her level. She responds with a smile and a hug. He even laughs at one point when Annalise points at him and says, "That's Daddy." I laugh nervously and explain, "You have dark hair like her dad." Thankfully, Mr. Dean just smiles and nods.

My employment with Gateway is going well. I am learning a lot about web copywriting and how to merge copy with design. I'm also getting to work with the content management system to learn how web pages are built. My hours are set, and my pay is steady. Plus, the people who work on my team are some of the smartest and most hilarious people I've ever met. I'm instantly friends with most of them and going to work every day is fun because I get to be around them. I've had the chance to hang out with my colleagues outside of work too and having this new set of friends has been so fulfilling. This part of our life finally feels somewhat settled, and I welcome this newfound happiness.

50

Another Trial, Another Test, a New Beginning

Anna
1989–1990

God has to be looking after me on my trip to Cancun, Mexico. I have no idea what I am doing or why. But there I am, checking into an ocean retreat, armed with plenty of books to read during my stay. I change into my swimsuit and head down to the beach. I am instantly smitten with the incredible beauty of the ocean and beach surroundings. I have never seen such clear blue ocean water. This feels so right! I want to just bask in this beautiful and peaceful environment.

For the first time in years, I feel like I can just sit back and totally enjoy myself without worrying about work or slaving over some course project. I think about my youngest child at camp; I feel comfortable knowing all my children are safe and secure. My oldest daughter is married, and that has come with another set of issues and problems. My son is working and hopefully is spending some quality time with his father. For the moment, I just want to just relax.

However, my peaceful moments are soon interrupted by a stranger who calls out, "Honey, you want to share my cabana?"

I look over, and there sits this man who is staring in my direction. Suddenly, something wells up from deep inside of me, and before I catch hold of myself, a rage of anger and bitterness spews forth. "Get lost!" I grab my towel and march past him as I head back to my room.

I sit there in my room and begin to cry. "God, please help me control my thoughts, words, deeds, and actions." *Why do I act this way?*

The next day, I meet a group of single women who are also staying at the resort, and it is fun to connect with them. Interestingly, we all share common stories, and it is good to be with others. My emotional defense wall is slowly crumbling. God is helping me to overcome the negative emotional barrier that has been around me for so long. Even with the issues in my family the past three years, I find a peace and strength that comes after I receive the Holy Spirit. I know that no matter what came against me in life, God was there. While I do not understand why suffering occurs in my life, I know that God is in control. That verse about God not letting us suffer more than we can endure is still hard for me to grasp, but for the first time in my life, I grasp what God is saying.

On my third morning at the resort, I meet my new group of ladies for breakfast. The waitress leads us to a table that is being occupied by a man sitting by himself. All of us ladies sit there, talking nonstop with one another. Suddenly, I realize we have not included this man in our conversation. He has sat there the entire time without making a comment. Maybe it is because I am feeling remorseful about being so nasty to the gentleman on the beach on the day I arrived at the resort, but I feel the need to try to be friendly. I ask him where he is from and what he plans to do today.

The man at the table mutters something about going on some all-day boat trip. Based on his abrupt manner, I feel no need to engage him in conversation.

The resort is wonderful in terms of having so many incredible things to do, such as sailing, parasailing, snorkeling, scuba diving, exercise classes, excursions, and so on. I love the fact that everything is on a schedule for those who choose not to lie on the beach all day. I go from one thing to another all day long. I discover that just lying on the beach is not for me. I need to be active and stay busy experiencing and learning new things. I must have had ADHD as a child because sitting still is not my mantra.

My thoughts are drawn back to the ladies at the table, who also make the attempt to include the man seated with us in some conversation. Well, after a few brief comments, the man asks to be excused and leaves the table. "Guess we frightened him off," I gleefully say to the ladies at the table.

That evening, we spot the man from breakfast. He comes over to us and asks if we want to join him at the evening entertainment show. This is a surprise to all of us. One of the ladies nudges me and says, "I think he likes you."

"I hope not," I reply to her. We are polite and sit with him for the evening show.

The next day, I am enjoying some leisurely floating in the ocean water. The waves carry me along as I lie on my back and stare at the bright blue sky above. I allow the waves to carry me out beyond the safety ropes. I spread out my arms, close my eyes, and just clear my mind of anything other than happy thoughts. Before long, someone grabs me by the neck and drags me through the water. The man from breakfast wraps his arms around my neck.

I try to scream and hit him with my fist to release me, but he is stronger than I am. I thrash about and take in large gulps of ocean water. I try to get away from him but to no avail. He keeps dragging me through the water. At one point, I spot a lifeguard on the beach screaming. Why isn't the lifeguard coming to help me? Is he going to continue to stand there on the beach and let this guy drown me?

After what seems like forever, the man drops me on the sandy beach. I begin screaming at him and the lifeguard. Have I come to Mexico only to be killed by some lunatic? I continue to hit him in an attempt to get some distance between us.

"Don't you realize what was happening out there?" The lifeguard is now yelling at me and waving his arms in the air. "This man saved your life. Look out there! It's a wonder that barracuda didn't attack you. He risked his life to save you."

I look at the man who rescued me. He just stands there quietly as he looks into my eyes. My first reaction is to be flippant, but this time I hold my thoughts in check. *Rescued by a man. How ironic.* Yes, I am tempted to say that but do not. God still has work to do in my life. I am saved and Holy Spirit filled but so far from perfect. My tongue is my weapon of choice, and daily I must bring my thoughts and tongue under submission to God.

I return home, and life settles back to its usual routine of work and rearing my two younger children. My son finishes high school and enlists in the navy, so it is just me and my youngest daughter at home. The man who rescued me in Cancun and I develop a long-distance relationship. We speak to each other on the phone every day. He comes to visit us in Arkansas. I joke with him that he wants to see how I live. I can only imagine what his perceptions are of the state. My youngest daughter and I visit him in California. Yes, California! He lives thirty-five miles from Los Angeles.

After much prayer, I agree to marry my future husband but only if I find a job in California. So I put out my fleece and apply at a couple of state universities. I have interviews at three universities, and after much consideration, I choose the offer to teach in Los Angeles. Yes, Los Angeles! To this day, I stand amazed at how God works out my life and His will is done, not mine. The one place I am determined never to go, and here I am. But for God go I.

I move to California a week before our wedding. My home in Arkansas is rented. My belongings are en route to my new home with my future husband. I am soon to begin my new job. All is well—or sort of. My ex-husband calls me on my phone at work a few days before I leave for California, begging me to give him another chance. Is he serious? What is going on, and why is he doing this? I learn later that his girlfriend has broken up with him. He is not one to be alone. But I know I cannot go back. He will soon find another replacement for me.

I am afraid. I am nervous about getting married again. Am I making the right decision for my daughter and me? Is it wise to relocate in California and place my daughter in such strange surroundings? So, what do I do? An hour before the wedding ceremony with all his friends and children present, I tell my soon-to-be husband that I need a half hour alone. I go into an adjoining room and shut the door. I begin to pray. "God, I need your peace about what I am about to do. If it be your will, let me go out there and marry this man. If it is not your will, give me the strength to go out there and tell him we will have a nice party and I will head back to Arkansas."

But what will I be heading back to? I signed an agreement to rent out my house before leaving Arkansas. I resigned from my job at the college in

Arkansas. I accepted and signed a contract to begin a new teaching position in Los Angeles. Do I really want to go back? Or am I just afraid? I love my church in Arkansas and wonder if I will find another church to feed me spiritually. What am I doing? Do I really want to get married again after all that happened in my former marriage? I am independent. I can take care of myself. What do I really know about this man? What do any of us know about another person?

All kinds of thoughts run through my mind. I am suddenly filled with so much doubt and fear. *I do not have to do this.* I look toward the door. Tears fill my eyes. *What am I doing? God, please help me make the right decision. This woman before you with a doctoral degree has made some incredibly unrealistic decisions in her life.* Then it is as if God reminds me of who I am. During a time of intense prayer a few weeks earlier, God whispers to me that I am a Deborah. I go to the Bible and read about Deborah being a warrior who fights alongside the men in battle.

My spirit soars as I think about this revelation. A Deborah marches forward as a brave and fearless leader. Deborah faces difficult challenges. She does not run or shirk under the weight of carrying out God's instructions. She allows God to direct her. She was a married woman, a wife.

After I pray, I walk out the door and announce I am ready to marry my future husband. At this point in the story, one might assume a fairy-tale ending. But once again, life is about to become quite interesting. And to this day, I know God has on several occasions reassured me that He has me in the palm of His hand. My Lord will show me time and time again that He is watching over me.

51

Halloween

Eliza
October 31, 2007

For the past few years, Annalise has wanted me to dress just like her for Halloween. She tells me what she wants us to dress as, and I go off in search of the perfect outfits. This year, she's into Disney princesses and has decided she would like for us to dress as Snow White. I'm not sure where the idea of dressing alike came from, but I don't protest too much. I figure I only have a few good years before she doesn't want to trick-or-treat anymore, and most likely even less time that she'll want to hang out with me on Halloween.

Tonight was Halloween, and it was the first time we'd made it all the way around our neighborhood. Annalise returned home exhausted but happy. She immediately plunked herself down on the living room floor and emptied the apple-shaped bag filled to the brim with candy all over the floor. I left the Crock-Pot cooking all day, so our meal of corned beef and cabbage was ready to eat. This was one of the dishes I'd learned how to make by watching my mom. She'd put the corned beef in the Crock Pot and stuff it until there was absolutely no room with cabbage, carrots, and celery. Then we'd relish in the scent of cooking cabbage and salty meat until dinnertime. It was a dish I loved, and one that Annalise did too.

We ate dinner at our small square table, which I'd pulled into the living room so Annalise could continue watching *It's the Great Pumpkin, Charlie Brown*. Annalise devoured her dinner and then ate two of the candies from her trick-or-treat haul.

I cleared the table of dishes and was just about to pull the table back into the kitchen when Annalise made a small sound that caught my attention. I turned to look at her, and she vomited. She fell backward on the carpet, and her eyes rolled back. I put her on her side the best I could and ran to grab the Diastat. When the emergency medicine didn't work and she was still seizing three minutes later, without even thinking, I scooped her up and ran to my car. I buckled her stiff body still dressed in her Snow White outfit into the front seat and drove as quickly as I could to the nearest ER.

I pulled up to the front, and without even turning off the car, I lifted Annalise out of the seat and ran inside the ER doors with her, yelling, "Help! She's having a seizure!"

Halloween is the worst time to have an emergency. It was crowded. Annalise was still seizing in my arms, and I was yelling at the admissions nurse to please admit her. I explained that she needed to have medicine injected to stop the seizures, that every passing minute was giving her brain damage.

The nurse looked at me and said, "You should have called the ambulance then, shouldn't you? She would have gone straight back if you'd called an ambulance."

As if on cue, Annalise vomited all over the admitting room floor. I held her head and whispered into her ear, "Such a smart girl."

The woman looked up at me, gasping in horror as I stared back at her and uttered, "Now can we go back?"

She immediately picked up the phone and called for assistance. The nurse who responded to the call took approximately three seconds to assess the situation before rushing me and Annalise to the nearest available bed.

Annalise spent three days in the hospital following the Halloween seizure. When we finally made it home, I surveyed the living room scene we'd left behind. Strewn candy on the floor, the table pushed to the side to allow the paramedics enough room to work, the red bow from Annalise's costume thrown to the side.

I sat on the floor and pressed my back against the couch. I had no idea what possessed me to drive Annalise to the hospital myself. *That is a mistake I vow not to make again.*

52

Pleading at Calvary

Eliza

My body and head ache from the week I just spent, sleeping upright in the chair next to Annalise's hospital bed. I hold her hand while I drift off, to make sure that I won't miss the start of any seizure activity.

That's my job, to monitor and alert the nurses the second she starts to seize, so they can mark the focal point of the brain misfiring on the EEG monitor. Because her seizures are focal in nature, meaning she doesn't go into a grand mal situation that most people imagine when they think of seizures, I have to keep a close eye on her. Annalise's seizures typically went like this: she'd be asleep, only to be jarred awake by something (an aura perhaps?), she'd call out "Mommy!" throw up, and then she'd be lost in this battle with her brain. Dr. Michaels calls it a "brain hijack" when the seizures take control, and while Annalise may understand that she's seizing, she can't do anything to stop it. The start of the brain hijack is so undercover in nature that I have to be on high alert in order to catch the onset.

It's been a week, and still nothing. Normally I'd rejoice for the lack of seizures, but we need to record the seizure data so we can figure out if Annalise is a candidate for a hemispherectomy.

Hemispherectomy: a very rare neurosurgical procedure in which a cerebral hemisphere (half of the brain) is removed, disconnected, or disabled.

Annalise's first surgery caused the seizures, and they were now happening every single month. Each time, they stole a week from her life because they lasted three hours on average and forced a 911 call and subsequent hospital visit so she could be pumped with Alivan to stop the seizure activity. Numerous medicines had been tried, as had the Keto diet, regular sleep schedules, lack of bright lights and definitely no strobe lights, multiple hospital stays—you name it, we tried it. A hemispherectomy was our last resort, the final solution to stopping the seizures. If it sounds like science fiction to you, imagine how I felt. At this point, Annalise had already survived two brain surgeries. This would be her third, and it would be to remove *half of her brain*. Obviously, this was no small decision.

I hadn't had a shower in a week or a decent night's sleep. Annalise's night nurse, who I hadn't seen since the first night we were in the hospital, had taken one look at me and insisted I go home for the night. I'd only agreed after demanding multiple times that she call me the second anything happened. She said she would and handed me my purse as she showed me out of the room.

As I pull off the freeway, I glance in the back seat at Annalise's booster seat. I miss the sight of her chubby cheeks and the sound of her giggles as we drive over speed bumps. Just ten minutes, and I'll be pulling into the car park of our Yorba Linda townhome. I specifically rented it because it was only a few miles from my mother's home in Anaheim Hills.

The stoplight at the intersection of Nohl Ranch Road and Imperial Highway is red. As I wait for the green light, I look around. Signs for banks and a grocery store light up the otherwise dark street. The grocery store makes me wonder when the last time I went grocery shopping was. *Do we have food in the house? If so, is it still good? Am I even hungry? When was the last time I ate? Let's see, I had a coffee this morning, courtesy of the EEG tech who was kind enough to bring me a cup during his morning rounds. That was really nice of him. Did I even bother to say, "Thank you?" Food. Am I hungry?* The light turns green, and I slowly cross the intersection.

The lights of Calvary Chapel East Anaheim catch my attention, a large white glowing dove. The church is tucked away inside an industrial park, surrounded by random office buildings. If you didn't know it was there, you could miss it entirely. But we'd been going there for a couple of years now, so I knew that if you looked between the overhang of the trees, you'd see it. A few years ago, Annalise had her dedication there. It was right after her father, Nick, and I separated, and he'd shown up and sat in the back row. I didn't even know he was there until I received a text message from him directly after the end of the service. "Those boots looked cheap," he'd remarked, regarding my choice of knee-length dress, black tights, and calf-high boots. I felt a chill go through me—not because he'd insulted me yet again but because he was there, watching us without my knowing. It felt like a pickax violently making an opening in my safe place.

On any given Sunday, the reflective glass of the church would gleam in the bright sunlight, and inside there was barely room to walk without having to maneuver around mothers holding brand-new babies or little girls and boys screaming gleefully as they ran through the halls.

I'd been lax in my prayers lately. I continued to say them, but my heart was heavy, and my belief was delicate at best. At my worst, I'll admit that I yelled at God more than a few times in the past five years. I learned never to ask God, "What now?" because He always answered me. Only it was never the answer I wanted.

It is a Wednesday night. I haven't been to church on a Wednesday since I was forced to attend as a child by my mother, a devout Christian. I've heard many stories about giving one's self over to God in the most desperate hours, and well, I am mighty desperate.

I make a left turn into the parking area of the church. There are a few cars scattered throughout the lot, and I assume that perhaps the service ended early. I figure that there will be a pastor there anyway, so I park the car and walk into the chapel. It is brightly lit inside but completely empty. Seeing the totally empty church on a random Wednesday night is a bit disheartening. I suppose I'm expecting a glowing white light to welcome me as I walk in, or a chorus to erupt out of the silence, but nothing like that happens. It is just me in this large auditorium, which is too brightly lit, with rows and rows of empty beige pews.

I'm already here, so instead of turning around and going home, I sit down in a middle pew to the left of the stage. I'm not sure what to do now. Pray? Sit and think? Talk to God?

The sound of silence in the church is the loudest silence I've ever heard.

It is bright and loud with nothingness. In that moment, I do the only thing I know to do. I call my mom.

"Eliza? Is Annalise OK?" my mom asks. I can tell she is getting ready for bed, since it is almost nine and she never stays up past nine thirty.

"Mom …" My voice cracks. "I'm at the church."

"What? Which church?"

"Down the street. Calvary."

"OK. Are you OK? Why are you at the church, honey?"

I pause, unsure of how to answer her. I honestly can't recall why I came and, more importantly, why I stayed. "I'm not sure why." Tears flood my eyes and start to roll down my cheeks. My face burns, and my nose runs.

"Stay there. I'm coming to get you."

"No, it's fine, Mom."

"Eliza." Her voice sounds stern. "Stay there. I'll be right there."

The church is at least a five-minute drive from her house, but I'm fairly certain my mom was there in two minutes, parking and walking into the church included.

My head is on top of my folded arms, lying on the back of the pew in front of me. I'm the picture of a woman defeated.

I feel my mom slide into the seat next to me. She says nothing but wraps her arms around me in a tight hug. While I have cried over the past few years, this moment, while my mom is holding me, I feel like I can finally let it all go. I not only cry. I weep—deep, heaving sobs that steal my breath away and force me to gasp for air. My entire body shakes.

At this moment, I say the words that are the most raw and true, "Mom, I'm so scared."

She rocks me. Here I am, a grown woman with a child of my own, and my mother is rocking me to soothe me as I cry.

Just then my mom whispers, "She's going through some difficult times." I'm not sure if she is talking to me or to God.

Then I hear a man's voice respond, "Does she need some prayer?"

I raise my head and open my eyes. The light makes me feel nauseous. I look at the source of the voice and see a man with gray hair and khakis.

"What's going on?" he asks me.

I'm not even sure where to begin. I just sit there in numb silence. The tears flow, and I don't have the energy to form actual words.

My mom answers for me. "Her daughter, my granddaughter, is in the hospital. She's been getting treatments for seizures, and it's been really difficult for her."

They begin to pray, asking God for healing for Annalise and peace of spirit for me. Maybe it is the calming nature of this prayer or the fact that I've just been rocked like a baby, but I feel lighter. Not like all of the problems have been solved but like I can go home and shower and sleep for a couple of hours. My tears slow.

I'm not sure what to do next, so I thank the man and tell my mom I'm ready to go home. My mom and the man exchange simpering glances. There is a pit in my stomach, growing larger with each passing second, and all I want is to go home and sit in a dark corner.

We walk outside, my mom holding on to my arm as if to steady me. I suppose I am unsteady, but only emotionally, not physically, at least not that I can tell. Perhaps my mom is anticipating a stumble or fall, but I can't allow myself to do that just yet.

"You sure you're OK?" My mom searches my face as she asks. I'm not quite sure what she is hoping to find and don't want to prolong the agony of being felt sorry for, so I keep my tone as flat as I can.

"Yeah, fine," I say, my voice barely above a whisper.

She stares back at me. Her eyes narrow. "You want to come stay at our place tonight?"

"No. Really. I just need to be home, in my own bed." The last thing I want is to have to see my stepfather, to hear his condescending voice that spits out offensive turns of phrase any chance he gets.

I hug her tightly. "I'll be fine. I'll call tomorrow."

"What time are you heading back to the hospital?" she asks.

"Around nine o'clock, after traffic dies down a bit." That is actually a joke, as traffic in Los Angeles is terrible no matter what time of day you leave.

We say our last goodbyes for the evening, and I start the drive home. I hover my hand over the radio for a moment and decide that I prefer the silence. Every song on the radio has annoyed me lately. All the songs are either too happy or too sad, and everything sounds like junk.

The silence in the car leaves me alone with my thoughts. My mind drifts to Annalise's hair and how it will be a mess upon her discharge from the hospital. They have to use glue to keep the leads on the EEG monitor attached to designated spots on her head. It is important that the glue be strong enough to ensure that the leads don't slip from her head, causing inaccurate readings to be picked up in case of a seizure. If they thought they'd captured a seizure from an area that it hadn't actually originated from, they could potentially remove the wrong portion of her brain, a healthy portion—as opposed to the unhealthy bits that are causing the seizures in the first place.

It may sound silly to think of the mess in Annalise's hair left over from the glue residue. But it is trite thoughts like these that help me not to focus twenty-four seven on the fact that another mistake could be made, one that would leave her with less of a healthy brain than what she currently has. I need the inconsequential "nothing" thoughts to survive.

Baby oil, apple cider vinegar, wet brush, leave-in detangler. That's what would be needed to remove the adhesive and brush out the knots. Annalise will hate it. She always has. But this is the routine to get back to our version of normal.

53

The Psychiatric Evaluation

Eliza
November 2007

Aside from seizures, hospitalizations, and figuring out the best way to help Annalise, I'm also trying to find out what's going on with Nick. His attorney finally got back to mine about the psychiatric evaluation and forwarded the following letter from Nick's psychiatrist.

Re: Nick Reza

Nick Reza has been in my care since March 2006. He initially sought treatment for anxiety and depression related to difficulties in his marriage and concern for his youngest daughter, Annalise. As you well know, his marriage has subsequently failed. Although Mr. Reza has been very unhappy about his failed marriage, his major symptoms have been anxiety/stress and insomnia. Both of these have been rather difficult to treat as previous treatments have either been ineffective or caused unacceptable side effects.

He has switched antidepressant medication several times, mostly due to GI complaints. I have been convinced that these complaints were not due to the medication, but rather a symptom of his high level of subjective stress. He has been seen by me on a monthly basis, in addition to a therapist here at the clinic.

I should also add that Mr. Reza has been reluctant to take meds. I have had to strongly encourage him to NOT stop his current regiment on at least one occasion as well as encourage him to make liberal use of "as-needed" medication. He has been reluctant to take anything that might be habituating or cause cognitive impairment.

Mr. Reza has never reported suicidal ideation to me. He was hospitalized in July 2007 after his family became concerned that he was going to harm himself. To be honest, I was rather surprised by this. He later told me that he has never had any intent to harm himself and feels that he would never do that to his children, especially Annalise. I have personally observed him with her on two separate occasions. He was very gentle and appropriate with her. He has always talked about her welfare as a major priority for him.

I will also add that Mr. Reza has described himself as the more stable parent. He has complained about his daughter's condition after he gets her from her mother but was quick to point out that he did not want to deprive his daughter of a relationship with her mother. He recently told me that she screams, cries and claws at him when he takes her back to her mother's house. Although I cannot claim to have done a thorough clinical assessment of his interaction with her, I feel comfortable in stating that I have every reason to believe that he is totally devoted to her and would not do anything to put her in danger while she was in his care.

The psychiatrist had given a glowing recommendation on Nick's mental state and in the process had thrown in an accusation from Nick that I was an unstable parent. I was livid. I had never met this doctor, had never spoken to her, and I certainly wasn't aware that Annalise had gone with Nick to his psychiatrist's office.

The entire situation made me want to call Nick and demand an explanation. I took a few deep breaths and decided against it. I knew that I was a good mother. I stepped back and took stock of the current situation. I had a steady job. Annalise had a stable environment at home, where we followed a daily routine. This routine in itself screamed stability. Every night, Annalise ate dinner with me at our kitchen table. She had a bath. I read her bedtime stories and the poems of Shel Silverstein. We worked together to lay out her clothes for the next day. She took her medicine on time, in the morning and in the evening. She was loved and adored.

I decided against calling Nick to discuss why he'd told his psychiatrist that I was the less stable parent, because it wasn't the truth. Lies may have been swirling around me, but I wouldn't succumb to them and treat them as if they were truth. Lies hold no gravity. They get thrown out into the environment, and others swarm them in an attempt to make them stick. But what they profess isn't real. Leave them alone long enough, and the truth will come out. I had to stand my ground and let the truth speak for itself.

54

The Intervention

Eliza
November 2007

Today was a good day. They're incorporating a new computer system at work, and I'm finding it really interesting. Since the letter arrived from Nick's psychiatrist, I've been trying to focus on the good in my life. I'm learning to be kinder to myself and allow positivity to influence my thoughts, instead of allowing negativity to drive me into the ground. So today, I decided to embrace learning something entirely new and feel pride about putting into practice this new thing that I've learned.

When I pick up Annalise from day care, she is excited to see me. She runs into my arms and gives me a giant hug. I stand there and let her wrap her arm around my neck, taking in all the love that she is willing to give. After dinner and bath, she isn't ready to go to bed. Since she is in such a loveable mood, I don't make her.

We sit on the living room floor with Chutes and Ladders, playing by Annalise's rules, which means sliding the game pieces up and down the ladders and slides on the board as she directs. With each slide, Annalise makes a loud "Whoop!" before crashing the game piece onto the carpet. This goes on for about thirty minutes, sliding and crashing, until she lays her game piece on its side and announces that it is going to take a nap.

Seeing this as my cue, I recommend that we put the entire game to sleep in the box. Annalise agrees and yawns deeply.

Tonight, there is no fighting against bedtime, no request for multiple stories or glasses of water. She only wants one Shel Silverstein poem, called "Everything on It," about a man who asks for a hot dog topped with everything and regrets it after it comes topped with a parrot and a front porch swing.

I finish reading the poem, kiss her three times (on her forehead and both cheeks), and turn off the light. I creep quietly downstairs and begin my nightly routine of cleaning up the kitchen. I made chicken tacos for dinner, which Annalise loved. I sweep the floor under the kitchen table, gathering bits of taco shell and shredded cheese that fell from Annalise's plate. Cleaning up in the silent house lulls me into a state of relaxed concentration, and my mind drifts from one random thought to the next.

When my phone rings, forcefully pulling me out of my deep thoughts, I am a little annoyed at the intrusion. I glance at the clock on the microwave; it's just after nine. When I see the name on the caller ID, I pause before answering it. It's Nick's daughter. She never calls me, and she wouldn't be calling this late just to talk to Annalise.

"Hey, Janie," I answer.

"Hey, Eliza," she says, her young voice sounding urgent. "Sorry to call this late, but my dad isn't doing well."

Over the last year, Nick has made frequent trips to the emergency room for "heart attacks," which in reality are panic attacks. They are serious, and he's been seeing mental health professionals and taking medication in an attempt to control them. It has been a few months since he was hospitalized for attempted suicide, and since then, Nick has been on a mission to convince everyone that he is fine.

"What's happening? Is he OK?" I ask.

"Not really. We're all at his house, my brothers and my mom and me. We're trying to get him to check himself into the hospital."

"The hospital? For what?"

"I'm not sure how much you know, but it's not good. He's been trying to commit suicide."

"I mean, I know about the fifty-one-fifty back in July. Is that what you mean?"

She inhales deeply and lets a small groan escape on the exhale. It isn't lost on me how awful this was for her. She is still a teenager. At her age, she should be worried about things like college admissions and final exams, not about whatever is going on with her dad.

"Not exactly. He's been talking about it, and there have been two more attempts since the one in July," she explains.

My head begins to buzz. "What do you mean *two more attempts?*"

"Well, you know how before I told you that he'd been sleeping a lot?"

"Yeah, I remember."

"Well, he actually took a bunch of pills. And uhm, my brother also caught him another time trying to take pills."

"Hold on a second. Annalise was with him, you said, when he was sleeping all the time. Was he taking these pills, trying to—he was with Annalise?" I sink to the floor in the kitchen, the realization of what I've been missing making my body feel heavy.

"Yeah, we just wanted you to know, you know … so Annalise was safe."

In the background, I hear Nick arguing with someone. He pleads, "Let me talk to her." "Hey, Eliza, my dad wants to talk to you," Janie says.

"Yeah, fine. OK."

The phone shuffles, and Nick's voice comes on the line. "Eliza?"

I close my eyes, trying to think of how to approach this conversation with him. A small "Hi" is all I can muster. I am having trouble understanding what Janie admitted, that Nick has been trying to kill himself, even while he was with our daughter. All the times Annalise returned home screaming and crying. Clinging to her dad. Was it because she was worried that it might be the last time she would see him? Did she comprehend what he was trying to do?

"Eliza, it's all lies," Nick says.

In the background, I can hear one of his sons and his ex-wife responding to what he is saying to me, "Tell the truth! She deserves to know what's going on." Nick shushes them, and I hear their voices fade out.

"Nick, what is going on? Tell me the truth. Are you OK?"

"They're trying to get me into trouble. I don't know what they're talking about," he says hurriedly into the phone.

"Why would they do that?" I ask.

"I don't know. They want something from me, money or something. Don't believe them. They're all lying." His voice is frantic and paranoid.

"Even your daughter? Come on. Tell me what's really going on. I won't get mad. I won't try to keep Annalise from you. Just tell me the truth. I want to make sure you're getting help," I say, running down a mental list of all the reasons why he might continue to lie to me.

"I swear to you. I wouldn't do anything like that. I wouldn't do that to Annalise. I love her," he says and begins to cry.

"This whole thing doesn't make sense, though. Why would you be pulled in by the police for attempted suicide, and now your kids are there with your ex, saying you're trying to take pills? And were you doing that with Annalise there with you? Was she in danger?"

"No. Why don't you listen? I just told you that I wouldn't do that to her." His voice is just above a whisper but firm. He has stopped crying.

"Tell me the truth."

"You're just like them," he says. "All you want is me gone."

"That is not true, and you know it. I want you here. Annalise wants you here. We need you to be healthy. All we want is for you to be healthy. That's all this is about."

He begins to cry again. "Annalise is my life. She's my little baby Boos. All I want is to see her. That little baby gives me life."

"Then get help. Get well for her."

"I'm trying. I swear I am."

I bite my lips together, trying to come up with the right words to say. My mind is suddenly blank, and all I can muster is a simple "I know."

In the background, I hear one of his sons knocking on the door and saying, "Dad, open the door."

Nick sniffles and says quietly into the phone, "I have to go."

"OK. I'll give Annalise a kiss for you." As soon as I finish saying those words, the line goes dead.

I sit there shaking my head and thinking how crazy this all is. After a few moments, I stand and walk upstairs into Annalise's room. She's sleeping and looks so beautiful with her dark curls falling into her face and tiny pink lips protruding into a sleepy pout. I lean over and give her a soft kiss on the top of her head. As I press my lips into her warm hair, I feel a sob rising in my throat as the thought that I've been trying to submerge rapidly floats to the surface. *He could have taken her with him.*

55

The Christmas Gift

Eliza

December 7, 2007

Since the intervention at Nick's house and my phone call with him, things between us have been extremely cordial. I'm not sure if he's just putting on a brave face for the purpose of appearing fine, but the fact that we're not arguing every time we talk is a welcome shift in our dynamic. He called this morning and asked if he could take Annalise to a basketball game. His friend Paul is going with him, acting as the chaperone per the court order for supervised visitation. I know Paul will keep an eye on Annalise, and that makes me feel better about allowing her to go.

The main reason that I agree to the outing, however, is that Annalise misses her dad. I wait to tell Annalise about going out with her dad until an hour before Nick's scheduled arrival, since he's cancelled or been a no-show a few times in the past two months. His reasons are always the same, that he is feeling sick or has a doctor appointment. I don't argue over the reasons why he has not kept his promises to see Annalise, but I do remind him that she's only three years old and doesn't understand.

This morning when he asks to see her, I reply to him in earnest, "I can't keep telling her why Daddy isn't showing up." When I tell Annalise that she will be going to a basketball game with her dad, she is so thrilled that she grabs me by the hand and drags me to her room to get ready.

When Nick brings Annalise back home that evening, she excitedly runs to the front door waving red and white pom-poms. "Look!" she squeals, shaking the pom-pom with all the zeal she can muster.

"Oh, my goodness! Are you a cheerleader?" I say, picking her up and kissing her cheek. She wriggles out of my hands, wanting to be put down so she can show me a cheer.

"Gooooooo tea!" Annalise says, giving the pom-poms a flourish.

I clap my hands and exclaim, "Best cheer ever!"

Annalise is beaming, and it warms my heart to know that she had a good day with her dad. I ask her if she ate, and Nick answers for her.

"She had part of a hot dog, some cotton candy, and some popcorn."

I look at Annalise, "Whoa! You ate all of that?"

She gives me a sly smile and nods.

"I bet it was good too, wasn't it?"

Annalise's eyes get wide, and she gives me a more enthusiastic nod.

I laugh at the gesture and turn to Nick. "Thank you for today. It's obvious she had a great time."

Nick picks up Annalise and asks her in Farsi for a kiss, "Boos?" Annalise responds by puckering her mouth and kissing him on the lips. He squeezes her so tightly she groans a little but doesn't wriggle away from him. Instead, she wraps her arm around his neck and squeezes back.

The sight of them together and the relaxed and easy exchange between Nick and me is a welcome shift. The normalcy of it all nearly makes me forget that Paul is sitting in the driver's seat of Nick's car, waiting for him to finish saying his goodbyes. I give Paul a small wave, which he returns.

Nick gives Annalise one more hug and kiss before gently setting her down on the ground. "Be good for Mommy, OK?"

Annalise looks at me and gives a mischievous grin.

I shake my head. "That means no naughty."

Nick laughs before bending over to give her one last kiss. "I love you, *khoshgel*."

Her mischievous grin is replaced with a sweet one as she hears him utter the words meaning "beautiful girl" in Farsi. She says, "Bye, Daddy!" and runs inside the house waving her pom-poms.

Left alone on the front step, I want to keep the mood light, so I reference Annalise's cheer. "Go tea? Is that a Persian cheer?" I say with a giggle.

He laughs. "I think it might be."

"I'm glad she had fun tonight. Thank you for that."

He shrugs and smiles. "I had fun too." He glances back at the car where Paul is waiting patiently. "I have to get going, but I wanted to give you something for Annalise." I follow Nick to the trunk of his car. He opens it and pulls out a large cardboard box.

My eyes go wide. "What in the world?"

"It's her Christmas gift. I hate to ask you to put it together, but would you mind?"

I look at the box and see a picture of a Strawberry Shortcake Big Wheel on the front. "For Annalise? But why don't you just wait and give it to her yourself?"

He stands quietly. "I just, uh, I'm not sure what Christmas plans are, and I want to make sure that she has a gift from me."

"Well, of course you can see her on Christmas." My brow furrows. "I mean, you will want to see her sometime during Christmas, won't you?"

Nick shifts his weight from one foot to the other. "Yes, but I'm just not sure about seeing her on the actual Christmas Day, and I want to, you know … make sure she has a gift to open on Christmas morning."

"Uh huh." I eye him suspiciously. "I mean, you could see her Christmas morning if you wanted to. I could bring her down and let her open gifts with you."

His eyes dart from my face to the surface of the driveway. He doesn't look me in the eyes when he says, "Can you just make sure she gets it?"

I bite my lips, knowing that once Nick sets his mind to something, there is little chance of changing it. "Sure," I say, not masking the disappointment in my voice. "No problem."

"Thank you, Eliza," he says, looking up to meet my eyes again. "And, uh, I'm sorry for everything."

I wasn't expecting gratitude from Nick, and it makes me pause. "Uh … it's fine. It's all good." I motion to the box. "Can you carry this in for me?"

He nods and lifts the box. We decide that I'll keep the gift on a high shelf in the garage until Christmas Eve, when I'll take it down to put it together. As he's leaving, something in me urges me to give him a hug. We never hug anymore, our exchanges typically strained due to the pressure of separation. But I do it anyway, and to my surprise, he hugs me back.

We say nothing more but smile and wave at each other as Paul reverses the car out of the driveway.

56

Bad News

Eliza
December 19, 2007

When I think of hard times, of those really gut-wrenching, soul-damaging, just flat-out painful times, I can't help but think of Nick.

Like a lot of marriages, we had our ups and downs. Neither of us were particularly great to the other, especially after our first couple of years. And it really is so hard to talk about him. Even now.

He passed away in December 2007. It was a Wednesday afternoon. A week before Christmas.

It was the week before Christmas, and Annalise and I had gone to the bookstore to peruse the shelves. I was looking for some small stocking stuffers or for any books that Annalise might want to add to her growing collection.

Around 6:30 p.m., as I pull into the driveway of our house, my phone rings. The name on the caller ID, Ashley, is one I haven't seen in a long time. Ashley is the girlfriend of Nick's eldest son. I accept the call and glance at Annalise, who is strapped into her car seat, examining a new book that she picked out on her own. She is in a happy place, and so am I.

"Hey, Ashley," I say, holding the phone against my ear as I put the car in park.

There is a slight pause on the line before Ashley replies, "Eliza?"

"Yeah. What's going on?" I ask.

"I don't know how to tell you this ..." Ashley's voice trails off.

"Tell me what?" I say, pausing for a reply. When one doesn't come, I say, "Ashley? Just say it."

"There's been an accident. With Nick."

"What do you mean? Is he OK?" My thoughts immediately flash to Nick lying in a hospital bed due to a car accident. We live in Southern California, and accidents on the freeway are a common occurrence.

"No. He's ..." Ashley takes a deep breath before continuing. "Eliza, he's dead."

My mouth drops open, and I'm sure I've misheard her. "Wait. He's what?"

Ashley hands the phone to Nick's ex-wife, who says, "Eliza, it's true. Nick killed himself."

"No. No. No! It's not true," I reply.

"It is true. Are you alone? You might want to call someone. I need to go now. The police are here," she says and hangs up.

My head begins to swim, my vision goes blurry, and I step out of the car. Annalise is still in her car seat and is looking at me with an odd expression. She is possibly wondering why all of a sudden her happy mommy has gone from smiling and trying to grab her toes in the back seat to screaming out, "No!" and crying.

I walk to the spot where Nick and I last stood together, where I felt hope that we might be able to work this whole separation and co-parenting thing out. I stand there stunned. And then I collapse. The steps are cold and hard. I lie on them and cry, my mind not wanting to grasp what has happened.

After what feels like an hour, I finally stand up and walk to the car. Annalise is still strapped in her car seat, and this usually chatty girl isn't saying a word. I open the car door and unstrap her car seat. I carry her inside, burying my face against the softness of her curls. Her clothes feel chilly, but her skin is warm. Once we're inside the house, I put Annalise down and call my mom. I'm hysterical and can't stop crying. My mom asks where Annalise is and tells me to stop crying because I might scare her. As she says this, I look over at Annalise, who is staring at me, studying my every move.

That night, I don't sleep. Images of the last conversation with Nick swirl in my brain, followed by so many questions, followed by pain.

When morning comes, I dress Annalise and bring her to day care. I call my boss, who tells me that I can take time off, approximately three days, as per standard procedure. Since this is Thursday, I am grateful that I can have the weekend to try to get myself together before heading back to work. Since it is the Thursday before the Christmas break, that means I have the Thursday and Friday before Christmas, then the weekend, and then an additional day on Monday, with Christmas on Tuesday being a holiday. I shake my head when a sarcastic thought enters my brain. *At least Nick planned it well.*

I can't recall the exact timing of when I told Annalise about Nick's death. But because she is a toddler, she keeps asking when she will see her dad again. One week after his passing, Annalise will begin asking for him on a daily basis. She will look at me, her little mouth pursed as she asks, "Where is Daddy?"

One month after his passing, I realize for the first time that I am raising this little girl completely on my own.

Three years after Nick's passing, I will find the Strawberry Shortcake Big Wheel as I am preparing to move out of our home. It had remained in the garage rafters, in the same spot where Nick had tucked it away.

I hadn't given it to Annalise because I couldn't bring myself to see it, to watch her on it, to explain to her why her daddy hadn't given it to her. I realize now how selfish that was on my part. And trust me when I say that I wish I'd given it to her.

One day, I'll have to explain to her what happened. And even now, it's so incredibly difficult to come out and say how he died.

But there is one thing that I really need my beautiful little girl to know. And that is this.

Annalise, your daddy *loves* you. He loved you, and he loves you still. You were so precious to him. If you want to doubt anything in this world, and you will doubt many things in this world, don't for a single second doubt the fact that your daddy thought the world of you.

One day, this will all make sense. One day, you and I will sit down and have a long conversation about life and death and hard times. But today, just know that you are not in this alone. I'm here. And I will do everything I possibly can to protect you, to love you, and to give you the most incredible and blessed life I possibly can.

And, just one more thing. I'm sorry that I didn't give you the Big Wheel. I was wrong in doing that. I honestly didn't know how to give you that gift.

I hope you can forgive me.

57

Lost Christmas

Eliza
December 25, 2007

I've had two Bloody Marys. Actually, make that three. I think. They were strong ones, one-third Kirkland brand vodka, four olives, a celery stick, lots of horseradish, splash of Tabasco, and mix. The man I have been dating has opened up his home for us, and he makes them spicy. I think the spice level is a failed attempt to get me to drink more slowly. I want the burn though. That's what he doesn't realize. I feel as if I deserve the pain.

I stare at the plastic ceiling of the bounce house I gave to Annalise as a gift this morning. I'm alone in here, but SpongeBob is currently staring back at me with manic blue cartoon eyes and giant buck teeth.

"Go ahead. Judge me. What do you know? You're just a sponge."

I imagine his reply, "Yeah, well at least no one ever committed suicide because I was a pile-of-trash person."

"Shut up, Sponge Turd," I slur.

"Mommy?" Annalise's sweet voice interrupts my boozy conversation with her favorite cartoon character. "What are you doing in there?"

I lift my head just enough to catch a glimpse of her poking her head in through the opening of the bounce house. I blew it up in the middle of the living room, and like a homeless person, I proceeded to squat in it for the last hour.

"Oh, just relaxing," I say as soberly as I can.

"You wanna bounce?" She jumps in, causing my body to become weightless for a moment upon the force of her impact.

The sudden motion makes me want to retch. I grab hold of her waist and gently tug her to a lying position with me.

"How 'bout we cuddle first?" I ask.

She stares at me, the sweetness of her big brown eyes a stark contrast to my red-rimmed and bloodshot green ones.

"Mommy doesn't feel good?" she asks me, pursing her lips.

I sigh heavily. "I'm just sad, baby."

"Did Santa forget you?"

A wave of guilt floods me. Some mother I am. Drunk on Christmas and taking up literal space in my kid's SpongeBob bounce house. I have officially reached loser status.

"Santa is for kiddos like you, baby. Mommy doesn't need anything."

"Besides vodka," SpongeBob taunts.

"Shut up, Sponge."

Annalise gasps. "Ooooh, Mommy said a bad word!"

It isn't the joyous holiday that I envisioned, to say the least. I spend most of the day drunk and in tears. My typically rambunctious toddler spends the day patting my head and repeating the phrase, "Poor Mommy."

58

Can't Sleep / Where's Daddy?

Eliza
January 2008

It's been three weeks since Nick has passed, and I am not sleeping. It's easy enough to drift off; overwhelming exhaustion makes sure of that. The problem is staying asleep, which I can't seem to do. I wake up at the same time every night, 3:00 a.m.

While cleaning the house one day, I have the TV on for background noise. The second the vacuum cleaner shuts off, I hear, "Three a.m. is the witching hour, the hour when the veil is the thinnest between our world and the ghost world."

Great.

Now, I'm lying in bed and staring at the time on my bedside clock. *Three a.m. The witching hour. Ghost world.*

Jesus, please be with us, I think, too tired to speak the words aloud.

My eyes dart from the doorway of my bedroom to the ceiling, as if I'm expecting to see Nick standing there. It's a horrifying thought.

Jesus, please. Keep us safe. Fill this home with Your protective light. The prayer echoes on repeat in my head, and I hope that God hears prayers that are thought as well as He does spoken prayers.

Every sound in the house frightens me. I hear the fridge begin to make ice, and the sudden crash of settling ice nearly causes me to have a heart attack. I'm scared. My heart is racing, and I can't seem to catch a good breath. My head feels light, but my eyes feel heavy, as if my eye sockets are being sucked into my brain. When I close my eyes, I see flashes of light and static.

I quietly succumb to a full-blown panic attack. As quietly as I can, I cry until it passes. My whole body is numb afterward. In my head, I hear, *You're not strong. You are so weak. Annalise deserves a better mother than you. What a shame. You are a failure at this, at everything. You are the one who deserves to die.*

Biting my lip, I begin to repeat the words *Help me, Jesus* in my head. After about two hours of this, I finally drift off. When my alarm goes off at 6:00 a.m., I'm exhausted, with extremely puffy eyes, but I'm thankful to see the light of day. The darkness didn't get me last night, and I thank Jesus aloud.

Annalise toddles into my room. She looks at me and says, "Where's Daddy?"

I don't know whether to laugh or cry. I choose neither. Instead, I grab her little body and swoop her up into a tight hug. "Not here, baby."

She is still for a moment and then begins to wriggle. "But where is he?"

"He's with Jesus, baby."

"No!" She squirms until I let her down. Then she hits me. "Noooooo! Daddy!"

"Baby, don't hit Mommy, OK?" I try again to hug her, but she's having none of it. She toddles off into her room and slams the door.

I hear another crash, only this time it's not the ice machine. I run into her room, anxious about what I might find. In my head, I panic, thinking that she's flipped her dresser over or tipped her bookshelf over. I fully imagine that this little girl, even at three years old and with a paralyzed arm, has the strength of Hulk. In many ways, she does. Opening her door, I don't find any flipped furniture, but I do find Annalise in her closet, throwing toys and books at the wall.

"Annalise! Stop!"

A book whizzes by my face; it's so close I feel the breeze of it against my cheek.

"Noooooooooooo!" she screams. "I want Daddy!"

"Annalise! Stop it right now!" I say firmly, trying not to lose my cool.

I fight the heat of a panic attack rising up through my arms and torso. My doctor has prescribed Xanax for me, but I haven't taken it, fearful of how it might affect my psyche. After what happened to Nick, I'm afraid of losing myself.

She pauses to look at me. She opens her mouth to yell again and then closes it. She puts down her ammunition of clothing, stuffed animals, and books. I feel triumphant and take a deep breath.

"OK, thank you," I say to her. "Now, come on. Let's get ready for day care."

Can I just say that three-year-olds are frightening? This precious baby girl who I carried and gave birth to is staring at me with the detached intensity of a serial killer.

"No," she says, her voice calm and cold while her gaze bores a hole into my forehead.

"Annalise." I say her name sternly, using my best mom tone.

"I said no," she repeats.

It's not lost on me that she's using my words against me. I mean, "I said no"? She's terrifying, and I'm certain that she will murder me in my sleep one day, probably very soon. I decide not to go down without a fight.

Briskly, I walk to the closet and swoop her up into my arms. I sit her on her bed, and in three short movements, I get her nightgown off, her T-shirt and leggings on, and carry her like a football down the stairs. I have her socks in my mouth, and my head is tilted away from her kicking legs.

We make it to day care, where I gratefully hand her over to someone else for a few hours.

59

Clinical Depression

Eliza

The last few months have been trying, to say the least. Annalise's temper tantrums have gotten worse, and we're still dealing with monthly seizures. On top of all of this, more information about what happened to Nick is now coming out. While cleaning out his house, his children found dozens of medicine bottles in his kitchen cabinet. There were a variety of antidepressants, anti-anxiety pills, and insomnia drugs, prescribed by different doctors Nick had been seeing.

Upon review of the labels, it appears as if he may have been taking as much as a dozen different pills to treat his mental health during the same timeframe. What's even more disturbing is the news that Nick had attempted to visit a mental health facility four days before he committed suicide, only to be turned away for not having an appointment.

According to Nick's friend Paul, he had driven Nick to Los Angeles on Saturday afternoon, at Nick's insistence. Nick told him he initially had an appointment on Friday, but it was raining so hard that he was afraid to drive the roughly forty miles by himself in bad weather. Nick had apparently called the mental health facility to let them know his concern, and they changed his appointment to Saturday. When both Nick and Paul arrived at the check-in counter, Nick was rudely turned away and told to return when he could obtain another appointment.

Hearing this straight from Paul, who had been a witness to the rejection on Saturday, absolutely tore me apart. I was so angry for Nick, knowing that he'd tried to get professional help and was turned away. Somehow Nick also managed to talk the doctors into giving him electroconvulsive treatments for his depression, which were to begin the week following his death. When I read more about this treatment that Nick wanted, my stomach sank. This treatment intentionally triggers seizures in order to alter the brain chemistry. I'm sure that this treatment works in some way for certain people. But I was just so floored that Nick would intentionally want to undergo this treatment, to force himself to have a seizure, after all we had been going through with our daughter.

60

Behavioral Therapy

Eliza

Annalise's mood swings have become more violent. She absolutely hates me and only wants her dad. In her mind, I am the person who is keeping her from seeing him.

Every day after work, when I pick her up from day care, I sit in my car in the driveway and psyche myself up to go in and get her. *It's going to be OK. Just walk in there with a smile and greet your daughter with a "Hi, kid." Deep breaths.*

Donna, the day care owner, greets me warmly as I walk in the door. "Hey! How was work?" It's nice to have someone ask me that. Looking back, I think she knew that I sat in her driveway every day, contemplating whether or not I'd actually come in and collect my child, and she was probably relieved that I always did.

"It was fine. Work, you know." My eyes scan the room of kids, looking for Annalise.

"She's outside, playing in the sandbox," Donna says, motioning toward the screen door.

"Ah, OK." I pause for a moment. "How was she today?" I ask timidly, afraid of the answer.

"Annalise was great," she says cheerfully.

"Really? No temper tantrums or anything?"

Donna looks at me and shakes her head. "Nothing. She was great."

I pause for a moment and think.

Donna looks at me and asks, "Is everything OK?"

"Uh, it's just that, um, Annalise has been ... a little ... upset lately."

"Really? Like how?" Donna seems genuinely surprised.

The realization that Annalise is a perfect angel with everyone but me sets in. My daughter hates me. "She's just ... she's been throwing things and, um, hitting me?" My statement comes out more like a question.

Donna looks at me, and her mouth drops open in shock. "You're kidding? Annalise?" She shakes her head. "She's one of the better-behaved ones."

I laugh. "Huh. Wow. So, just me then." I inhale sharply. "Awesome." I shrug and open the screen door to collect Annalise. I smile and say, "Hi, kid." Annalise ignores me. I say it again, a bit louder, "Hi, kid!" She still ignores me.

Donna walks out and says, "Annalise, your mom's here. Time to go."

Annalise looks up at Donna, smiles at her, and then looks over at me. The smile drops, and she walks right past me into the house without saying a word. At the same time, some of the other mothers are coming to collect their children and are met with sons and daughters who run joyfully into their arms.

I'm embarrassed and look back at Donna. She's eyeing both Annalise and me. I'm sure Donna thinks I'm abusing her. The thought makes me want to laugh. If only she knew that the one being abused was me.

I buckle Annalise into her car seat, and she spits at me. I take my shirt and wipe the spit away from my face. *Only three hours until bedtime.*

This week, I begin the search for a behavioral therapist. I find a therapist named Dr. Scott, who is located near my work. The first meeting is with both Annalise and me so that Dr. Scott can meet both of us and assess the situation. Every subsequent meeting will be with only Dr. Scott and me.

The office is small but inviting, and there is a doorbell that allows you to announce your arrival. I let Annalise push it, and then we stand in the waiting room. Annalise doesn't want to sit; she wants to run around and throw magazines. So, I stand and hold her to keep her from destroying Dr. Scott's tidy waiting room.

That first meeting lasts about an hour. Dr. Scott and I sit on the floor with Annalise, while he attempts to talk to her, using toys to grab her attention. I can see that he's waiting to see the behavioral issues, and Annalise does not disappoint. Within moments, Annalise is pulling my hair, spitting at me, and slapping me.

Dr. Scott sticks his hand in his pocket and clicks something inside of it. The noise distracts Annalise, and she turns her attention to Dr. Scott. For a moment, I think she's about to attack him. Instead, she pauses to listen. Not hearing the sound again, she turns her attention back to me. She slaps me again, and Dr. Scott clicks the device in his pocket.

This goes on for a few more minutes. Annalise would attack me, Dr. Scott would click his pocket device, and Annalise would go on the hunt for the sound.

Dr. Scott asks me to stand up. He removes the device from his pocket and shows it to me. I look at it and then look back at him.

"Is that …" I begin.

"A dog clicker," he answers. "Yes."

I laugh. "I can't use a dog clicker on my daughter."

"Why? It worked," he says, with no humor in his voice at all.

"Because. She's not a dog." I'm trying to figure out if he is serious or just kidding around.

"Listen, here's your first assignment," he says, unfolding his plan to me. "Go to Petco, pick up a few dog clickers—they're about a dollar each—and put them around the house out of Annalise's reach. Keep one in your car, one in your pocket."

I stare at him, still waiting for the punchline of this joke. "OK …" I reluctantly agree.

"And every time she starts to hit, or spit, or throw anything, you click it."

"That's it?" I ask.

"Try it out, and then you and I will meet again, without Annalise, next week."

I realize he's serious. "So, I'm treating my daughter like a dog?"

"No, you're training her not to hit or spit," he corrects me.

"Using a dog clicker," I add.

"Yes," he says, nodding once.

Annalise and I leave the office, and I feel as if we are both a bit confused. Within moments, Annalise begins throwing a temper tantrum in the car.

The next day, I stopped at Petco during my lunch break and bought a handful of dog clickers. I put one in my car, one in my pocket, and the rest I scattered around the house. There were dog clickers everywhere—in my bathroom, in Annalise's bedroom, in the kitchen. Whenever Annalise would act up, I'd pull one out and click it. And much to my surprise, she would stop. She was so desperate to find the source of the noise that she would focus her attention on locating the clicker instead of on hitting or spitting or slapping me.

I'm not one to normally exhort any perceived or literal dominance or intelligence over anyone, but this victory over my child's awful behavior felt awesome. It felt so awesome that I started using other techniques that Dr. Scott recommended. Here's the thing: all of his methods were *strange*. During one session, he filled me in on how he'd trained his cat to use the toilet—as in, a toilet meant for a human. I laughed so hard when he told me that, and then it dawned on me. If this guy could train a cat how to use a commode, I could train my child to be nice to me. As long as his advice was producing results and not hurting her, I was all ears.

61

Mommy Throws a Tantrum

Eliza

The way therapy worked was simple. I'd take notes of terrible behaviors that Annalise was eliciting during the week, and then I'd bring my notes to share with Dr. Scott and get tips on how to handle them.

One week, I brought up how impossible it was to go to a store with Annalise. Since every minute of every day was spent working, taking care of her, or in therapy, the only way I could get any grocery shopping done was to take Annalise with me. The problem was that the second we'd get halfway into the store, Annalise would take this as an opportunity to throw King Kong–sized temper tantrums.

"I've talked to her beforehand and have asked her to act nicely while we're in the store," I explain to Dr. Scott, who listens politely. "But the second we get halfway through the store, with a cart filled with groceries, she will have massive meltdowns."

"And what do you do when she's throwing a tantrum?" Dr. Scott asks.

"Panic," I say with a laugh. "Bribery, pleading. Anything to make her settle down."

"Do any of those techniques ever work?"

I sigh. "No. It seems to make her scream even louder."

He smiles and sits back in his chair. "This is what I want you to try next time Annalise starts throwing a tantrum in the store."

I listen intently to his set of instructions, and when he's done, he asks, "Well, do you think you can do it?"

"Honestly, I don't know if I can," I say sheepishly. "I mean, everyone will think I'm nuts."

"I don't think so. I think anyone who is there and who is a parent will completely understand."

Four days pass. I'm nervous to try the experiment that Dr. Scott recommended I try, but it is down to the wire for accomplishing this week's goal, and we've run out of toilet paper, which means I'm forced to go to the store.

It's a crowded Saturday morning at Target. As I'm parking the car, I begin my usual prep talk with Annalise, "OK, we're going into a store, which means we *behave*. No screaming, no tantrums. Got it?" She nods in earnest.

We walk into the store, and I seat belt Annalise into the shopping cart. Once again, I warn, "Remember what Mommy said. *Behave*." Annalise looks at me, a naughty expression fanning out over her cherub face.

One of Annalise's favorite things to do in Target is to look at the toys, and I promise her that we could look at the toys but only after I've been able to collect the items on my shopping essentials list. The problem is that Annalise knows where the toy section is, and when we start heading in the opposite direction, she begins chanting, "Toys! Toys!"

Shaking my head, I remind her of our deal. "We can see the toys after we finish getting what we need. That was our deal. Remember?"

She looks me dead in the eyes, pinches me, and screams, "Toys! Now!"

"No, Annalise. Toys after, but only if you're a good girl."

She replies by pinching me again. I move away from the cart and say as calmly and firmly as I can, "Annalise. You're being naughty. Stop or you don't get to see the toys."

I barely get the words out before the screaming begins again. Her vocal attack is loud, and several people appear to be stunned as they pass by. My head begins to pound, and I feel the heat of a panic attack encompassing my chest, neck, and face. I remember Dr. Scott's instructions. It is now or never.

So, in the middle of quite possibly the most crowded Target I've ever been to, I begin to throw a temper tantrum of my own. It starts out small, embarrassed, and restricted by shame. And then something inside of me snaps. My voice begins to rise to the point that I am rivalling the volume of Annalise's own tantrum, and then I surpass her. I get *loud*.

I look at my daughter, taking in all twenty pounds of her, and begin to yell. "Oh, you think that's a tantrum?" I say, throwing my head back in a forced laugh. "That's not a tantrum! *This* is a tantrum!"

Annalise screams for about five seconds. Then, realizing that her mom has absolutely lost her mind, she stops. She stares at me in utter confusion. Then she begins to plead with me to stop.

Her pleas come about five seconds too late. *Oh, no, little girl. I'm in the zone now.* I yell out, "Annalise, you have to scream louder, so the people at the back of the store can hear you!" I turn my attention to the onlookers whose shopping carts are at a standstill as they take in the lunacy unfolding before them. "Don't worry, everyone! Temper tantrum in progress! Just showing the kid how it's done!"

Annalise is mortified. "Mommy, no. Mommy, please. Mommy, stop!"

I stop and look around. Mothers who are passing by throw me air high fives and laugh. One woman in her fifties exclaims, "Oh, honey, I remember those days!"

It was then that I realized *I have the power.*

We finish up our shopping trip without making a detour to the toy section. Annalise doesn't make another peep as we shop. In subsequent trips, she will quickly cease and desist with any tantrums the second I say, "Oh, is it tantrum time? Let's do this!" She will grab my hand, apologize, and even become (gasp) *loving.*

When I tell Dr. Scott about the experiment, he stands and applauds my performance.

62

A Hedge of Protection

Anna
1990–1993

My first three years in California are a time of testing. I find myself asking God on more than one occasion why I moved here. And so many times, I remind myself who really placed me here and reprimand myself by saying, "Oh, ye of little faith." Actually, in every place I have lived, I have questioned God as to why I had to move there. Looking back, I see how He orchestrated my life in every season and every situation. It is because of where I have been that I have become who I am, through God's grace and hand of protection upon me throughout my life's journey.

Obviously, someone or something is going to try to stop me from the plan God has in mind for me in my new state. The first year in California, I head to a doctor's office for a quick routine surgery on my earlobe before heading for work. Suddenly, I hear all this commotion in the parking lot. I spot all these police cars converging on the parking lot. I am walking up the outside steps to my doctor's office, which is located on the second floor. Behind me, two men come running up the stairs. I notice they hold guns in their hands. I begin running faster up the steps. I crash through the door of the doctor's office. For the next four hours, we are taken hostage in that office until the men eventually surrender.

What happens during that time? The doctor remains calm as the police are outside on their bullhorns telling everyone to stay away from the windows. As for my scheduled appointment, the doctor continues treating his patients. The day is so surreal. When I get home, my husband questions me regarding my whereabouts. Apparently, my office secretary at work calls my house, wondering why I have not shown up for my classes. When I share with him what happened, his reply is "Only you. Things like that just don't happen normally."

The next year, one of my female colleagues and I are in Northern California to make a presentation. My presentation is scheduled in the morning, and her presentation is scheduled for the afternoon. I am glad to finish my presentation and inform her that I am dying for a cappuccino. Almost my famous last words. We head over to the local galleria, order our coffee, and sit at a small table in the mall lobby area.

After a few minutes, I tell her we should leave and mention having an uneasy feeling. She looks at me and responds, "You and your uneasy feelings. I am not ready to go yet. Let's look at a few shops."

So, we get up from the table where we are sitting, and I follow her to look at a display close by. The next thing I know, she is lying flat on the ground. A woman knocks her over as she passes her, screaming and running for the back of the store. I look back, hearing the commotion in the mall lobby, and see a crowd running past where we were sitting, knocking over our table and chairs.

I think I hear them yell, "Fire!" But then I hear, "Gunfire!" About then, two store clerks grab me and my colleague and lead us to a back storage room. They lock the door, and we wait. I spot the lady who knocked my colleague over. She is huddled in a corner, crying and grasping what looks like a toilet. My colleague goes into shock and begins repeating over and over, "I have a presentation to make."

The next thing I know, my colleague opens the door and walks through the store into the mall lobby as she heads for the mall exit. I run behind her, telling her to stop, but she doesn't appear to hear me. She keeps walking, as if she is in a trance. As we exit the mall, we see the SWAT team on the roof. I get chills thinking they could mistake us for the criminals and shoot us. People are asking us in the crowd if it is safe to go back inside. I never reply as I follow my colleague back to the conference hotel. The whole way back to the conference hotel, I am behind her and saying, "In the name of the Father, the Son, and the Holy Spirit," as I make the sign of the cross. My old Catholic practice of protection bursts forth. My colleague, still in a state of shock, makes her presentation as if nothing happened earlier. As soon as she finishes her presentation, she sits down in her chair in the conference room and begins to cry. I want to hit her for the way she is acting but realize she has been on autopilot.

The third year in California, I probably should be used to life being anything other than normal. My husband, youngest daughter, and I are preparing to leave on a trip that morning for Huatulco. Since I am always the early riser, I finish packing and am ready for our trip. While everyone else is getting ready, I take my little cockapoo for a walk before we are to leave. My son is going to stay with my fur baby while we are gone. Almost as soon as my dog and I come around the corner on our street and head toward home, I spot two dogs coming toward us. Again, I get that uneasy feeling that something is not right.

Before I can run, the two dogs attack me and my dog. The dogs begin to tear at my dog from each end. I try to pull my dog away as they tear him in half. I scream and beat at the dogs. That is when one of the dogs lets go of my dog and jumps on me, knocking me to the ground. The dog is on top of me. I try to scream again, but nothing comes out. All I can do is stare at this dog, just knowing I will be savagely attacked at any minute.

Luckily, one of the neighborhood women comes to our assistance, waving a large towel and broom at the dogs. The dogs, both startled, run a little distance up the sidewalk, allowing enough time for my little dog to seek cover under a car. This also gives me a chance to get off the ground. About this time, the owners of the dogs come out of their house and whisk the dogs away.

My little dog survives but comes within a quarter of an inch of being completely disemboweled by those dogs. My little dog has to have more than one hundred stitches to close his wound. The police show up and inform me that I am truly fortunate. If I had been able to scream when the dog pinned me down, it is likely the dog could have torn my jugular to silence me. Also, I learn that these neighbors harbor what are considered killer attack dogs. I am angry to hear that such vicious animals are allowed in our neighborhood. This news is disarming. I learn that these dogs dug through their fencing a week earlier and killed two other dogs who were on a walk with their owners. This information provides further proof that my fur baby and I were protected that day from further harm or possible death.

I am reminded of that day each time I pick up a pen to write or I grasp something with my right hand. The thumb on my right hand was torn away when I fell to the ground with an outstretched hand. The fall caused a tear to the ulnar collateral ligament, which is referred to as a gamekeeper's thumb.

My third year in my new state ended with more proof that God's hand of protection is on my life. I begin my usual commute to Los Angeles one morning. I am driving in the farthest left lane. Driving on these freeways with eight lanes of traffic is a nightmare at times, although I am now quite skilled driving on those freeways. I still hate that it takes me almost two or two and a half hours to commute to work. I spend four to five hours of my day on the road. I live only thirty-four miles from work. My grumbling will take on a whole new outlook after what happens this morning.

I notice something strange happening with a large semitruck a few cars ahead of me. The siding on the right side of the truck appears to be flapping in the wind. I continue to watch as the siding rolls back, similar to opening a can of sardines. The next thing I know, the siding breaks free and is flying through the air. I stare in disbelief as the large metal roll looks like it is hurling straight toward my car. I expect this large object to come crashing through my windshield any minute. I look for a way to get into the next lane of traffic, but it is nothing but back-to-back traffic. I put on my blinker to switch lanes, but no one gives me an opening. "Oh, Lord," I cry out as the large object falls to the road directly underneath my car. What happens next is only God and God alone, who does the miraculous.

My car runs over the large metal object. The next thing I hear is a loud crunching sound under my car. I just know something bad is happening. Suddenly, a clear path opens on the road. Somehow, I am able to get across all lanes of traffic to the side of the road. What is even more amazing is what the emergency crew says when they inspect my car before hauling it off. "Your car is cut completely in half underneath. It is amazing how you were able to steer that car because there is no steering. We even have to get another vehicle to haul your car away. You are one lucky lady."

My insurance agent confirms their statement as well when he says, "If the metal object stayed airborne, you would have been decapitated if it came through your car window. You are incredibly lucky to have escaped that incident unscathed. It is a good thing you ran over the metal instead and cut your car underside in half." He smiles and states that the good news is that I am OK. The bad news is that because I ran over the metal object, it is my fault. What! What kind of insurance is that? I try to rationalize all this. *Well, he does say it would not have been my fault if it stayed airborne and hit my car, but it's not likely I would be here to enjoy that fact.*

Time after time, the enemy does all he can to keep me from accomplishing the plans God has for me. But each time something happens, God's hand of protection is on my life. This just proves that nothing will prevent you from doing what God has planned for you until He says it is finished and calls you home.

63

Greek Life through a Window

Eliza
November 2008

One thing that cannot be understood until it is experienced is just how boring it can be sitting in a hospital room for days on end. Annalise has been staying at UCLA Medical Center for over a week while we wait patiently for a seizure to occur. We need a total of three reported episodes caught on the EEG. We have one recorded, with two more to go. One perk of being in the UCLA system is that their children's hospital is sponsored by the toy company Mattel, which means tons of new toys for Annalise to play with.

Every day, one of the play life volunteers comes by with a cartload of toys, still pristine in their boxes, for Annalise to choose from to her heart's content. This awesome perk holds her focus and keeps her calm for about a week, and then she wants nothing more than to be out of that hospital room. This is when the constant crying starts—all day, every day crying. She is so miserable that she throws herself against the bed, kicking and wailing for someone to come and rescue her.

This is why I'm thankful when the parties across the street start. It is the week of Thanksgiving, and I thought that the university would be a ghost town because of the holiday, but it turns out to be the opposite. One sunny day, late in the afternoon, I watch from the hospital window as a trio of young men haul giant speakers from inside a home onto the front porch. The house is white with a black roof, a zigzag of stairs trimmed in red brick, and Greek letters spelling out SAE. Within moments, loud music and heavy bass can be heard pouring from the speakers and lightly thumping through the thick glass of the hospital. Within the hour, young collegiates spill out of the house and onto the lawn. It's as if the speakers are a honing system using its sonar to guide students who have remained on campus and are looking to party.

The unfolding scene is such a welcome change from the monotony of sterile walls and beeping medical equipment that even Annalise is enthralled. She kneels beside me on the small couch that I have been using as a bed and watches as the students dance. Every once in a while, she will point at the scene and look at me with a curious expression of wonderment on her face. It's as if to say, "Mom, I wanna go there." I laugh and reply, "Looks fun, huh? You wanna party?" Annalise then bounces up and down on the couch, letting me know that is exactly what she wants to do.

The party scene lasts until after we've already decided to turn in for the night. I chuckle as I close my eyes. I'm thinking about all of the Thanksgiving celebrations that will take place the following day and how so many of them will include bleary-eyed UCLA students who may or may not be getting any sleep tonight.

Around 7:00 a.m., the EEG technician we have gotten the opportunity to know well appears in the doorway of Annalise's room. He peeks in after giving a soft knock.

"Nothing yet?" he asks, his white hair matching a thick white mustache.

I shake my head. "Nothing."

He grimaces. "I'm sorry. And having to be here today of all days. Well, happy Thanksgiving." He presents me with a large cup of hot coffee.

I let out a quiet shriek, taking into consideration that Annalise is still sleeping. "You. Are. Awesome!"

"It's the least I can do, considering you have to be here," he says, gingerly lifting a few of the leads that trail from the crown of Annalise's head into the EEG machine. "I'm hoping today is the day, so we can get you guys out of here."

"That would be nice, although at least I don't have to do any Thanksgiving cleanup today," I say with a shrug.

"True. Doing all of those dishes is a chore. Luckily, I'm going to my mom's house, so I don't have to worry about that."

"What? You should help her!" I say with a laugh. "You know, moms—we do a lot."

He considers this for a moment. "True. OK, I'll help with the dishes."

"You're a good son."

"Eh, I'm okay." He clicks a few keys on the computer monitor and looks at his watch. "Well, sorry again you have to stay here. I hope you get a turkey burger or something at least."

I tip the coffee cup toward him. "Thank you so much for this. You're a lifesaver."

He smiles. "Of course. Anytime."

64

She May Never Use Her Hand Again

Eliza

Annalise's walking was a miracle in itself, especially because we'd heard early on in her medical journey that the possibility of walking again would be slim. We held the same belief for her to regain the use of her left hand. When Annalise began eating solid foods as a baby, she used her left hand frequently, even favored it over her right. After her first surgery, we'd hoped that her left hand would one day just wake up and start to move.

Stretching exercises, night splints, day splints, serial casting (where Annalise's left hand is placed in a cast to keep the stretch for weeks at a time), restrictive therapy (where Annalise's right hand is placed in a splint in order to encourage her to only use the affected hand), and Botox (to loosen up tight muscles) have been tried over the years. By the time Annalise is five, she's tried all of the above, multiple times.

In 2009, while staying at UCLA medical center for EEG testing, I engage in a conversation with an occupational therapist about Annalise's baseline and past treatments on her hand. During this discussion, I repeat a phrase I've used dozens of times in reference to Annalise's hand, or "Emma," which is the name that Annalise gave her left hand a year earlier.

"Emma's become more of a helper hand," I tell her, motioning to Annalise, who is scowling at the therapist from her bed. "We keep waiting for Annalise's brain to catch up so that Emma can be more than that."

Confusion spreads across the therapist's face. "You say the hand's been paralyzed since …" She trails off, checking her notes.

"Since her first surgery, when Annalise was fifteen months old," I say, filling in the blanks for her.

"Oh, I see," she says.

I've learned that when a therapist or other medical professional says, "Oh, I see," it typically means they're about to drop a truth bomb on me. I ask her a question that deep down I already know the answer to.

"Have you seen kids like Annalise ever use a hand again after this long?" My arms are crossed in front of me, bracing myself for the truth.

"I mean, it's true that the brain is more pliable in children, but …" She looks down at her notes again. "In most cases that I've seen, if the child hasn't regained the use of the affected hand by now, it's most likely not to return to full use again." She looks at me, that same sympathetic look that I've seen on the faces of therapists over the years.

I can feel the tears welling up in my eyes but lift my head and blink rapidly to keep them from falling. Annalise's watching me, and if I cry now, I may scare her.

"Right. Well …" I begin. "New baseline then?"

"New baseline," the therapist repeats, giving me a sad smile.

She finishes up her analysis with Annalise, gives me a quick rundown of what she's found, and turns to leave. Before she clears the doorway, she changes her mind and turns back to me.

"You know, I see a lot of mothers in here with their kids," she says. "And I just want to say you're doing a great job with her. She's lucky to have you."

The words cause my tough demeanor to break, and fully formed tears flood my eyes and run down my cheeks. The therapist hugs me, letting me sob into her shoulder for a few moments. The force of the truth collides with years of hope for recovery and worry for Annalise's future. I had feared that this news would come one day, and now that it has, all I can do is cry.

My heaving sobs grow weaker, and I break the hug. I mouth the words *thank you* to the therapist and duck into the adjoining bathroom to blow my nose and make sure I don't frighten Annalise with my appearance. The truth about Annalise's hand was hard to hear. While in the bathroom, I say a prayer.

"God, please. If there is any compassion at all for Annalise, please heal her, Father. Please. You are the Great Physician and can do anything. Annalise's just a child, my baby. You entrusted her to me, and while I don't know why You would give her to me, an imperfect mom, You know the reason. Please, Father. Heal my baby."

It's pleading that I've uttered a variation of many times over the past several years. This truth about Annalise brings back the same feelings I had when I first learned of Annalise's paralysis, delivered by a different young therapist in a different hospital.

Over a decade of weekly occupational therapy has given Annalise certain skills. She now uses her left hand as a helper, such as to hold papers as she writes. However, it is still paralyzed and will most likely always be used as a helper hand. She still calls her left hand Emma.

65

Breakthrough—Seizures

Eliza

February 2010

After two years of rotating through UCLA, trying to capture at least three strong seizures on the EEG, we are finally rewarded with the final piece of the puzzle. Overnight, Annalise had a seizure.

Around 2:00 a.m., Annalise lets out a faint cry for me, saying only "Mommy," which wakes me from my sleep in the chair next to her bed. I jump up, press the call button for the nurse, and frantically scream, "She's going to have a seizure!" Within seconds, the nurse runs into our room, and as if on cue, Annalise vomits all over the bed. I reach out and grab the receptacle for her to continue vomiting, and Annalise bends forward at the waist, her entire body going stiff. Thirty minutes later, she has resisted two rounds of IV medication, and it is declared that she is in status epilepticus—or, in my terms, a stubborn seizure that refuses to quit.

It takes an adult dose of a cocktail of medications to bring Annalise out of the seizure, but she finally breaks free of its horrific hold. By the light of day, after the seizure has gone and the room has been sterilized, we are able to grab a few moments of rest before the doctors make their rounds into Annalise's room.

Dr. Jason is young, handsome, and kind. He'd introduced himself to us during Annalise's last weeklong visit to UCLA and has come by to see us a few times in the two-plus weeks that we've been here this time around. He is the one to break the update about Annalise's seizures to me.

"I hear we had a good night last night," Dr. Jason jokes.

I rub my eyes and grab my glasses from the window ledge. "Yeah, uhm. She had a seizure, and it lasted about an hour."

"Mmhmm," he says, checking Annalise's chart. "Well, I have some good news and some maybe not so good news. Which do you want first?"

I groan. "I hate having bad news before I've had coffee but give it to me."

His eyebrows raise. "Bad news first? OK. The bad news is that it appears from the EEG that Annalise's brain is always firing off." He pauses to let me process the information, but I don't quite understand.

"Meaning?"

"Meaning that she's always seizing, albeit most of the time at a very low level. What we've been witnessing, or rather what you've been witnessing, are breakthrough seizures."

I close my eyes, trying to process this new information. "Hold on. You are telling me that Annalise ... that all day, every day ... she's ..."

"Seizing. Yes. On a low level, which is why she's able to walk, talk, etcetera."

"But how? I mean ... how does she not have permanent brain damage?" I look at Annalise, who is still sleeping off the effects of the medicine she was given the night before. She's still, and her face is peaceful. She shows no signs of any kind of distress.

"She's a very lucky little girl."

"But this has been going on for five years?" I ask him.

"Quite possibly. Since we've only seen her for the last two years, we can only go by what we know from her time with us."

"I'm just stunned." I think of all the times she's had meltdowns, all of the behavioral issues. Could it have all been a result of this?

"Did you want the good news now?" Dr. Jason asks.

"Right. I'd forgotten that there was a second part to this. You sort of distracted me with the bad news, which, by the way, I'm glad I heard first."

He smiles. "The good news is that we have enough data to go on to make a decision about surgery."

I nod and bite my lip. "Can I just tell you that I hate the fact that this is our version of good news?"

He lets out a burst of laughter. "You're so right. But hopefully this means we can get rid of these seizures."

66

New Vocab Word: Hemispherectomy

Eliza

The day after learning that Annalise's seizures are in fact occurring on a consistent basis and that the seizure activity that has been captured on EEG are actually breakthrough seizures, we are given the all-clear to head home. Before we leave the hospital, we are introduced to Dr. Michaels, one of the leading neurosurgeons who specializes in epilepsy surgery. It is during this initial meet and greet that I'm reminded of a particular word, one that I researched before I even allowed Annalise to set one foot into UCLA Medical Center: hemispherectomy.

Hemispherectomy surgery is when a neurosurgeon removes the portion of the brain that is causing the misfires, the place in the brain where the seizures originate. Once the area is pinpointed, there can either be a partial or full hemispherectomy performed. In real talk, this surgery meant removing either part of a half or an entire half of the brain.

Hemisphere = half of a sphere

Ectomy = surgical removal

If the first time you hear this term and understand its meaning, you gasp, then you will understand my initial reaction. Add a gaping mouth, repeating the words *science fiction*, and a trip into denial, and you have my full reaction.

I still haven't made up my mind about allowing Annalise to have the surgery. In the past two months, I have spoken to the founding members of the Hemispherectomy Foundation, as well as their daughter, who was the catalyst for their starting the organization. I've met with a trio of mothers who all have sons who had the operation and who introduce me to the term "Hemi Mama." I've read every research article, watched every YouTube video, Googled Dr. Michaels, and read his reviews, his resume, and pretty much everything else short of a background check.

Dr. Michaels sends me a two-line email reminding me that it has been nearly two months since we last spoke and asks if I will be making a decision soon. My reply to him is an email that includes a list of twenty questions pertaining to everything from the state of Annalise's healthy hemisphere to the percentage rate of her going into early puberty. This is not a small decision I'm making. Once again, I'm placing my daughter's life in the hands of a neurosurgeon. The fear of the unknown sends my emotional and mental state into a cluttered mess of heavy static and panic.

The reason it takes me months to decide on the hemispherectomy isn't because I want my daughter to continue to suffer through the seizures that are ravaging her brain. It's because I simply cannot make this decision. I have no problem going to work at my eight-to-five job and taking care of Annalise's needs at home. But the logical decision-making side of me that needs to focus on the hemispherectomy? All thoughts around that decision are just static on a TV screen.

Dr. Michaels's response to my lengthy email is less than comforting. His emailed response informs me that we have already discussed all of my concerns in detail during an in-visit clinic over two months prior to my email. His answer is so brusque that, upon reading it, I vow to never allow Annalise to be operated on by him. And then my phone rings. The caller ID lets me know it is UCLA Medical calling, and for a moment I consider that perhaps Dr. Michaels is calling me to apologize. I answer the call and discover that it is not the doctor but his surgical RN, Sharon.

"Are you OK?" she asks.

I respond with a tense laugh.

"I know. I saw your email and then his reply. I figured you might need to talk," Sharon says, her voice gentle and oozing kindness.

"Well, I guess it's my own fault for asking for his candid responses. He most certainly was straightforward with his opinions."

"That's him, all right," she says with a laugh.

"I have to be honest with you, and if this could stay between you and I, that would be appreciated."

"Of course," she agrees.

"I'm a little put off by his attitude. I'm not sure if it's because that's just how he is or if it's because he's friends with the doctor at the other hospital who caused the brain damage in my child in the first place. But either way, I am just looking out for the best interest of my child. I want Annalise to be seizure-free, and I've heard that Michaels is the best possible person to perform this surgery. But I sincerely hope that if he has some sort of animosity toward me, because of what occurred with the other doctor, that he won't allow it to affect the surgery performed on Annalise. Our family, she … we've been through enough," I explain, my voice beginning to crack. "I'm nervous and stressed and scared. Annalise's life and well-being are my only concerns. I hope he understands that."

"I can't tell you what his feelings are about Annalise's prior procedure, but I can attest to the fact that he cares for these kids, every single one of them. And I have seen him completely turn with his attitude once the surgery is successful," Sharon says.

"I hadn't thought about that," I admit. It had to be difficult to deal day in and day out with children who were suffering and families who were desperate for solutions. One mistake, and a life could be lost. Still, Annalise was my primary focus in life, and I needed to be sure about this decision.

"Did you want to come back in and discuss the surgery again in the clinic?" Sharon asks.

"I think so, yes. I know this is just his way of doing things, but this is *my child*," I say firmly. "I can't take another chance without being totally sure."

We meet with Dr. Michaels once again in the clinic, and the meeting goes much better than I anticipated. He answers every single question that I have and pauses several times to make sure I'm able to process what he is saying, as much of it is extremely technical. Annalise sits on the examination table wearing headphones and watching *Dora the Explorer* videos on my phone. Every once in a while, she looks up at me and cocks her head, as if to let me know that she is paying attention and taking in every single word we are saying. While I know she doesn't fully comprehend the entirety of the conversation, she definitely understands that the focus is around her.

The media relations office for UCLA has been approached by an Australian news outlet, who express their interest in highlighting the hemispherectomy surgery. Since Annalise is the next viable surgery candidate taking place during their desired timeframe, I am asked if we would like to participate. I ultimately decide that we should participate in the filming of the episode since it will be a good video diary for Annalise to view when she is old enough to understand.

Erik, the producer, shows up on the doorstep of our home along with reporter Sara, cameraman James, and a very attractive lighting and sound hunk named Derek. It makes me nervous to have a professional camera crew in my home. I'm not sure how they will spin the story. Mostly, I'm worried that when Annalise does see this as an adult, she will feel as if I'd made the right decision. The enormity of the situation and the fears are gently assuaged by the Australia news crew. Erik is warm and funny, with a comforting grin. Sara is gorgeous and kind, taking Annalise's hand when it is offered and following her up to Annalise's bedroom to see her toys and books. James is intimidating at first, as he is all business, setting up places to shoot and moving my living room furniture around to better accommodate the lighting. After a few hours, he shows how incredibly humorous and joyful he is to be around. And Derek, well, he is six feet tall, ruggedly handsome, and has an adorable accent and a wicked sense of humor. Even my mother, who is rarely impressed by men, falls prey to Derek's charms and before long is giggling at his jokes like a smitten teenager at a Justin Bieber concert.

We shoot a segment in our home, Sara getting all of the sixty-minute style interview questions out of the way. At one point during the interview, Sara mentions to me that Dr. Michaels isn't even sure himself if he'll be removing the correct portion of Annalise's brain. If you watch the video, you'll see my eyes dart quickly to one side. Two things about that moment. First, that was news to me. And second, Annalise had crept onto the landing of the stairs with her babysitter Jan and had dropped a load of toys with a loud crash.

Within hours, I put in a call to Dr. Michaels, who reminds me that nothing is ever 100 percent accurate, as they can only be as accurate as current medical technology allows. He offers some reassurance by stating that while nothing is guaranteed, Annalise's case has been discussed very carefully with an entire team at UCLA, and this decision is one made in cooperation with the doctors and myself.

Am I sure? No. Am I hopeful that this will mean a better life for Annalise? Yeah, I am. I also pray. A lot.

67

Belle

Eliza
March 2010

In an attempt to get Annalise socializing with other kids, I enroll her in a VIP soccer league for kids with mobility issues. She looks adorable in her black and red soccer uniform, and she even lets me put her hair in pigtails for the games. They don't keep score during game play, but the kids don't seem to mind. There is just one problem. Annalise is not a fan of the heat. And since soccer is a sport that is primarily played outdoors, and as we're in Southern California, this has presented some challenges. While the other kids are perfectly adaptable to running around in the sun for forty-five minutes (with a ten-minute break thrown in the middle), Annalise instead saunters onto the field, waits for me to set up my chair, and promptly retreats to the nearest shade tree.

She doesn't care that the coach is calling for her to come join the fun, doesn't care that her teammates are yelling for her, doesn't care that there is a goal about to be made. The only thing she cares about is her spot in the shade. I have found a workaround though. Annalise loves M&Ms. Something about milk chocolate in a crunchy candy shell speaks to her very soul. I've started bringing a small bag of them to every game.

"Annalise ..." I singsong her name, waving the brown bag of candy in the air.

She sees the bag and does her trademark run-hop over to me. "Gimme."

I jerk the bag away and hide it behind me. "Nope. Not until you go … and … play."

She sulks and doesn't move.

"Go. And then you can have M&Ms."

Knowing this is a battle she won't win; she reluctantly goes out onto the field. Annalise can be very stubborn, and when she doesn't want to do something, it can be a frustrating ordeal to get her to comply.

The game goes by fast, and it looks like even Annalise is having the tiniest bit of fun. Whatever joy she's shown on the field goes away quickly when she approaches me during the break. She holds out her hand for her reward.

"Drink water first," I tell her, handing her a plastic bottle.

She whines. "M&Ms!"

"Water," I say. "Come on. Take five sips. It's hot out."

She takes the bottle and lifts the bottle five times, taking obviously small sips each time. She thrusts the bottle back at me and holds her palm out.

I roll my eyes at her as I count out four of the candies. "Just a few. You have to go back after the break and finish the game."

She shoves the candy into her mouth and chews. The look that comes over her face is one of pure enjoyment. "Mmm. More?" she asks.

"After the game. This is only halftime, or break, or whatever they call it in soccer."

"It's a half," one of the other soccer moms who is sitting nearby says.

I nod and laugh. "Oh, thank you. A half."

The coach blows her whistle, and I make Annalise take one more sip of water before waving her back onto the field. This time, she goes willingly. I turn my attention to the other soccer mom who is sitting in a chair with a canopy. A beautiful golden retriever is sitting patiently at her side.

"He's so well behaved!" I say.

She looks down at him. "Bogie is the best."

"Bogie? Like Bogart?" I ask.

She nods. "Yup. He was part of a Hollywood-themed litter. His sister was Hepburn, another one was Monroe."

"OK, that is awesome. Where did you get him?"

"We got him for Nathan. He's from a local charity that raises puppies for kids with special needs."

The wheels start spinning in my head. "Really? How does that work?"

"It's pretty straightforward. Fill out an application, and they do a home visit to make sure you can keep a dog. Did you want their contact information?"

"Absolutely, yes." I glance out at Annalise, who is standing to one side of the goal. "I think a dog might be the best thing. She only has me at home. It might be nice for her to have a little friend."

The following Monday after I drop Annalise off at day care and get to work, I type out a quick email to the organization that the soccer mom provided to me. Within thirty minutes, I get an email back from the charity's outreach coordinator, who attaches a preliminary questionnaire that will be used to determine the right type of dog for our family.

The week before Annalise's birthday in February, a duo of representatives from the canine charity are touring our home and getting to know both Annalise and me. They ask a series of questions about our backyard, whether the pool's fence latches securely, and my personal plans for any pending relationships. The man I had been dating and I broke up over the holidays, and I haven't dated much, although it would be nice to be back out there. I tell them as such. It's the only part of the interview that makes me feel uneasy, and I jokingly say this to the woman who I've been corresponding with since the start of this process. She laughs and places a hand on my arm.

"Don't even worry. We're mostly just making sure that you'll be around for the puppy. That's all. We just want to make sure that you won't take in a dog and then turn around and have to give it up. That's all."

"I promise. We will love the pup like a member of our family."

"Then you're fine. We love Annalise. She's adorable and funny. And we think you're a great mom."

"She is a great kid, a bit headstrong, but I think that's going to turn out to be a good thing," I reply.

She nods and looks at one of the other women. "Well? Do we have news?"

The other woman smiles broadly. "We have good news. You're getting a dog!"

I squeal and grab them both in a crushing hug. I then pick up Annalise and repeat the news. "Did you hear that, Annalise? We're getting a new puppy!"

Two weeks later, Annalise, her babysitter, and I all pack into my Jeep and drive up to San Francisco to pick up our new family member. The moment I see her, I know she's meant for us. She's sweet yet a bit anxious. Her golden fur is curly, and her eyelashes are the longest I've ever seen on a dog. She's only a year old but completely trained. When the trainer calls her over, she comes immediately and sits directly in front of me.

"Meet Belle," the trainer says.

I bend down and gently rub her head and ears. "Hi, Belle. You are coming home with us today."

The trainer hands me her leash, a bag of dog food, and a file folder filled with Belle's pedigree papers, her training information, and vaccination records.

"Is that it?" I ask, amazed at how quickly this process actually went.

"That's it. Let us know if you have any questions."

I take Belle's leash and make sure the babysitter has Annalise's hand. I take Belle to the back seat, where I have placed some blankets for her to sit on.

"Uhm. Belle, can you jump?" I motion to the seat.

Belle looks at me.

"Hmm. Jump, Belle!" Belle stands next to me, staring. Her big puppy eyes seem to be saying, *Wow, they're sending me home with this clueless human?*

I purse my lips, wondering if I should just pick her up. An idea pops into my head. "Belle, up!"

The command works, and Belle easily jumps into the car and settles onto the back seat.

"OK, we know a command." I rub her ears with both hands and praise her for being so smart. "Good girl, Belle! You're going to have to be patient with me, OK? I haven't been trained yet."

On the drive home, I keep glancing in the rearview mirror to make sure that Belle and Annalise are getting along. It dawns on me that there is a strange dog in the back seat with my toddler.

I mention to our babysitter, who is sitting in the passenger seat next to me, that she should keep an eye on them while I focus on the road. She assures me that Belle is harmless, while I keep getting images of rabid dogs biting children's faces in my mind.

About halfway home, I pull over to fill up the gas tank and take Belle for a quick bathroom break. On the greenway in front of the gas station, a couple is walking their small Chihuahua. They see Belle and immediately head toward us. I look down at Belle and say, "Easy, girl. Let's not do anything crazy." Belle, who is about thirty-five pounds, is easily three times the size of the Chihuahua. I grab her leash tightly and brace for her to lunge. What she does instead lets me know exactly what kind of dog Belle is. Instead of lunging, she bows down to the small dog, lifts her butt in the air, and pants excitedly. She wants to play! Of course, the Chihuahua does not share Belle's excitement over the prospect of play and immediately snarls and lunges at Belle. I'm so taken aback by this that I give a strange look to the Chihuahua, say, "You know, she could eat you if she wanted to," and tug Belle away from this obviously wild beast.

When I get her back into the car, using our new favorite command, "Jump!" I commend Belle on her demeanor. "You are quite possibly the most amazing animal I've ever met." Belle looks at me while I speak to her and plants her very first doggie kiss to me on my face.

The rest of the way home, I don't worry as much about what Belle might do to Annalise and instead start to worry about how Annalise might treat Belle.

68

Another Surgery, Another Early-Morning Check-In

Eliza
June 24, 2010

Five a.m. It doesn't escape me that the last time we had such an early-morning check-in at a surgical ward, Annalise came out of surgery paralyzed.

"I know what you're thinking." my mom says, staring at me.

"Oh yeah? What's that?"

"Five a.m. Early-morning check-in."

I place my hand over her mouth and issue a warning, "Mom. No. Don't even say it."

My mom nods her head and reaches out to rub my back. "It's all going to work out," she assures.

I made the effort to appear fine today. I showered. Put on makeup.

In the waiting area, Annalise sits quietly. She mentioned to me over the past few weeks what her understanding of the hemispherectomy was.

"Mommy, no seizures for me." To which I'd reply, "That's right. No more seizures."

To pass the time and calm Annalise's fears a bit, I begin taking pictures. I brought the camera to document the day, to show Annalise when she's older. And honestly, I'm afraid of not capturing the final moments of the time I have with her before she goes off to surgery. Dr. Michaels had stated, "It's a big if. If we're removing the correct damaged portion of the brain. We won't know until we're in there." In there, meaning in her brain. If they take the wrong portion out, Annalise could be lost. Not just as in deceased, which is also a possibility, but lost as in they could remove the portion of her brain that governs personality. My Annalise could go in and come back a completely different person. It is a possibility, and no matter how small a possibility, I've come to accept that we currently exist in the realm of small possibilities. After all, it was a small possibility that robbed Annalise of a typical life.

We thumb through picture books, and I attempt to read to her. We don't get through more than a couple of pages before Annalise's name is called and we have to make our way into pre-op. I snap a few final pics of Annalise before I have to get her dressed in a surgical gown. She smiles at me, her right hand clasped protectively around her left. Her hair has recently been cut into a short bob in preparation for the procedure. Her shorter hair will make it easier for the surgeons to shave a portion of her head in order to saw her skull open and access her brain. Such a gruesome task for such a small girl.

I help Annalise change out of her street clothes, including her favorite short-sleeved gray T-shirt with an embroidered pink bow on the chest, and help her into the surgical gown the nurse provided. The nurse has also provided me with a surgical jumpsuit so that I can make the trip with Annalise all the way to the operating room door. Annalise laughs as I pull the white, hooded jumpsuit over my clothes. She laughs even harder as I zipper the hood completely over my head, concealing my face, and begin a tickle attack on her as "Fred," the name that Annalise calls headless store mannequins.

I'm trying very hard to hold it together for the sake of my daughter. On the inside, I'm shivering and hiding in a dark corner. My exterior strength begins to crack the second the surgical team wheels her into the operating room. Dr. Michaels hugs me, and I weep into his shoulder and beg him to take good care of her. The hours that she's in surgery are long and excruciating. At one point during Annalise's surgery, I find myself on top of the hospital's roof, ready to take my own life. It's a well-timed phone call that keeps me from doing so.

69

Happy Birthday, Mommy

Eliza

Annalise's lips are pink, and half of her face is a purplish blue. I look down at her, watching while she sleeps. It hurts to see her like this, her head wrapped in gauze, her right eye bruised and swollen shut. She came through the surgery missing only the part of her brain that was causing the seizures. And now she sleeps. As I look at her sleeping, I wonder for a moment if her dreams have changed.

Everything seemingly remained intact, just as I had hoped it would be. She was still very vocal and was communicating. She had even gotten on the phone with my mom, telling her over and over again that she was watching Disney Channel shows, at one point looking over at me in exasperation when she felt that her grandma wasn't listening. Her personality that I was so afraid of losing was intact, strong as ever. Her vision had remained too. I tested it myself, walking around the room, asking Annalise to point to me. I asked her about colors, shapes, and numbers on the whiteboard in her room, all of which she dictated to me accurately. She hadn't lost any remaining motor function, which was a common side effect of the hemispherectomy surgery.

As a standard form of practice following hemispherectomy, Annalise was being transferred from UCLA Medical Center to a rehabilitation hospital in Orange County. She would stay in the rehab center for approximately one month.

I watch as a duo of nurses stroll into the room, carrying sterile surgical scissors and gauze. They greet me warmly and begin their task of carefully removing the bandage around Annalise's head and taking out the ICP tube that has been monitoring the pressure inside of her skull. Annalise is not thrilled about being woken up, even more so now that she is in recovery and needs her rest. I cringe as I watch the removal of the ICP tube. Memories flash back to the last time nurses removed it and got a mouthful of brain fluid. This time is less dramatic. I hear a small pop, and the tube is neatly wound up and tossed in a biohazard receptacle.

I think perhaps this fussing about within her skull will put Annalise off on the entire nap idea. Instead, she glares at the nurses and turns her back to them, settling into the fetal position and going right back to sleep.

As we wait for the medical transport team to take Annalise to her new room at the rehab center, I snap a picture of my napping daughter. Earlier that morning after I'd gotten word that she was being transported, I changed her into normal clothes—leggings and a T-shirt, both with hearts emblazoned on them. Her thick brown hair has fallen forward, covering the T-shaped scar that will remain for the rest of her life. Above her, courtesy of my friend Kristin, a large bouquet of balloons creates a helium-filled archway. I stare at her and wonder if this will be the last time a surgeon will have to cut into her brain. I pray that it is.

The rehab center looks less like a hospital and more like a retirement community. There are several buildings, yellow with white trim, connected by a series of shaded walkways. To one side, there are picnic tables where families sit with paper bags of various takeout. And on the other side, there is a garden and a tool storage that looks like a doll house. Annalise is placed in a wheelchair and rolled up a ramp, past a quartet of porch swings and into her new room. While she is settled with the help of a young nurse, I'm escorted to the business office where I sign a dozen papers about liability and billing responsibility.

Being a single and working mom is not an easy task. I'm thankful for insurance, even at the rate of being responsible for a hefty out-of-pocket and then 20 percent of a bill after that. I don't even want to try to do the math on what the bills would be without insurance. I'm so grateful that

Annalise is facing a future in which she won't be ravaged by ever-present seizure activity.

Since I can't sleep at the rehab center with Annalise, we are adapting to a new schedule. In the morning, I wake up at five and drive to the rehab center to sit with Annalise and make sure that she knows that I'm nearby. I then hop on the freeway to get to work by eight thirty and log off right at five. After work, I take side streets back to the rehab center, stopping along the way to pick up some healthy foods at the grocery store. Annalise and I have dinner, and I help her shower and get dressed in her jammies before helping her to bed before leaving at ten.

This is the schedule, day in and day out, unless it is a holiday or a weekend. Then I pack up a cooler bag of goodies and bring them to Annalise, along with a handful of movies. We take walks in the garden, eat our snacks outside at the picnic tables, relax for a while on the front porch swings, and finally retire to her room to watch a movie before bedtime. During the weekdays while I am at work, Annalise gets several hours of therapy. They even casted her arm and leg to see if it will help with her tight muscles.

A month of this schedule has taken its toll on both of us. One evening after I help Annalise into her jammies after a shower, she grabs my hand and whispers, "Let's just go. I'll be quiet." She is dead serious.

I look back at her and without a hint of irony in my voice say, "Soon. Very soon." I look around, making sure we haven't been heard, put a finger to my lips, and whisper, "Shhhh." Annalise nods and reclines back onto her pillows.

This becomes our game. We are the secret agents, and our mission is going home. In order to complete our mission, Annalise has to cooperate with all of the therapy that she is being asked to do. It may seem odd, but this tactic works wonders. Annalise participates in every single therapy session they want her to. And as a reward, she is given the all-clear to go home a few days earlier than scheduled. Her release date is July 22, 2010. My birthday.

I show up at eight in the morning to pick Annalise up. I spent all morning cleaning the house and making sure she would see all of her favorite things upon entering the house—her toys, her books, and of course our dog, Belle.

Once the discharge papers are signed, I help Annalise into the car. As I buckle her seat belt, she leans into my ear and says, "Happy birthday, Mommy."

I look over at her and smirk. "How did you know it was my birthday?"

"I just know," she says with a smile.

I kiss her cheek. It is soft and warm. "Best birthday gift ever."

70

Stroke on the LA Freeway

Anna
1994–2000

After those first few years in California, life goes somewhat smoothly. I can share other stories one day, but they are not related to the focus of this book. My husband will smile at this comment and say something to the fact that I am always at the center of something. He will further add that he finds life in California peaceful and quiet. He likes to share how he's lived here almost his entire life and never encounters such issues. I keep reminding him with a smile of "But for God, go I."

I remind him of this not long after our tenth wedding anniversary. As I mentioned earlier, I am super active and always undertake new adventures. If I am not up by sunrise, I feel like I am missing part of my day. So, it is not enough to commute five hours to work each day, teach, and serve as the first female head of my department. I get a brainy idea that since I am in a school of business, then I need to use my business skills and work in the business world as well.

Soon, I find myself enrolled in a beauty school to get a state-certified skin care license. Life becomes super busy as I balance my commute to work, my full-time job, family responsibilities, and evenings at beauty school. As soon as I get my license, I open my own med spa and hire people to work and manage my establishment. One of my workers includes my youngest daughter. I expand the storefront location by adding an e-commerce site. All is going well, and the business is growing.

Then life throws me another curveball. I am on my way across the business campus courtyard when I spot two of my colleagues approaching me from the opposite direction. For just a second, their images appear to double. My first thought is *That's kind of weird*. I think no more of it and head to my classroom. My students are giving presentations this day, so I proceed to set up the classroom for their presentations and then take a seat among the students. Again, just for a brief second, the image of one of the students presenting at the front of the room doubles. Once more, I let it pass without another thought.

After working the entire day on the campus, I get into my car and head off to do a radio interview. The radio station is ten miles away. I am running late, and traffic is already backed up for miles. As I enter the 710 Freeway, a typical fast-moving and busy freeway, my world takes a sudden turn. The road appears to curve, but I know from driving that freeway each day that this road is not curved in this location. The palm trees on the side of the road appear to flash across my windshield. What happens next is truly God's protection on this foolish woman's life and those around her. I shut one eye, and everything comes into focus. Do not ask me how I know to do this; I do not have a clue as to my strange eye movements. I cannot explain how or why I close my left eye. I just do, and everything comes into focus.

At this point, I probably need to pull off the road. I do not. I keep driving. I become disoriented, and at one point I am driving across the San Pedro bridge. I am not able to tell the difference between the bridge and the ocean. I feel I am about to plunge my car into the ocean. I cry out to God. I am so afraid. Again, in my disoriented state, it never occurs to me to pull off the road. I have an interview to go to, but the route I am driving takes me miles from where I intend to go. After hours of mindless driving, I somehow arrive home that evening. I somehow also call the radio station while driving with one eye closed. I tell them I cannot keep my appointment that day due to a minor inconvenience that has developed.

For some reason, upon my arrival at home, my vision comes back into focus. So, I get on the computer and research what is likely causing double vision. I think I find my answer—diplopia. I read the symptoms, which describe double vision (diplopia) is caused by dryness of the eyes, certain medications, and straining eyes for long periods. I believe I have my answer. My eyes are certainly dry a lot, and I spend hours each day and evening on the computer. With that confirmation, I shut down the computer and go to bed. I am exhausted after such a crazy day. Besides, tomorrow is going to be one busy day of meetings on campus.

The next morning, I wake up and am ready to start my busy day. I breathe a sigh of relief to open my eyes and see everything quite clearly. I am grateful for not seeing double images. This morning, I decide to drive by my business before getting on the interstate and heading to the campus. That decision is also a blessing because as soon as I park in front of my business location, everything turns double again. I surprise everyone when I make an appearance this early in the day. Everyone knows I spend my mornings and afternoons in Los Angeles at the campus. Without revealing what is going on with me, I ask my office manager to accompany me to the campus for the day. She is perplexed as to why she is going to accompany me to my campus. I joke about her being my chauffeur that day.

My double vision continues to come and go that entire day. The large intercampus business meeting I chair that day is unlike any I have ever convened. I cannot very well close my right eye with all those people from departments across campus sitting in the room. Each time I have to direct a question or answer at someone, I do not know if I am talking to them or their double.

Again, that evening upon arriving home, my vision stabilizes. This time I convince myself it is stress related because once I am home, I feel fine. I go to bed early to make sure I am ready for another busy day tomorrow.

The next morning, I wake up but feel anxious about whether my double vision is gone. I decide to stop by my ophthalmologist. Maybe I need some stronger eye drops or some new glasses to wear while I work on the computer. Possibly, I just need a better computer screen to reduce the glare. However, seeking eyecare help ai my first plan of attack.

Luckily, that day I can be slotted in to see my ophthalmologist very quickly. After a very quick examination, he tells me I need to check into the emergency room at the hospital immediately. What is he saying? ER?

I head over to my doctor's office first and inform them about the symptoms I am experiencing. I mention my visit to the eye clinic and tell them what the ophthalmologist said. Before I know it, they put me in a wheelchair and whisk me over to the hospital ER, which is located adjacent to the doctor's office. After a few hours of tests and scans, I am admitted to the hospital. What is going on?

I decide not to contact my family. My independent nature is such that I do not want to alarm them. It is too soon for them to know what I am doing or where I am until I specifically have more information. My daughter who works for me part-time at the business tries to call me. She left me here this morning after I went to the eye clinic. I mention to her that I have a doctor's appointment. I tell her I plan to call her when I am done with my doctor's appointment. I call her once they transfer me from the ER area to a hospital room.

I share with her that I am having some usual tests done. I do not want to alarm her or contact my husband until I know what is wrong. I tell her not to worry and I will call her back when the tests are completed.

The neurologist enters my hospital room and briefly looks over my chart. I am perplexed by the first question he asks me. "Do you teach theology?"

"No," I reply as I look at him strangely.

"Do you believe in God?" He continues to stare at me as he stands beside my bed.

"Yes," I reply as I stare back at him or his double.

"You have to because you had a blot clot that exploded in your brain, which should have resulted in instant death or severe impairment. And you tell everyone this has been going on for three days?" His voice is now to a pitch that he is practically yelling at me.

"I had places to go and things to do," I reply. "I thought I had diplopia."

"You are one hardheaded and stubborn woman," he says. "And for some strange reason, you were saved." He then smiles as he looks down at my chart, writes something down, and starts to walk out of the room.

"Wait! Can I go home now?" I ask. I know my family is probably getting worried about me. I notice that my daughter has called and left several messages.

"Go home? You better plan to spend a couple of days with us. You forget about going anywhere right now. We need to run some further tests and determine what is going on." With that said, he quickly leaves my hospital room.

My family is in a panic when I share with them what is happening. They become furious with me when they hear my story involving the last several days and my so-called double vision. They all agree with the doctor about me being stubborn and hardheaded. I try to tell them that I am not one to worry others about something like that. They all shake their heads in disbelief. Besides, I emphasize, God once again has things under control. I do not need them worrying or fretting about the small things I encounter.

"What if this happens again? Don't you think we will now worry about you not telling us when you are experiencing something like this?" My family is becoming a real pain, I tell them. Again, they just shake their heads in disbelief.

Well, it turns out that the blood clot that exploded in my brain is due to my taking hormone replacement therapy (HRT). I learn that women who take HRT more than double their risk of developing blood clots. Why do doctors give this medication when there is such a risk? A few weeks later, I return for my follow-up doctor's visit, and my doctor discovers I am no longer taking the HRT drug. She informs me that I need to get back on the medication. I look at her, trying to control my anger.

"Why do I need to take this drug when it caused my problem in the first place?" I take a deep breath as I try to control myself, wondering what she is even thinking to suggest such a thing.

"You need to be on the medication, or it could lead to your having a heart attack if you don't take it." She relays this statement to me so matter-of-factly.

"Don't you understand what happened to me? A blood clot exploded in my brain due to this medication!"

Obviously, that is the last time I plan to see that doctor.

But the journey is not yet over. Due to what has happened, I am placed on a blood thinner medication. This medication is to prevent another blot clot. The medication is also given to prevent platelets in blood from sticking together and forming an unwanted blood clot that could block an artery.

A few weeks after my return to work, I suddenly find myself leaving class one evening and barely able to walk. Until that point, I am very mobile and moving around the classroom just fine. I am so thankful class had ended and the students left for the evening. I drag my left leg down the second-floor hallway, into the elevator, and exit the underground garage where my car is parked. I manage to get into my car and notice that my hands cannot grasp the steering wheel very well.

What now? What is going on? Please, God. Please help me! I manage to get home, determined to go back to the ER the next morning.

Early the next day, I leave the house without mentioning anything to my family. I head back to the ER. After being examined, the doctor informs me that I have developed severe rheumatoid arthritis.

"Are you kidding me? Overnight?" I look at the doctor in disbelief.

The doctor gives me a steroid and sends me home. I am in utter disbelief. The issue continues for a few days; therefore, I make an appointment with another doctor who wants to put me on yet another blood thinner. I want an answer as to what is going on. I do not need more medication to mask the problem.

The doctor places a sample of the medication in my hand. I look at it and throw it across the room. As I often say, I must pray often for patience.

"No more medication," I reply as I leave his office. I stop taking the medications, and that "severe rheumatoid arthritis" I supposedly had disappears. Once again, I give God all the glory for intervening on my behalf. The Great Physician has once again done the healing work in my body.

Through this journey, I want to again emphasize that there are incredible medical staff. God has given so many the skills needed to intervene and heal. I continue to faithfully go to some fantastic doctors for my wellness checks and any other issues that arise. But I also believe in the power of prayer as my first line of defense. I pray for those who treat me and others. I did not realize at the time when God planted in my heart that Jeremiah 29:11 was my life verse just how often I claimed that in my times of trouble. "For I know the plans I have for you, plans to prosper you and not harm you; plans to give you hope and a future."

My life settles down once again in my job as professor and department chair at the university. Or so I think. Serving as department chair is definitely full of challenges. I really enjoy my work and am able to build the department in both reputation and ranking. The work done in this position eventually leads to my becoming an associate dean of student services in the business college in which I work.

All is going so well. I have a high regard for all the faculty I supervise, both the full-time faculty—tenured and tenure track—as well as the adjunct faculty. Life is good. I am so blessed to once again have the chance to overcome another hurdle in my life after facing the stroke scare.

Why is it when I get comfortable, it seems another trial or test comes along? I find the position of associate dean of student services challenging. My charge is to revamp the entire student service center in one year. While I miss working directly with the faculty, I love being able to assist the students in an even greater way. So, why am I sitting at my office desk one afternoon asking myself this question? I just received a bit of information that involves my youngest daughter.

My youngest daughter and I are remarkably close. She is a student at the university and loves her studies and role in the journalism program. She is a student in the liberal arts college. I learn she has been seeing one of my former adjunct faculty I once supervised, and this is unsettling news to hear. She has not told me about the relationship. He is old enough to be her father. He is a nice enough guy and a particularly good adjunct teacher. The students love his classes, which I experienced firsthand during the times I visited his classes when completing faculty performance reviews.

By the time I learn of their relationship, it is too late. They eloped and are now married. She is expecting her first child. I am upset on so many levels, both as a mother and as an educator. While she is not his student, he is still a professor. I am even more upset that neither of them came to me and shared with me what was going on. Those old feelings of betrayal and lies surface within me. Our relationship is now distant and fragmented. I am thankful I am not her husband's supervisor in the administrative position I currently occupy. This rift between my daughter and me is difficult. We do not communicate with each other for several months.

I do not attend her wedding party. I know how much I hurt her and deeply regret this. This breakdown in our relationship led to my not being there for the birth of her daughter, Annalise. I regret that as well. I fail her in those areas due to my own hurt and pride. I allow the school gossip to affect my relationship with my daughter. I weigh the costs of my professional and personal responsibilities and allow the professional responsibility to take first place above all else.

Then one day I spot my daughter on campus pushing a baby carriage. I attempt to call her on the phone at one point, but she will not take my call. She is very hurt and angry at me for not forgiving her and being there for her. She has every right to be angry at me. I fail to forgive my daughter and her husband, not acting like the Christian I claim to be. Looking back, it still hurts knowing I failed her at a time she needed me. I see a similarity in the actions taken by my mother and me regarding my relationship with my ex-husband. Didn't I lie and keep secrets from my mother? And yet my Father, my Lord, has forgiven me time and time again.

But that day in that university courtyard when I spot her, I feel led by the Lord to take the first step back to my daughter and the child in that baby carriage. Hesitantly, I ask her if I can see the baby. I cannot describe how I feel upon seeing her daughter, Annalise, for the very first time without crying. That memory will be with me forever. My heart just breaks. It is everything I can do to fight back the tears and not break down crying in that courtyard. Annalise becomes the bond that brings us back together. She becomes my precious little granddaughter whom I love so fiercely. My relationship with her mother grows to become stronger than it ever was. Nick proves himself to be a very good father and in time accepts Jesus as Lord. That is truly God.

I want to say that all turns out great and, just like the fairy tales, "all lived happily ever after," but we are about to take one journey after another in the months and years ahead. This faith journey is about to test the very core of our reliance on God Almighty.

My other children are experiencing problems in their lives, and it seems like once we overcome one issue, another issue arises somewhere else. However, the biggest battles regarding our faith and trust in God are about to be tested once again.

A year after I moved to California, my mother died. I went back to Massachusetts for her funeral, which occurred during the week of Palm Sunday. I never got her to share her secret regarding my biological father with me, but as the family went through some old photographs, we came across some startling pictures. We all looked at one another as we stared at a picture of my mother. The picture was dated several years before I was born. It was clear in the picture that she was pregnant. As time went on and we were able to pull together some information, we learned she had apparently had a miscarriage and then had also given birth to a child who was given out for adoption.

For the first time, I truly understood the shame she carried within her all those years. She lashed out the only way she knew how. What she did to herself and me did not make it right, but I grieve that she may have gone to her grave not accepting Jesus, never finding forgiveness and peace, and believing all those years "her torment was right here on earth."

71

Rising from the Ashes

Anna
2001–2007

After my stroke, I expect my life to once again settle down. I run the business for another year and then make the decision to close the med spa. Being in the college of business, I love being able to share with my students the real-life hands-on approach of running a business. However, the stroke is also a warning sign. I become a lead administrator and take the position of associate dean of student services at the university in addition to serving in my role as a professor. I do not need or want any distractions from what is most important to me. I laugh at this because when I started my educational journey, I never dreamed that my initial desire to focus on a business career would become secondary to working in education.

My heart is full of gratitude to be able to serve others in the field of education. Just to see these students walk across the stage at graduation and receive their degrees is incredibly rewarding. I see myself in so many of these students and the journey they take to arrive where they are at this stage in their lives. The greatest legacy I can ever leave my firstborn son is living a life that honors him. I wish I could tell him I do what I do for him.

Little do I realize at the time just how drastically our lives will soon change in so many ways. Our faith is about to undergo tests and trials beyond anything we can imagine. Once again, I find us on our knees crying out to God in the months and years ahead.

"I think it's time for us to make some plans about moving to Georgia," my husband states one day.

Georgia? My oldest daughter, Tammy, now lives there. My son Trent and family move to New Hampshire. My youngest daughter, Eliza, lives in California. I feel torn about moving; I am needed right where I am and am not ready to suddenly just move. So much is going on with all that Annalise has recently been through. Eliza is trying to balance working and caring for her daughter. It doesn't make any sense for us to move away.

We are like gypsies; we have lived in our new home less than four years. After living in so many states and relocating so often in my life, I am not eager to move again so soon. I am comfortable, and after these California adventures and trials, I do not want to go anywhere. I really like my job, and my family has just endured a major trial that has once again rocked our world. And my husband wants to move! I pause for a minute. Oh, no! Did I say comfortable? Why do I always find myself uprooted when I am comfortable? Comfortable is not really the right word. There is a lot going on in our lives with what is happening with Annalise right now. This is the wrong time to leave California.

Once more, I put out a fleece regarding another job and am interviewed by a couple of schools. Soon we are on our way to Georgia. And to get totally indoctrinated in my new state during my first week on the job, another event proves once again God is at the helm. As I drive the back country road in Georgia to my new main campus, I hear an explosive sound. Next thing I know, a bullet hits the passenger side of my front windshield, which quickly shatters. I am shaking all over. A bullet is lodged in the lower part of the windshield.

I am told later that someone has obviously been target shooting too close to the road. The stray bullet found its target, my car windshield. It looks like life is not going to be dull in my new state. *God, You certainly keep reminding me of my 911 verse (Jeremiah 29:11) and that You are my protector.*

Of course, there is no way I become too content or too comfortable with all that is happening with the family in California. Another test, another trial, but nothing compares to what lies ahead once again in my family's journey of faith. I believe God is giving me a chance to catch my breath before the next journey is about to begin. This next journey will be one that again tests my faith, my patience, and my ability to love and forgive.

A few months after our move to Georgia, my daughter Eliza calls me to tell me Nick is dead. Our world is rocked once again. Back in California, the seizures in Annalise's life continue to ravage more and more of her brain. The decision finally comes to remove half her brain. Eliza is back there in California, battling these day-to-day trials without family around now that Nick has died. I fight being angry at myself and my husband for what I feel is our desertion of Eliza at a time when she needs us most. Again, I ask God, *Why this is happening?* I cling to knowing and believing He will never give us more than we can bear, but I am struggling.

During these times of tests and trials, we cling to our God as the battles within our lives rage. Annalise continues to face life-threatening seizures. More operations are forthcoming in the months and years ahead for her. Eliza is beyond remarkable in her ability to remain calm during the storm raging in her and Annalise's life. We grasp every blessing that comes our way. Our house in California does not sell after being on the market, and I, too, take that as a sign that the house is meant for Eliza and Annalise.

My life in Georgia goes on, but my heart is torn between wanting to be in California with Eliza and Annalise and starting my new life in Georgia. I fill my days with work. I love the opportunities and challenges to build enrollment on a new extended campus.

Some who hear or read my family's story of three generations of medical mishaps of death, stroke, and brain removal, among other tests and trials, refer to this story as a modern-day Job story. I will let you be the judge of that. One thing we know is that our Lord has loved us and forgiven us each time we faltered in our walk, loving us back to Him and showing just how much He is a God of second and third chances. Like Job, we always know He is God, even in the darkest times of our lives. More importantly, like Job, we always know there is a God who never leaves us and carries us when we are too weak to take one more step without His mercy and grace covering us in our bleakest hours.

72

Taking Next Steps

Anna
2007–Present

For some unknown reason, I decide to apply for a position with a larger university in Georgia to build the academic programs on that extended campus. Soon, I am moving once again into another house, another city, and finding a new church.

I relish the small blessings that come my way. Two of my three children and their families live in Georgia. Annalise is making incredible progress after her most recent surgery. Eliza is living closer to the family in a neighboring state.

Life goes by so quickly. Each day, I try to undertake what I call my Jericho walk of prayer, which consists of a six- to ten-mile walk. Every mile, I pray for specific areas, such as family and friends, missionaries/pastors/evangelists, church staff/missions, nation/leaders/issues, children/soldiers/veterans, and so much more. There is not a day that goes by that I am not thanking God for His many blessings and the incredible way He has answered so many of those prayer requests.

Recently, I retired from my position as an administrator and professor to begin what I call my next phase of life. No one told me how busy this retirement life could be when one asks for God's will to be done. The Lord continues to place so many new people in my life. I love each new adventure and have traveled to more countries in the last two years than I ever imagined possible. I am going to places I never anticipated going to serve. God is opening doors for me to undertake mission projects—in the U.S. and abroad, serve as a layperson on the Assembly of God US Missions Board, undertake intensive multiyear Bible studies, and so much more. My heart is overflowing with gratitude for all that my Lord has done.

That "sin child" is blessed beyond measure. God had me in the palm of His hand from before time began and knew the plans He had for me. Yes, I encountered being tested and went through trials I would not want anyone to go through in life. But God never left me in the valley. One only gets to the top of the mountain a step at a time. The way to the mountaintop can often be treacherous, dangerous, weary, and uncertain. Yet, as long as we keep our eyes on our Lord and heed His call, we will make it.

Looking back on my life, I have regrets. I cannot go back and change the things I did that caused me and others so much pain. All I can do is ask my Lord for His forgiveness for those times I chose a different path due to my own willful disobedience. No one else is to blame for those actions except me. God gives us free will. I sometimes had trouble understanding that. God loves us enough to show us the right way but does not treat us like a servant who must obey their master. We have the freedom to follow God or turn away from Him. We are either for God, or we are not. The choice to turn away means we chose to follow the one who will lead us down a path of destruction.

My ex-husband and I had the chance to speak a few times before he died from cancer. We were both at fault for what transpired in our relationship. We were both so incredibly young and ill-equipped for marriage. Even when we were given a second chance, we blew it. I believe he tried so hard to make peace with his life before he died. I was so proud of my children and the way they were there for him in his final year of life on this earth.

If you have gleaned anything from my story, I pray it is the knowledge that in this life, you will have trials, but God is a faithful and loving Father. Open your heart, mind, and soul to the only one who will give you a peace that surpasses all understanding. I continue to pray for so many family, friends, and former colleagues on this journey we call life. My heart grieves knowing they are where I once held residence. I pray for the lukewarm individuals who know there is a God but have no relationship with Him.

Some of them say they do not believe in organized religion, which is just an excuse for not giving God their time, talent, or resources. My heart grieves for those individuals who try to be so politically correct they are morally bankrupt. My heart grieves for those who are incredibly brilliant by world standards but so blind to the truth of believing in a Creator.

I so readily remember what it was to be lukewarm. I knew there was a God. I believed in God, but that is all. I did not have a relationship with God. When my firstborn son died, I did not turn to God for comfort. The seeds of bitterness in my life took over and controlled my every waking hour. Even after my other children were born, I was convinced that if I did not love them too much, then God would not take them away from me. I loved my children, but a part of me was so afraid of what would happen to them if I loved them too much. I allowed the enemy to take control of my life until the day I totally surrendered my life to Jesus and the Holy Spirit took up residence in my heart, mind, and soul.

Not a day goes by that I am not thankful for the Lord, who rescued me and set me free from the bondage of sin. I am reminded of how Jesus called Peter the "rock," even then knowing that Peter would deny knowing him three times. Jesus knew who Peter was to become regardless of his failures. I believe the Lord knew who I was meant to be and that I was a life worth saving even when I felt worthless, unloved, bitter, and confused.

Lastly, I am a work in progress. I must pray daily for God to help me control my thoughts, words, and actions. But this one thing I do know—I was gloriously saved at a time in my life when only God could take a broken vessel and repair it to be used for His glory. My prayer each day is that God will help me to love others as He loves me and forgive others as He has forgiven me.

Finally, I whisper, "I love you, Mom. Thank you for giving me life when you could have chosen not to. Thank you for enduring the disgrace of giving birth to an illegitimate child and people abandoning you. Instead of loving you at such a time, people treated you as an immoral woman and sinner. Forgive me for taking so long to realize the emotional pain you endured in your life." As I write the end of this book, God reminds me of a memory of a three-year-old little girl. This little girl was mesmerized as she watched the joy on her mother's face as she listened and swayed to the song "The Tennessee Waltz."

As I reflect on this memory, I remember the radiance on my mother's face as she recalled a time when she danced and was held in the arms of someone she must have loved very deeply. I never saw that look or longing in her eyes other than when she was held captive by her dreams and her possible longing for what might have been. My heart aches for a woman who built a wall in her life that no one could penetrate. Oh, Mom! If only you knew just how much you were loved. My prayer is that you met the One who was there to wash all your tears and pain away.

To my firstborn son, I love you yesterday, today, and forever. It took me a long time, my son, to realize the greatest legacy I could give you. Each life I touch in some way is a tribute to you. My desire is to live my life in a way that would make you proud that I am your mom. I shudder to think how close I came to allowing my anger and bitterness to consume me. If it had not been for the Lord, I could have missed heaven and spending eternity with you and Jesus.

To my son and daughters, I love you so very much. I spent so much of the time you were growing up trying to build a career and give you all the things I never had—a nice home, nice clothes, toys, and other things. The whole time, what you wanted most was for me to be there with you rather than so consumed with things that were not as important as you. I thank God every day that you children turned out to be amazing adults in spite of me. My prayer each day is that God will continue to give you the wisdom of Solomon and the strength of Sampson to handle all that is before you—spiritually, emotionally, physically, and financially.

As I bring this story to a close, God has honored a desire of my heart that I believed was impossible. But once again I am reminded that nothing is impossible for God. In God's perfect time, He has given me something I never, ever expected to see or discover in my lifetime. There is more to come. God is so faithful! My story is not over. Recently, during a prayer service at my church, a woman I did not know prayed over me. Her words, "God is about to restore to you the years stolen from you. You are about to do great and mighty things for the Lord. Don't be afraid to go and do what He has planned for you."

Never give up on what God has planned for your life. The enemy is a liar. Don't let him rob you of what God has in store for your life. Let go and let God take control of your life. It took me a long time to embrace this and there is no greater joy than walking in the power and might of God and the Holy Spirit.

73

God First: Listening When He Speaks

Eliza

June 2019

Forgiveness. God gave it to us in the ultimate way, by sacrificing His only Son. But when it comes to us, as humans, we are slow to forgive. We can't help it; it's part of our inherent flaw. We are slow to forgive sinners. Yet God forgave us for all of our wrongs, for all of our faults, for all of our mistakes.

I serve every other Sunday at Elevation Church in Charlotte, North Carolina. This is where Annalise and I live now, and we absolutely love it here. It feels like home, and we have discovered a wonderful tribe of people who we call friends and who love us just as we are.

As I've been working on this book, a lot of emotions have come to the forefront. Anger is the strongest of the bunch. I really thought that I had gotten over the hump of devastation. I can recite what has taken place in Annalise's life, with three brain surgeries and the death of her father, with absolute clarity and minimal emotion attached to it, and I thought that signified that I was doing fine. Put me in front of a new doctor, and I can give a bulleted list of surgery dates, staying perfectly calm when they look up in surprise when I get to the part about how Annalise had a hole punctured through her brain with an endoscope at age fifteen months. I got over crying about that years ago. Or at least I thought I'd gotten over it.

Last summer, I decided to start serving at Elevation. Every other Sunday, I pray with others who need guidance from God. I've taken leadership classes at the church. I begin to pray fervently, with Annalise and by myself. I read my Bible almost every day. I read a devotional almost every day. I begin praying to hear God's voice, to know when He is guiding me, to trust in Him completely—to put God first.

A couple of days ago, while reading a devotional by David Villa entitled "Walking in Favor," I finally heard God.

What I read was this:

> The word of God came to Jonah to declare unto him his destiny ... the presence of the Lord goes before you to prepare your place of blessing ... Walking in favor is just that, walking. It is an action. A movement. A decision that you have to make on your own. It isn't always the easiest decision. In fact, sometimes it's the most difficult decision there is. But it's the best decision that you will ever make.

I read that passage and immediately thought of Dr. Henry. *Forgive him.*

I'm sorry. What? Forgive him? This man lied to me about what happened to Annalise in that operating room, only to admit it years later while under oath during a deposition. He completely changed the course of our lives, completely shattered any chance of Annalise living out a normal life, and You want me to forgive him? God. You must be joking.

I try to push the thought out of my mind and go to sleep.

The next morning, I wake up and go to the gym. The entire time that I'm walking on the treadmill, all I can think about is Dr. Henry.

Forgive him.

God. You can't be serious. I cannot do that! After what he did to my child!

Jesus.

I'm groaning. Partially because of the workout but mostly because

I can't believe what God is asking me to do. I head home, put my purse down, and walk into the hallway.

"For God so loved the world that He gave His one and only Son ..."

The scripture is quoted in the art on my wall. I bought it because I believed it. And now it is asking me to prove it.

I close my eyes and shake my head. *God, please. Please don't make me do this.*

June 23, 2019

> We have a volunteer meeting before church begins on Sundays. Today, our associate campus pastor, Ashley Babika, is teaching us about a season in her life that she's been going through. She is trying to understand that in order for God to be able to plant His goodness in her life, she must first allow Him to till the soil. God has to remove all of the weeds (sin, doubt, resistance, stubbornness, hate, spite, unwillingness to forgive) so that He can fill us with His light, with His love, with His Spirit. If we hold on to all of the weeds, we cannot experience His growth in our lives.

I hear God again. *Forgive him.*

I ignore the voice.

In the service, we have a guest pastor, Robert Madu. He speaks about Matthew 15:21–28. The story of the Canaanite woman who approached Jesus, asking for Him to heal her daughter. Jesus heard her but ignored her initial request. She repeated her request, and the disciples urged Jesus to send her away. This mother cried out yet again. Jesus responded, "It is not right to take the children's bread and toss it to the dogs." The mother, insistent upon getting help for her daughter, replied, "Yes, it is, Lord. Even the dogs eat the crumbs that fall from their master's table." Upon hearing her, Jesus replied, "Woman, you have great faith! Your request is granted." Her daughter was healed at that moment.

Pastor Madu was making a point that this mother had to first be ignored, then bullied by the institution (the disciples asking Jesus to turn her away). Then she was made to feel insignificant and insulted (being called a dog by Jesus, of all people).

What's the point of this? That there is power in persistence. And by getting over the multiple offenses, that woman was granted the miracle she was asking for.

The entire time, I feel God persisting. *Forgive him.*

I talk about what I'm struggling with to a friend at church. Erika was one of the first people who made me feel truly at home at Elevation. When I moved into a new home, I asked her to come over and help me anoint the house with oil. When Annalise started suffering from migraine headaches earlier this year, I asked her to pray for Annalise. She knows Annalise's history, so I tell her what I feel God is persistently telling me to do.

"I'm really upset with God right now. How could He ask me to do this? I mean, I can do a lot of things, Erika. But this? How could I ever forgive Him for what happened to Annalise?"

Erika looks at me with her beautiful blue eyes, the color of them not concealed by the large-framed glasses she always wears. She shakes her head and says, "I don't know. But I do think that God sometimes asks us to forgive people not for their sakes but for ours. Maybe this is God telling you that in order for you to get over it, you need to do this."

When I get home from church, I speak directly to God. "God. If this is what You really want me to do, then make it possible. I know Dr. Henry is retired, so I can't get a hold of him at his old office. If you want this, then help me find some way to contact him. A phone number, an address, an email address." Then I add, "And if You really and truly want this, then let it be on the first page of Google."

I pull out my phone, open the Google app, and type in Dr Henry's name. On the first page, I am presented with his phone number, his address, and his email address.

I pick up my phone and call my mom. I tell her about the sermon and about what God has placed on my heart.

"Mom, He can't be serious. How can I do this?"

"It takes a lot to forgive. I had to forgive the doctor after what he did to your oldest brother. But you have to remember, God gave His only Son. Sent Him here to die for all of the things that we needed forgiveness for."

"I know." I sigh into the phone, tears streaming down my face. The idea of actually forgiving this doctor, this man, for the lies, for the damage he caused. It's a lot to process.

My mom's voice becomes firm. "Eliza, think about it. If God is asking you to do something, you need to listen. I wouldn't want to be the one to say no to God."

I open my Bible. I want to listen to God but need one more push. In my heart, I fight against the words I now see every time I let my eyes close. *Forgive him.*

"If you follow my decrees and are careful to obey my commands, I will send you rain in its season, and the ground will yield its crops and the trees their fruit." My Bible had opened to Leviticus 26:3.

If there is a blessing for following God, then there is also a punishment for not doing so.

Outside my bedroom door, I hear the sound of Annalise and her friends doing karaoke. They laugh and scream into the mics, clapping for each other after every song. I grab a box of tissues and my cell phone and walk into the closet.

I sit on the floor, the closet door providing just enough privacy for the phone call I am about to make. I dial the number, thinking there is no way that anyone will answer. In this day of massive amounts of robocalls, does anyone answer their home phone anymore? Two rings are all it takes before a woman answers with a simple "Hello?"

I swallow hard. My heart is thumping in my chest. "Hi, uhm. Can I speak to Dr. Henry, please?"

"Uh, sure. Can I ask who's calling?" There is a note of suspicion in her voice. She must think I'm calling to sell something.

"Yeah, this is Eliza Reza."

"And can I ask what this is regarding?" she asks.

I sigh deeply, quickly thinking about how I should answer her question. I close my eyes. "I'm calling ... to forgive him."

There is silence for a moment. "Uh ... OK ... hold on a sec."

I hear feet shuffling as she moves from what appears to be one room into another. Sounds of children's laughter and mumbles of conversations taking place three thousand miles away from where I now sit reverberate through the phone. I hear a woman say, "Dad? It's for you. Eliza Reza? She says she wants to forgive you?" The mumblings suddenly go quiet, and I hear another shuffling of feet as Dr. Henry heads toward the phone and takes the receiver.

"Hello?" It is a voice that sounds not at all as I remember it.

"Uhm, Doctor Henry?"

"Yes?"

All of the things that I had always imagined saying to this man over the years just disappear from my mind. I can't think of a single thing to say. I pray quickly, *Lord, send Your Holy Spirit to me now please. Give me the words because I have none.*

I begin to cry. "Doctor Henry, I'm not sure you remember me. This is Eliza Reza, Annalise Reza's mom?"

He pauses. "The name sounds familiar. Can you remind me?"

My insides jump. It sounds familiar? I thought of this man every single day for fifteen years, and he can't even recall who I am or who Annalise is?

"You and Dr. Lin operated on my daughter, Annalise Reza, when she was fifteen months old. It was an endoscopic procedure that paralyzed her on one side and caused seizures," I explain.

"Oh." He pauses again. "Yes. I remember."

"Annalise just finished her freshman year of high school," I explain. I'm not sure where this is going, but I just keep talking and hoping that God will get me through this phone call in a way that provides closure.

"Oh good, uh huh," he says.

I continue. "I didn't think that I would ever want to talk to you again, but I've been doing a lot of soul searching, and uhm, but I just want you to know that Annalise has had issues her entire life. I've been really angry at you for a very long time. I just felt that I needed … that God wanted me to … give you a call to let you know that I forgive you. I don't forget, but I do forgive."

"It was tough for all of us, you know," he says.

"Right." I feel anger rising. My mind flashes to Annalise in a hospital bed, unable to move. Being lied to about what happened to her. It was tough for her, for her family. *God, please. Why are You wanting me to do this?*

"It was tough for all of us, very hard for everybody, for the doctors and the family. It's not easy when something like this happens," he explains further.

"You know, Annalise is my only child. I've dedicated my life to her, to taking care of her. And I want you to know who she is. She's a good kid, an amazing person. She has dreams of college, of Clemson. She wants to be a writer. She's joyful and loving. She has no hate in her heart whatsoever. And I need to forgive you, because that's who I need to be, for her. I really hope that you will remember Annalise."

"Of course, I remember. When surgeons get together, we of course all have nightmare cases that we remember unfortunately. And she is most certainly one of them. Dr. Lin and I still talk about it, you know. It's the type of thing that you wake up in the middle of the night … it's not easy. I know it's not over."

I tell him about Annalise's hemispherectomy in 2010. How she had half of her brain removed to stop the seizures that started after the surgery he and Dr. Lin performed on her. He is surprised to find out about that. I tell him that she still doesn't use her left hand and that she uses an AFO to help her walk.

"You know, it took a lot of courage to call you," I say. "I hope that you don't ever forget about her. And I hope that we can both find some sort of peace."

"Will you give her a kiss for me?" he asks.

I pause for a moment. "I will. I will do that."

After we both hang up, I sit against the closet door and close my eyes. I take deep breaths, inhaling through my nose and exhaling forcefully through my mouth. About five breaths in, I begin to feel the weight of what I've just done come over me, and I begin to sob. I let the tears wash over my face and run down my neck. I pick up the phone again and call my mom.

"Mom?" I cry into the phone.

"Honey? What is it?"

"I did it." A whine escapes as I tell her.

"You did?" she asks. "OK. I'm so proud of you. So, so very proud. I know that wasn't easy. How do you feel?"

"Uh, right now? I feel … I don't know." I perform a quick scan of my emotions. What do I feel? Relieved? Sad? Angry? Nothing? "I honestly don't know how I feel. I just feel … ugh."

"Just let it sink in. What you just did was so brave. And I'll tell you something else. What you did was obey God. That's no small feat. I'm sure that there is a chorus of angels rejoicing for what you just did. You set yourself free, honey. Be proud of that."

Maybe it is my mother's words or maybe it is the fact that I just let go of something. But I do begin to feel lighter when she says those words.

"Thank you, Mom. I love you. I'll call you tomorrow, OK?"

"OK, honey. I love you so very much. I'm so proud of you."

74

Pressure Made Us Precious

Eliza

The next day, I wake up and open my Instagram. The very first post I see is a quote from C. S. Lewis that says, "To be a Christian means to forgive the inexcusable because God has forgiven the inexcusable in you."

I realize that by actively forgiving the inexcusable act that had been done against my beloved daughter, I've also forgiven myself. All of the years of guilt and bitterness had been eating away at me. I'd taken the knife out of my own back. I'd let it go. I wouldn't forget, but I could forgive. I feel lighter. It is the single most important thing that I could have done for the sake of my own heart and soul. All I had to do was listen to God. He hadn't been steering me wrong. He wanted me to forgive so that I could allow His healing to begin. He knew I could be brave, knew I had the power within me to take the broken path and repair it. He gave me the choice.

I hope that one day when Annalise reads this, she'll understand that she, too, can continue to do hard things. That she only has to listen to God. I hope that she understands that God's pressure makes us precious.

NOTES

Chapter 1
Jeremiah 29:11 (NIV)
Romans 10:17 (KJV)
Matthew 18:21–22 (NIV)
John 16:33 (NIV)
2 Corinthians 4:8–9 (NIV)
1 Peter 5:9–10 (NIV)
Luke 23:34 (NIV)
Psalm 147:3 (NIV)
Psalm 150:6 (NIV)
Revelation 21:4 (NIV)

Chapter 3
Romans 8:28 NRSV
Galatians 5:22 (NIV)
Ephesians 6:1–3 (NIV)
Ezekiel 36:26–27 (NIV)
Matthew 18:10 (ESV)
Psalm 139:16 (ESV)
Proverbs 18:21 (NIV)
Mark 4:22 (NIV)

Chapter 4
Ephesians 1:11 (NIV)
Isaiah 44:2 (NIV)
Psalm 139:16

Chapter 5
Proverbs 14:12 (NIV)
Matthew 7:13 (ESV)

Chapter 6
James 4:16–17 (NIV)
Psalm 139:13–16 (NIV)
John 10:10 (NIV)
2 Corinthians 1:3–4 (NIV)
Psalm 37:25 (ASV)
Jeremiah 29:11 (NIV)

Chapter 7
Genesis 4:7 (NIV)

Chapter 10
Isaiah 1:16 (NIV)
Psalm 34:14 (NIV)
Ephesians 4:31–32 (NIV)
Proverbs 24:8 (NIV)
Proverbs 20:22 (NIV)
Proverbs 24:29 (NIV)
1 Thessalonians 5:15 (NIV)
1 Corinthians 10:12 (NIV)
Proverbs 4:23 (NIV)
Psalm 139:13–16 (NLT)

Chapter 13
Exodus 20:12 (NIV)
Ephesians 4:14 (NIV)
Job 22:2 (NIV)
Galatians 6:4–5 (NIV)
Job 18:4 (NLT)
2 Corinthians 5:17–18 (ESV)
Psalm 73:21–22 (NIV)
Psalm 22:1 NLT
Isaiah 43:2 (NIV)

Chapter 17
Isaiah 41:10 (NIV)

Chapter 30
John 3:16 (NIV)

Chapter 73
John 3:16 (NIV)
Matthew 15:21–28 (NIV)
Leviticus 26:3 (NIV)

SOURCES

American Standard Version Bible (ASV). https://www.biblestudytools.com/asv.

Babika, Ashley. Personal communication. June 23, 2019.

Baylor, Helen. "If It Had Not Been for the Lord on My Side." February 28, 2015. Lyrics, https://genius.com/Helen-baylor-if-it-had-not-been-for-the-lord-on-my-side-lyrics.

The Daily Walk Bible (NLV). Tyndale House Publishers, Inc. Wilkinson, Bruce H. (Editor). Wheaton, Illinois.

English Standard Version Bible (ESV). www.ESV.org

Life.Church. 2019. Bible App (Version 8.13)

Lewis, C.S. 1960. *Essay on Forgiveness.* New York: Macmillan Publishing Company, Inc.

Lucado, Max. 2013. *God Will Use This for Good: Surviving the Mess of Life.* Nashville, Tennessee: Thomas Nelson Inc.

Madu, Robert. "Get Over It." Sermon, Elevation Church, Charlotte, North Carolina, June 23, 2019.

National Revised Standard Version Bible (NRSV). https://www.biblestudytools.com/NRS

The Quest Study Bible (NIV). Zondervan Publishing House. Grand Rapids, Michigan.

Valimont, Randy. 2014. *Betrayed*. Lake Mary, Florida: Charisma House.

Warren, Rick. 2003. *Daily Inspiration for the Purpose Driven Life*. Grand Rapids, Michigan: Zondervan Corporation.

ABOUT THE AUTHORS

Dr. Anna Ray is a retired university professor and administrator. She has written or contributed to many books and journal articles in both the educational arena as well as the literary marketplace. She enjoys traveling and has credited those trips with the inspiration for what she writes. She also keeps busy traveling on mission trips and serving on the Assemblies of God US Missions Board, as well as volunteering in her local church. She has lived in many states and has used those experiences as backdrops for the fiction books she has written. She lives in Griffin, Georgia, with her husband and three fur babies. She considers this stage of her life the best yet because it affords her the freedom and opportunity to share her story with audiences all over the world.

Eliza Harrison lives in Charlotte, North Carolina, with her daughter, a goldendoodle, and a newfiedoodle. She works in digital communications as a content strategist for a global financial institution. On the weekends, you'll find her volunteering at her church or taking road trips. Eliza is involved with the local improv scene in Charlotte and is an improv student with The Groundlings. In her free time, she writes for blogs such as Feminine Collective, Thrive Global, and her own blog, and she is a cohost for a parenting podcast. She considers writing this book an opportunity to share her belief that no matter what happens, God is faithful.

Printed in the United States
by Baker & Taylor Publisher Services